Springer Series: Focus on Women

Violet Franks, PhD, Series Coeditor
Carole A. Rayburn, Series Coeditor

**Vera S. Maass, PhD,** born and raised in Berlin, Germany, is a clinical psychologist, licensed in Indiana as Health Service Provider in Psychology and as a Marriage and Family Therapist. She is a National Board Certified Counselor and a diplomate and clinical supervisor on the American Board of Sexology. She received her PhD from the University of Missouri-Kansas City and served a 1-year clinical internship at the University of Kentucky Medical School in the psychiatry department, under the direction of Maxie C. Maultsby, Jr., MD. During her training, she had individual supervision by Albert Ellis, PhD.

Dr. Maass owns Living Skills Institute, Inc., a private practice agency in Indianapolis, and directs psychological services in a clinic that addresses sexual dysfunction issues. Dr. Maass is a member of Zonta International, a worldwide service organization of executives in business and the professions working together to advance the status of women. In her spare time she volunteers at the Indianapolis Museum of Art and provides guest lectures at a local university.

Sonja Maass, PhD

Women's Group Therapy

Creative Challenges and Options

 Springer Publishing Company

Springer Publishing Company, Inc.
536 Broadway
New York, NY 10012-3955

Acquisitions Editor: Sheri W. Sussman
Production Editor: Sara H. Yoo
Cover design by Joanne Honigman

01 02 03 04 05 / 5 4 3 2 1

Library of Congress Cataloging-in-Publication Data

Maass, Vera Sonja.
    Women's group therapy : creative challenges and options / Vera Sonja Maass.
        p. cm. — (Springer series, focus on women ; v. 23)
    Includes bibliographical references and indexes.
    ISBN 0-8261-7383-7
    1. Women—Psychology—Case studies.   2. Group psychotherapy—Case studies.   3. Decision-making—Psychological aspects—Case studies.
    I. Title. II. Series.

HQ1206 .M27 2002
155.6'33—dc21   2002017622

Printed in the United States of America by Maple-Vail Manufacturing Group.

Contents

Preface

The idea for this book came from the many female clients I have seen in psychotherapy and counseling over the years. The recurrent themes of searching and struggling that women experience in deciding on a life course, or changing their paths, or abdicating authority over their own destiny have impressed me again and again. And I have been equally impressed by the courage, resiliency, strength, talents, and competence women have demonstrated while engaged in the struggle.

There are reports about women who have been able to successfully combine fulfilling personal and professional lives, who seem to have it all. For that reason and to offset the impression gained from clients, I decided to involve and interview as many female volunteers from the community at large as possible.

There is no claim that the material discussed in the book is part of any structured research. The women who are described in this book are composites of White heterosexual females and are not representative of all women in the general population. Neither the volunteers nor the clients have been selected on a random basis. No attempt at statistical evaluation of the obtained information has been made. The purpose of this book is to give women a voice and to provide a sense that self-determination is a prerogative that needs to be pursued wisely. Although the book is intended for use by professionals and advanced students in the mental health field, I tried to avoid the use of professional jargon to make it accessible to readers not trained in psychology or counseling, without watering down theoretical or professional concepts. In writing this book, it has been my goal to make it readable and enjoyable for both professionals and lay persons.

Acknowledgments

The women who volunteered their life stories have become a significant part of this book. They were generous with their time and the information they shared. All of them were excited about this project. Their enthusiasm was encouraging and contagious. For reasons of confidentiality, their names have been changed and some of their circumstances have been disguised. Some of their stories have been combined to form composite characters. My gratitude goes to all the women volunteers. Although I cannot list their names, they know who they are, and they know the impact of their generosity on this book.

CHAPTER ONE

Background

For a generation or more, women's roles have changed, at least on the surface. Pioneers in the area of equal rights for women have done a lot to pave the way and create opportunities for the self-actualization of modern woman. Job advertisements and college recruitment activities encourage women and minority groups to apply. To the superficial observer, the high number of women in the workforce and on college campuses may indicate that women are finally actively involved in shaping their own destiny. However, these changes are often only skin-deep.

BIOLOGICAL INFLUENCES ON WOMEN'S LIFE PATTERNS

Although many women no longer follow the path of previous generations, such as being a permanent full-time homemaker, their lives are still affected by the discontinuities that are inherent in the female biology. Childbearing and childrearing are episodes in a woman's life in which she is forced to balance conflicting demands. These periods are often instrumental in emphasizing traditional female values rather than strengthening desires for individual autonomy. Young women expect periods of withdrawal from their careers when anticipating parenthood, whereas men consider family life to be a relatively minor factor in their career development. In women's perception, family and career operate in a zero-sum equation. Being socialized to function as the nurturing caregiver for the family, women may perceive efforts invested in their career as taking away from the caregiver responsibilities (Apter, 1985).

1

Considerations of the various responsibilities connected with giving birth to and raising children may be a reason why women who want to combine marriage and career consistently choose to embark upon traditionally female career paths. Bandura (1986) suggested that women's beliefs regarding the difficulties of combining the dual workloads of a successful career and managing a household keep them from pursuing traditionally male careers. Recognizing that progress in a career demands persistent efforts to achieve professional advancement and personal fulfillment, women are not convinced that they can combine those necessary efforts with the efforts required to fulfill home and family responsibilities. A study, examining the preferences of 120 women and 92 men regarding either traditionally female or traditionally male occupations (Bonett, 1994), found that married women scored higher than married men and unmarried women scored higher than unmarried men in favor of traditionally female occupations.

CHANGES IN THE CONFIGURATION OF WOMEN'S ROLES

During the 20th century, the configuration of women's roles has undergone overt dramatic changes. During World War II, almost 20 million women were in the workforce, constituting 36% of the labor force. With the end of the war and the veterans' return to reclaim their jobs, women were displaced from industry. By then many women discovered that they were able to make good wages and that they liked their independence (Langer, 1996).

In the 1950s, some day nurseries providing care for children of working mothers attempted to supply realistic toys (Price, 2000). A photograph taken at that time shows three little girls and one boy, playing house. One girl is standing in the background ironing clothes. The boy and the other two girls are sitting around a table with play dishes. Each of the two girls sitting at the table attends to a doll representing children to be fed and taken care of. The little boy appears to just sit at the table, enjoying a cup of tea. Thus, the children of working mothers were trained for traditional roles of mothers serving husbands and children with fathers looking on. The values and attitudes of those children were shaped through the influences of sex-role models of past generations as long-established attitudes and values were passed on (Maass, 1995).

Although to a lesser degree, women remained a part of the labor force and their roles continued to change from homemaker, wife, and mother to a shift in increased importance of wife and mother, separating them somewhat from the role of homemaker (Lopata & Barnewolt, 1984). Perhaps the shift in emphasis was due to technological advancements that found their applications in households and made it easier to manage household chores.

The roles of wife and mother increased in specialized significance. Lopata and Barnewolt (1984) asked women which of the roles—wife, mother, employee, or homemaker—they would regard as the most important one. The authors conducted interviews with 571 women and found that women who were employed but not also wives and mothers ranked their current role priority as employee. Women involved in family roles in addition to being employed gave their family roles highest priority. The combination of roles as wife and mother decreased the importance of the employee role to the point that only a small percentage of the respondents who carried out all three roles assigned first place to the importance of a role external to the family. Employed married women without children concentrated most heavily on the role of wife.

The investigators found an interesting division in responses between women in blue-collar and white-collar work situations. Married blue-collar workers were more likely to continue listing the role of worker first, whereas white-collar employees dropped their job emphasis when marriage was added to the situation. Some professional and managerial women were the exception. For the married women, the higher the status and income of the husband, the stronger they associated with the role of wife. In cases where the husbands held low-status and low-income jobs, their wives were more likely to identify their own primary role as that of employee.

Women who identified more strongly with the role of mother most often had a child under the age of 3 years at home. Surprisingly, an increase in the number of children seemed to decrease the orientation toward the role of mother. Overall, child-oriented women tended to be of a lower socioeconomic background and not living with a husband.

PUBLIC BELIEFS ABOUT GENDER-BASED LABOR

Public beliefs about a division of labor based on gender have been investigated again recently (Brewster & Padavic, 2000). Expanding on an earlier examination of attitude change between 1977 and 1985 (Mason & Lu, 1988), the authors conducted face-to-face interviews gathering information from 13,966 White and African American respondents. Although in 1977 a majority of women worked outside the home, most respondents then disapproved of women holding jobs in addition to carrying out family responsibilities. Two decades later, in 1996, attitudes and behaviors were more approving of women's dual roles. Thus, the overall trend reflects increasing egalitarianism, but the pace of change appears to be slower than it was during the earlier period, particularly with regard to mothers' participation in the workforce.

Explorations of the obtained results regarding differences in the pace of attitude change based on educational level and sex of the respondents demonstrated that college-educated participants held more egalitarian attitudes in 1977 as well as in 1996, but on the average there was little change over the 2-decade period. For both sexes, attitude gaps between the college-educated and the general population were significantly smaller in 1996 than in 1977. The liberalizing effect once linked with education became more generally diffused throughout the population, and at each educational level women showed a greater degree of change than men.

Another variable impacting attitudes was church attendance. People with weekly church attendance held more traditional gender attitudes. Though the average level of church attendance was lower among recent cohorts than for those 20 years ago, the importance of church attendance in differentiating between those with traditional and those with egalitarian attitudes had increased. The more liberal attitudes about women's roles found in participants reaching adulthood between 1985 and 1996 were probably consequences of exposure to mothers who first flooded the labor force in the 1960s and 1970s.

CHILDBEARING AS A "CAREER CHOICE"

In the 1970s, it was not unusual to have two generations of women living on welfare assistance. Betty, a White, divorced 48-year-old woman with two adult children and a young son whom she described as her "menopausal accident," came to therapy because of relationship difficulty with her male friend. Betty had never worked outside the home. She married at an early age and stayed home to raise her two children. After the divorce from her husband, she was able to remain a full-time mother. When her two older children left home, she was eligible for public assistance due to her school-age son. Although financially not dependent on her male friend, she had become emotionally dependent on him and struggled with her feelings of jealousy.

Later Betty referred her daughter Cathy who experienced difficulties with her 11-year-old daughter Lori to the same therapist. Cathy was the divorced mother of three children, who had never been employed outside the home and currently lived on a combination of child support from her former husband who was the father of her oldest two children and public assistance for her youngest child who was born out of wedlock. Cathy complained that her daughter skipped school, hardly ever studied, and spent most of her time reading magazines and trying out different hairstyles. Lori's answer to the therapist's question regarding thoughts about her future was simple: "I am going to be a wife and mother," she said. The young therapist responded with a statement that indicated that being a wife might not be a lifelong career because husbands can die or leave the family. In fact, the girl's mother and grandmother were examples of these possibilities. Lori agreed that both her mother's and grandmother's situations were relevant examples when she stated, "Both Mom and Grandma don't have husbands, but they don't have to worry about jobs. They are mothers and mothers don't have to work!"

Almost 20 years later, investigators (Merrick, 1995) reported that adolescent childbearing was considered a "career choice" and an alternative, normative life path among lower socioeconomic-status African American girls, aged 16 to 21 years. Attempting to reduce the high rates of adolescent pregnancy and childbearing, social programs had focused mainly on education about reproduction and contraception, assuming that lack of information was to blame for the situation. But lack of knowledge or access to contraceptive methods were not reasons for the adolescent pregnancies. Apparently, most of the young girls had decided not to use birth control methods in order to become pregnant.

CORRELATIONS OF MOTHERS' AND DAUGHTERS' WORK ATTITUDES

Some authors (Gerson, 1985) expected that the gender role revolution over the past 30 years would introduce young women to new norms and expectations about work and family roles. Transmission of ideologies, attitudes, and behaviors occurs across generations mainly through parents' role modeling. Because women's gender-role attitudes are shaped through their mothers' attitudes and beliefs, women whose mothers worked outside the home were expected to hold less traditional attitudes about women and work than women whose mothers were not employed. Timing and consistency of mothers' employment were considered as significant aspects for the shaping of their daughters' attitudes about paid employment. Maternal employment during children's earlier years was seen as most influential (Parcel & Menaghan, 1994).

Amity Shlaes, author and one of the editors of the *Wall Street Journal*, explained that her career success was inspired in part because her mother was not a "stay-at-home mom" (Tanenhaus, 1999). Similarly, another author (Goldman, 1993) reported that her own mother started to work as a reporter when she was 17 years old and did not discontinue working when she had children. The mother, author Lois Wyse, pursued all her interests, and even though she was very busy, she made sure that she spent time with her children. She wrote commercials, the most popular one "With a name like Smucker's, it has to be good," articles for magazines, her own syndicated newspaper column, novels, and musicals. Early on her daughter learned that pushing and doing and working could get people some place.

Whether young women's attitudes regarding career or work are based on what their mothers did or what they said about their own work-related beliefs poses another question. The effects of maternal employment on their children's attitude might be influenced by other variables, such as the mothers' expressed attitudes concerning their employment rather than just the mere fact of their working outside the home.

Ellen, the youngest of four sisters, entered therapy because of a suspicion that her daughter may have been molested by a male relative. At the time Ellen was married to her third husband and there was a concern about her own restlessness and emotional lability. In her family of origin, she was the only one who did not attend college and instead married at a very young age. Both her parents were professional people, and her oldest sister stepped into their mother's footsteps, becoming a registered nurse. The next oldest daughter embarked upon a teaching career, and the third daughter studied languages and eventually became a translator-interpreter for the United Nations. Ellen, however, never entertained the idea of a career. When her marriage ended after the birth of two children, she soon entered into another marriage. Several years and one child later the second marriage ended in divorce. Ellen's financial situation became strained and she obtained several low-paying jobs to make ends meet. Her physical beauty and pleasant manner made it easy for her to meet eligible young men and soon she met her third husband, a computer hardware engineer by profession. Several years after the birth of her fourth child, Ellen became restless again. She was a wonderful mother and housekeeper, but as her children gradually became more independent, she felt unfulfilled.

Ellen's husband suggested that she take some college courses to develop other interests. Although intellectually capable, Ellen had no interest in further education. Finally, her restlessness exerted too much strain on the marriage and divorce was inevitable. Ellen's fourth husband remained supportive of Ellen, but very little financial assistance came from the fathers of her other three children. Ellen had to work two jobs to keep the family fed and clothed.

In therapy, Ellen began to explore why she as the only one in her family had been so resistive to continue with her education. Because her three older sisters had chosen professional careers almost automatically, she could not understand why she had never been interested in a career. Through the exploration Ellen remembered that during her formative years, her mother had been disenchanted with the physical demands of her nursing career. Almost daily, Ellen heard her mother complain about the hardships of her work. Many household chores were left for Ellen to do because her mother was too tired after coming home from her stressful job. Obviously, Ellen had formed a different picture of a career woman than did her older sisters who had been exposed to more of their mother's job satisfaction. By the time Ellen was old enough to consider her own future, her mother had been burned out and disappointed in her career.

Similar experiences seemed to have accounted for Lilly's disregard for a professional career. Lilly was an only child. She remembered her father as being ill for most of his life and her mother working as a nurse. Lilly was a shy little girl who avoided upsetting her mother because her mother was always tired and complained about the hard work she had to perform in her job. During her senior year in high school, Lilly was courted by one of the wealthiest young men in town. Comparing her mother's life of complaints with the luxuries offered in a marriage to this young man, the decision was easy. Soon after graduation she and Paul married and started a family. Over the many years of her marriage, Lilly became increasingly more dependent on her husband. She hated it because her husband treated her like a child, but she saw herself as unable to make a life for herself, even after her children were grown.

Although her mother had been a professional woman, she never encouraged Lilly to think about a career for herself. In fact, her behavior indicated the opposite. Her behavior communicated that if it had not been for her husband's illness, her mother would not have to go out and work. While Lilly's mother thus criticized her husband for his inability to provide sufficiently for the family, she also instilled in Lilly the belief that it was not desirable to have a career. For Lilly, security was equal to having enough money rather than to be independent.

Susan's story describes a different attitude about employment. Her parents separated when she and her brother were quite young. Susan's mother had earned a two-year college degree prior to getting married. It seemed natural for her to stay home and raise the two children. After the divorce she found it necessary to earn extra money as a part-time sales clerk. She decided to return to college, taking one or two classes at a time. Finally she obtained her teaching certificate. In her new career as teacher, Susan's mother found great satisfaction and excitement. Although tired at the end of the day, she described her daily experiences in glowing terms to her children. She also communicated her happiness in being able to make enough money for the family so that they did not have to depend on the help of others.

In therapy, these three women explored and recognized how much their values and beliefs had been influenced by their mothers' attitudes and behaviors without having been aware of the influences at the time. Thus, significant decisions about their future lives were based on factors that were unrecognized and poorly understood by these young women.

Perhaps outcomes of studies on mechanisms of family socialization, comparing the importance of parental defining influence and parental modeling influence on educational aspirations and transmission of beliefs can be generalized onto the area of attitudes about employment. Parental defining effects have been found to have greater impact on educational attainment; but transmission of beliefs appears to be facilitated more through parental modeling than parental defining influences (Simons, Beaman, Conger, & Chao, 1992). Applying these findings, we can understand how the attitudes of the young women described above could have been shaped through maternal modeling. Mothers who are excited about their employment and the freedom it provides for them pass on that excitement to their daughters through their behaviors. Women who perceive their mothers as being drained of energy and joy because of their outside work will not likely be persuaded to seek a career for themselves.

PARENTAL SOCIALIZATION: DEFINING INFLUENCE VERSUS MODELING INFLUENCE

Influences of parental socialization on their adolescent offspring's plans for family formation was the focus of a study conducted by Starrels and Holm (2000). Their findings showed that daughters' plans for marriage and parenthood were related to their mothers' intentions—but not mothers' age at first marriage or birth. The authors interpreted these findings to support their first hypothesis that parents' defining influence has more impact than modeling influence. The fact that the teenagers' attitudes were obtained at their average age of 13.6 years—at least 15 years after their parents' actual behaviors—raises the question whether or not the mothers' behaviors qualified for modeling because the daughters did not actually observe the behaviors. The daughters did not observe their mothers' weddings, conceptions, pregnancies, childbearing, and childrearing activities and the effects thereof on their mothers' lives at those times. What the authors identify as modeling information appears to be historical information.

On the other hand, a study on the intergenerational transmission of gender attitudes, based on a life course perspective to explore the relationships between mothers' and daughters' attitudes and employment experiences, found that social change over a 30–year period resulted in greater mother-daughter congruence in gender-role ideology and work-role identity (Moen, Erickson, & Dempster-McClain, 1997). In 1956 the investigators interviewed a random sample of 427 women, who were wives and mothers. Thirty years later the investigators were able to interview 246 mother-daughter pairs from the original sample. The results indicated that daughters who worked continuously in professional jobs tended to see themselves as paid workers, regardless of their mothers' attitudes about employment. In those cases in which socialization processes through mothers' beliefs were effective, actual role modeling through mothers' participation in the labor force did not produce a significant effect in the attitudes of the daughters. In summary, the investigators explained their findings to show that due to the gender revolution over the past 30 years, women now are more likely than their mothers were to work continuously, to hold professional jobs, and to delay marriage. They regard themselves as paid workers rather than as homemakers.

WOMEN'S ECONOMIC VULNERABILITY

In this book, when discussing women's self-concept as homemakers or as paid workers, the purpose is not to assign any values to one or the other view. As in Erma Bombeck's opinion (Colwell, 1992), being a housewife or "stay-at-home-mom" is not less worthwhile than working as a secretary or teacher or executive of a big company. The contributions that homemakers make to society by caring for their families should be considered equal to anyone working in a paid job. Concerns expressed here about women who mainly focus on raising children and maintaining a home to the exclusion of a career are associated with the vulnerability these women face. As long as they live in an intact marriage they may be well protected financially and socially.

With the destabilization of marriage the economic uncertainty of young women and mothers increased in the 1970s. Economic uncertainties combined with changing commitments to marriage constitute a realistic threat for women. For instance, between 1969 and 1987 singleness for mothers of preschoolers more than doubled (Edwards, 2001). In cases where the marriage is deteriorating, husbands engaged in any kind of business can find many ways (often with help from their attorneys) to siphon off funds into the "business" before these funds become part of the marital assets. The division of community property may translate into the wife's possession of the house but there may not be enough left for her to live on. Women who find themselves abandoned through divorce or widowhood would be better equipped in keeping control over their lives if they had a job to go to and an income they could depend on. In times of loss, a work environment can provide financial as well as social support.

EMPLOYMENT AND THE DIVISION OF HOUSEHOLD LABOR

Another aspect worthy of attention is that women—even though they may see themselves as paid workers—in addition, they still perform the major part of the household chores. Studies exploring husbands' and wives' participation in domestic labor (Atkinson & Boles, 1984; Brayfield, 1992; Demo & Acock, 1993; Greenstein, 1996) have found that although husbands of employed women contribute more hours of household work than the husbands of nonemployed women, the overall differences are small. Even in households where wives earn more money than their husbands and in households where husbands are not employed, wives perform by far the greater share of the household tasks. Unless both husbands and wives share similarly egalitarian views about domestic labor and beliefs about gender and marital roles, husbands perform very little household labor.

The interesting implication here is that women may be less traditional than their mothers in their attitudes regarding outside employment (see Moen et al., 1997), but they are more congruent with their mothers in their beliefs regarding the performance of domestic chores. Studies reported in the relevant literature concur in suggesting that the revolution of women entering the labor force in the past several decades has not brought about a definitive shift in the practices of men at home. In most American families, the primary responsibility for household tasks and child care remains in the hands of the wives— even if the wives spend as many hours in outside employment as their husbands (Hochschild, 1989).

HOUSEHOLD CHORES REFLECTING GENDER IDEOLOGIES

Marriage is thought to set the stage where gender ideologies are played out. Husbands and wives are expected to behave in ways that confirm their gender identities as male and female and thus reflect their gender ideologies. Routine performance of household chores is thought to be an expression of the spouses' gender ideologies. In households characterized by breadwinner husbands and dependent wives, the amount of household labor performed by the wives is predicted to be a positive monotonic function of economic dependence. When the situation is reversed, with wives being major breadwinners and husbands being economically dependent on their wives, the amount of housework performed by both the wife and the husband is expected to decrease as the wife's share of the income increases (Greenstein, 2000).

A sample of 2,912 marriages formed the basis for Greenstein's (2000) study. The average duration of the marriage was 17 years, the couples had an average of 1.5 children, and the mean total family income was about $38,000. The average age of the husbands was 40 years and the wives were about 2.5 years younger. Approximately 8% of the couples were African American and 6% were Hispanic. Educational level was 13.3 years for the husbands and 13 years for the wives. The wives performed an average of 38 hours of housework and about 24 hours per week in paid labor outside the home. Husbands' work hours averaged approximately 40 hours and they spent an average of 17 hours performing household chores.

For most couples the wives tended to be economically dependent on their husbands. On the average, wives earned 28% of the couples' total income. In 31% of the couples the wives' incomes were at least 40% of the couple's earnings and in about 6% of the couples the wives' earnings were at least twice that of their husbands. As expected, the findings showed that wives with no earnings performed a weekly average of 45 hours in household labor. But wives who were the sole earners spent 30 hours doing housework, compared with 18 hours performed by economically dependent husbands. This is only approximately 3 hours more per week than the 15 hours of chores done by husbands who were sole breadwinners.

Greenstein's evaluation of the data showed a linear relationship for the wives between economic dependence and hours of housework performed but a curvilinear relationship for the husbands. As husbands' economic dependence increases, their housework participation also increases, but only to a point. The husbands' housework contributions start to decline around the midrange of dependence. Greenstein's findings are not surprising compared with other studies in which the household division of labor strongly reflected the system of gender inherent in the majority of families. Current social structural conditions still support male privileges. Anderson and Hayes (1996), in a self-esteem poll, found that 78% of women respondents agreed that their partners do not share childrearing responsibilities equally.

ECONOMIC CONTRIBUTIONS AND POWER OF GENDER

Other investigators (Hochschild, 1989; West & Zimmerman, 1987) proposed that men and women through their daily interactions re-create the gender structure that gives men more power than women, regardless of who has the greater fund of resources. Wives with greater resources often defer to their husbands to show that they are not seeking power in the relationship. Similarly, Tichenor (1999) found that wives with higher job status and higher income than their husbands placed higher values on their gender-appropriate contributions to the household than on their economic contributions to the family. Even though they may be the major financial providers, they think they should do more of the household labor. They seem to rate their success as wives and mothers by the work they perform around the house instead of by how much money they bring in through their jobs.

In traditional marriages, husbands had greater control than wives. It was thought that the husbands' power was based on their income and status of breadwinner. As demonstrated, this power base does not operate when wives have greater resources. Instead, the balance of marital power seems to be gender based and still reflects the effects of generations of gender-role socialization in which men are expected to be emotionally inhibited, assertive, independent, and powerful, whereas women are socialized to be emotional, nurturing, and deriving their awards through affiliation with others, particularly men (Gilbert, 1987).

ATTENDING TO POSSIBILITIES OF SOCIAL CHANGE

However, as pointed out by Lorber (1994), human beings do not only follow social rules, they also create them. In order to change the social gender-based dictates, the power of gender in families needs to be made visible. Whenever a reduction in the gender power system occurs it should be emphasized, calling attention to the fact that social change is possible. Some investigators appeared puzzled by the findings that although women did the majority of household chores, even when employed full-time, they generally perceived or expressed little conflict with significant others about the inequity. One explanation offered was that women might not consider expressing dissatisfaction or anger with husbands because of their economic and emotional dependence on the husbands (Kane & Sanchez, 1994; Pyke & Coltrane, 1996).

According to Hochschild (1989), spouses strive to accommodate their gender beliefs, emotional needs, and actions by fitting the demands of the structural realities of life into daily gender-oriented strategies that maintain the gender advantage of men. Both spouses corroborate gender beliefs that family work is women's work and maintain the questionable perception of fairness even though wives do most of the family work. Assigning symbolic meaning to the performance of housework may have paved the way for the maintenance of economically irrational, gendered expectations for housework and suppression of women's complaints of unfairness. When housework is considered to be part of the woman's natural desire to care for her family, the quality of her housework can be viewed as a symbolic reaffirmation of her standing as wife and mother (Berk, 1985; Thompson & Walker, 1989). Strategies such as those may reflect family harmony and mask conflict for a while, but do little to help spouses in their progression toward equality. Often underlying conflict or dissatisfaction in one spouse will express itself in different and subtler ways. A wife's sexual desire may dwindle because she does not feel loving toward a husband who criticizes the quality or amount of housework she does.

EFFECTS OF DIVISION OF HOUSEHOLD LABOR ON MARITAL SATISFACTION

Amy, a young mother of three children running a successful business from home, recently explained her lack of sexual desire with stored-up resentment toward her husband's criticism of her housekeeping. Amy's sexual desire had drastically declined over the past several years. Her husband had always been critical of her, but it had become even more disturbing after he quit his job and started a business at home at about the same time that Amy had made the first significant profit in her business. At first it seemed logical to operate both businesses from home. Office rent was high in their East coast town. They would not need to hire secretaries but could help each other in answering telephones and taking messages and orders. They also eliminated child care worries because at least one of them would be present in the home.

As Amy's business became more successful, she had less time for household chores, and she decided to concentrate on chores that were absolutely necessary and to spend what time she could make available with her children. Jim, her husband, made critical remarks about the quality of her housekeeping. He reported to Amy that on his parents' most recent visit his mother had taken him aside and asked him about his marital happiness. She remarked that, judging by the way Amy had left clean laundry sit on top of the dryer instead of in the family's closets, she did not seem to care much about her husband's and the children's well-being. Embarrassed about his mother's questions, Jim had made some vague excuse about Amy not feeling well lately. He was not prepared for Amy's sudden outburst of anger. She did not need any excuses, she told him. She was working as hard as she could on the business and the home. It would not have hurt him to put the laundry away if he thought his mother would be disturbed by it. Jim, surprised by her outburst, left the room without responding.

Jim's surprise was understandable because Amy had not complained in the past, even when he criticized her for some undone task. In fact, she had always encouraged him when he felt disappointed about the lack of success his business had demonstrated so far. He reluctantly admitted that she brought in more money than he did. On those occasions Amy downgraded her own achievements to "just being lucky," adding that his type of business was much more complicated and needed more time to develop. She had always been careful not to upset the traditional power balance between them. A few days after Amy's outburst, Jim rented an office in a nearby business building, explaining that it would be better for the business if his clients did not come to their home. Amy was not sure if he meant that her house-keeping was the reason for it. She was afraid to ask. His criticism had taken on another shape. Now he couched it in the form of questions, such as, "You are going to pick up the living room before my parents come, aren't you?" Her sexual desire did not increase.

Expecting inequalities in gender and parental roles to cause frustration and stress leading to anger, Ross and Van Willigen (1996) explored telephone surveys conducted on a national probability sample of U.S. households. Respondents were questioned about their feelings of anger and behavioral expressions of anger. The sample consisted of an overrepresentation of women. The investigators found that parenthood significantly increases anger, especially in women. Generally, women do more of the work associated with caring for children and often do so under more difficult economic conditions. Women have the responsibility for household chores, shopping, taking care of the children, and arranging for reliable and appropriate child care. In this sample, mothers had the highest levels of anger, and each additional child in the household seemed to increase the anger. The investigators were surprised to find that mothers were also the most likely to express their anger.

Investigations about the relationship between spousal division of both paid and domestic work and marital satisfaction also involved assessment of 382 two-earner married couples' attitudes about their value preferences for the gender division, the balance of power, and perceptions of equity and empathy (Wilkie, Ferree, & Ratcliff, 1998). It was found that personal preferences regarding the division of domestic and paid work have a significant influence on marital satisfaction for both spouses. Wives who enjoy being efficient in their jobs and wives who prefer a conventional division of household responsibilities are generally more satisfied with their marriages than wives who do not receive intrinsic rewards from their jobs and wives who prefer to share more domestic work with their husbands. Husbands in these dual-earner couples who prefer sharing in the domestic labor were more likely satisfied with their marriages than husbands who preferred a conventional pattern of domestic work. In general, performing the greater share of the housework and not receiving credit for it is more common for wives than for husbands and has a significant negative impact on the wife's perceptions of fairness and empathy.

Spouses who see themselves as able to determine the agenda of chores more likely think that they do a fair share of the household labor. The person who has the power to determine what should be done by whom and when also perceives himself or herself as sharing equally. The apparently gender-neutral effects of perceived fairness and marital satisfaction are misleading due to the deeply entrenched gendered nature of the division of labor. More often than not, husbands' personal preferences have more power than those of wives in determining the nature of division of labor. Husbands' priorities more significantly impact perceptions of equity and empathy and thereby indirectly affect marital satisfaction—at least for a period of time until wives' awareness of their own gendered perception comes into play.

These findings would not come as a surprise to Amy and Jim, the young couple described above; they are living proof of the dynamics. When they started out in their marriage, both adhered to the traditional pattern of employment and domestic labor, even though at the time Amy was employed outside the home. When their children arrived, both spouses decided that Amy should quit her job. Although Jim's willingness to criticize was always there, Amy did not openly react to it. Her own gender-based values influenced her to repress her displeasure with Jim's criticism of her household activities and to work even harder to gain his approval.

When she became successful in her own business, Jim offered to keep an eye on their children, provided he was not busy. In his opinion, he shared the household responsibilities and it was his schedule that determined when he was available to supervise the children's activities. Amy did not have the control over those times and, therefore, could not schedule her own activities independently. Only then did she realize that she worked twice as hard as Jim did, and only then did she express her anger overtly. No wonder Jim was surprised at her angry outburst. Previously, her displeasure found covert expression in her lack of sexual desire.

ESTABLISHMENT OF GENDER ROLES: CAN THEY CHANGE?

Although gender roles have been a way of organizing the world, they are not divinely ordained. People have established gender roles over history; and, therefore, people can challenge and change them to accommodate the process of growth for both men and women (Scher & Good, 1990). As long as developmental models stress that women are different from men because women are basically relational beings and their development of self is bound to take place within the context of relationships, women will have a difficult time developing a sense of self within themselves and independent of others. Thus, girls and women will be trained to look to others for confirmation of self as well as for a place defined for them by others. On a superficial level, such training may not appear harmful because most people live in relationships to others. And indeed, women's relationship skills are often considered to be advantages they have over men who have been deprived of such training. The "advantage" comes at a high price though. The energy that is diverted from learning about oneself and one's wishes in order to focus and concentrate on others, leaves the person's overall energy supply seriously depleted.

Feminist writers have warned about portraying women as victims who are passively oppressed (Harding, 1986; Westkott, 1979), because the victim stance serves to foster resignation and to keep the oppressive conditions intact. Instead, women should be encouraged to acknowledge themselves as active agents in their lives, even though the conditions of their lives might not be of their own making (see Harding). Perceptions of living the lives of victims within one's family and society at large, expectedly lead to feelings of anger, resentment, self-blame, blame of others, fear, low self-esteem, insecurity, and a host of other negative emotions. These powerful emotions often drain energy away from planning and executing goal-directed actions. These feelings also bring about emotional withdrawal and distance between spouses and significant others. This is hardly an atmosphere conducive to the creation of trust, respect, and intimacy, characteristics that are considered to be vital to harmonious marriages and family life.

UNDERREPRESENTATION OF WOMEN'S CONCERNS

Other voices have expressed opinions that historically, women have been underrepresented in psychological and in biomedical research (Fox-Tierney, Ickovics, Cerreta, & Ethier, 1999; Gannon, Luchetta, Rhodes, Pardie, & Segrist, 1992; Rodin & Ickovics, 1990). American psychology at the turn of the century, in exploring associations between the cultural context of gender and the practice of psychology, professionally marginalized women in psychology. Early women psy-

chologists did not express themselves and their ideas in a strong feminine voice (Minton, 2000).

This opinion was shared and expressed by psychotherapist and art
collector Helen Kornblum. In an interview with Susan Fisher Sterling
for *Women in the Arts* magazine (1999), Kornblum stated that during
her service on a medical school's review board that focused on protection of the rights of human subjects involved in medical research, she
observed that women were excluded from most clinical trials and that
repeatedly in medical research men were regarded as the norm while
women were ignored. Similarly, most work on personality, identity
formation, and developmental theories, which provides the basis for
psychotherapy, was based on the understanding of White, middle-class
men or male college students (Freilino & Hummel, 1985; Gilligan,
1977; Miller, 1986; Peck, 1986), even though women participate more
frequently in psychotherapy than men. Historically, in the mental health
field, underlying diagnostic assumptions and the resulting classifica-
tions have been developed by males with little awareness of female
experience and little input from women. Feminist psychologist Han-
nah Lerman (1996) responded by formulating criteria for the development of a feminist theory of personality.

Kornblum's observations in medicine led her to turn her attention
to art. Looking at art historians and directors of museums, she realized that here too, most decision-making positions were occupied by
men. Since then, she has focused exclusively on women photogra-
phers for her collection. Although in another aspect of art, screenwrit-
ing in the past has utilized female talents in equal proportions. Of all
the films produced before 1925, half were written by women, and the
highest paid screenwriter in America from 1915 through the mid-
1930s was a woman, Frances Marion, who wrote 200 produced films
and received two Academy Awards (Beauchamp, 1998).

Returning to the field of medicine, Nechas and Foley (1994) in
their book *Unequal Treatment* have wondered how women could be
ignored in every area of health care when they constitute at least half
of the population. Women had become invisible to science and research, the authors state, because in this culture women's lives have
not been important enough to notice. Apparently, women's monthly
hormone fluctuations and the possibility of becoming pregnant were
some of the reasons why scientists had systematically excluded them
from medical research—even though 60 to 70% of all doctor's office
visits involve female patients. For a long time, coronary heart disease
was believed to be mainly a man's affliction, yet since the early 1900s
it has been the leading cause of death in women.

In the past, women's lives demonstrated higher morbidity rates but lower mortality rates. With the recent dramatic changes in lifestyle and social roles for women, mortality rates have shifted and have decreased this advantage for women. The National Institutes of Health task force on women's health predicts increased and broadened research focus on women's health. The full biological life cycle, including the physical, mental, and emotional changes, should be included in the research (Volz, 2000). Advocating greater inclusion of women in health research, Rodin & Ickovics (1990) have suggested that future trends will have significant impact on women's health, such as the spread of AIDS, the extension of the life span, and the development of reproductive technologies.

Although for women HIV infection is greatest through injection drug use, when considering heterosexual transmission, male-to-female transmission is significantly greater than female-to-male transmission. Gender difference seems to play an important role because for most women sexual activity occurs in the context of unequal power. Female drug users often trade sex for drugs. Also, in sexual behavior, men can decide whether or not to wear a condom; but women have to persuade men to wear a condom or refuse to engage in sexual activities if the male partner is not compliant. Thus, condom use is a sexual behavior that is under the male partner's control (Amaro, 1995). Refusing to participate in unprotected sexual intercourse—although strongly recommended—is difficult for some women because of intervening variables, such as emotional and social factors or fear of resulting physical violence. Amaro cited her own earlier research (Amaro & Gorneman, 1992) as evidence for the importance of gender roles in inability to affect risk reduction decisions among Latina women. Women reported feelings of powerlessness and low self-esteem in the face of men's unwillingness to wear condoms.

SOCIAL-ROLE PERSPECTIVE AND EVOLUTIONARY EXPLANATIONS

Exploring the compatibility of social-role perspective and evolutionary explanations, Archer (1996) concluded that both evolutionary theory and social-role view predict widespread differences in the social behavior and dispositions of women and men. Social-role theory considers sex differences to stem from the division of labor between the sexes, while evolutionary theory attributes sex differences to the consequences of sexual selection and the conflicting reproductive strategies between men and women. According to sexual selection theory, characteristics, such as assertiveness, toughness, not showing emotion, and seeking to control the reproductive decisions of women enables men to compete in the social world of inter-male contest. The predicted pattern for females is to create interpersonal networks and to exercise choice over their own sexual and reproductive decisions.

Similarly, in contrasting approaches of evolutionary psychology and social structural theory, Eagly and Wood (1999) concluded that while occupational sex segregation is still prevalent and the homemaker-provider division is still evident, the answer to the question whether social structural origin theories of sex differences or evolutionary psychology approaches provide the best explanation for the origins of sex differences in human behavior will have to wait for future observations. Continuing attitudinal shifts toward increased endorsement of equal opportunities for women in the workplace and role sharing at home between spouses might lead to convergence of men's and women's psychological attributes and the traditional sexual division between paid labor outside the home and domestic labor may disappear. Until then, issues of gender equality remain the responsibility of the individual to decide and act upon.

As interesting as the various theoretical explanations are, today's women need to consider more actively what part they want to assume in leading their own lives. That is not to say that explanations of the reasons that have led to the current conditions are not important to consider. But equally important are the next steps. After explaining and blaming, individual action is as essential as social action to achieve increased awareness and resolution and transformation of women's roles and women's lives—if that's what is desired.

AWARENESS RAISING EFFORTS AND WOMEN'S SELF-ESTEEM

Alington and Troll (1984) proposed that the changes in the status of women have not been in response to the collective efforts of 20th-century women, but the foundation has been the economic needs of the nation rather than the sociopolitical needs of its women. Similarly, Bergmann (1986) stated that women's liberation from exclusive domesticity did not originate in feminist books or wars or inflation. Although these factors contributed to the progress, the increasing participation of women in the labor force came as a consequence of the industrial revolution of 200 years ago. The rising enrollment of women in paid work started drawing public attention only toward the end of the 1970s because by then employed women had become the majority.

In the late 1960s and early 1970s, consciousness-raising was the single activity most universally associated with women's liberation (Hewlett, 1986). Rather than to politicize the personal aspects of people's lives—as it was meant to do—that transition did not occur completely. Women were still wrapped up in their relationships and their interior worlds. Connections to the public world of institutions were rarely made. In consciousness-raising there is a tendency to shift the responsibility for change to the individual woman and away from society. Women are encouraged to look to themselves as the source of their liberation instead of expecting broad-based social action.

Women with low or insufficient self-esteem will not be able to act in their own best interest, as stated by Sanford and Donovan (1984) in their book *Women & Self-Esteem*. The authors go on to explain that high self-esteem is an exclusively male prerogative. A man who lets the world know that he values himself is considered to be well-adjusted and emotionally healthy. The same situation looks different for women. A woman who openly admits to liking herself is often considered by others to be vain, immodest, and conceited and—interestingly enough—the "others" include women as well as men. Family backgrounds, childhood experiences, schools, churches, workplaces, and society in general have been pointed to for years as sources for women's low self-esteem. Awareness-raising groups and assertiveness training have attempted to remedy this significant problem—without much success.

Perhaps these approaches have not been effective because the explanations for the causes had an element of accusation in them—at least, in the eyes of the accused. When accused of any wrongdoing, most social institutions and individuals alike will defend themselves more or less vigorously. Energy spent in defense and in showing the accusers how wrong they are is not available to be used in assistance or empathy with the accuser. When the literature focuses on the injustices done to women in our society and suggests that feminine views of reality are equally as important as those of "the White Male System" (Schaef, 1981, p. 2), certainly these are valid points, but the language used can be interpreted as accusatory and might only serve to widen the gap between males and females.

If we want to obtain empathy, understanding, and support for women's struggle for equality, we would fare better by showing the rest of the world how they can benefit from alteration of present conditions.

In general, people are more likely to help when there is something for them to gain than when their assistance is motivated by feelings of guilt. For instance, if Jim in the previously described case history had come to understand that helping more with household chores instead of criticizing Amy would have made her feel happier and more sharing toward him, her sexual desire might have increased. This is not to be confused with any situation of trade, such as trading sex for help with chores. But someone who does not feel defensive because of criticism and not physically fatigued because of double loads of work can be expected to have more energy, time, and inclination to engage in lovemaking.

PAST EFFORTS IN THE PURSUIT OF EQUALITY

Many writers have eloquently exposed connections between women's unequal achievements or treatments and various agents in the environment. Covering a broad spectrum of women's lives from the earliest decades of the movement to liberate women, Cassandra Langer (1996) answered the question of what is feminism and describes how feminism has changed American society, culture, and the way we live. Others scrutinized what feminism has become following the contributions of the classically liberal feminists (Sommers, 1994) and explained how women have been sidetracked in their quest for liberation, that things are getting worse, and that the claim of "women can have it all" is nothing more than a pacifying illusion. Although women have come a long way in the last 30 years, the contradictions that women are faced with now are more bruising than ever before (Greer, 1999). To some, feminism seems to be more embattled than ever as the sociopolitical backlash of the 1990s followed the economic downturn of the late 1980s. Female authors have realized and explained how and why women have been evaluated negatively relative to men (Valian, 1999) and have warned that the basic reasons for women's distress are the inequities and ambiguities about "woman's place" that are built into the structure of our lives and society (Tavris, 1992).

Alington and Troll (1984) cautioned that because of the external development of the change in women's status, the consequences will be less permanent, less significant, and less beneficial than commonly pronounced. The authors presented some compelling evidence in support of their argument. Inability to attain ratification of the Equal Rights Amendment has been considered a conspicuous failure of feminist organizations. Liberationist-feminists complained that the ideal of liberation was fading out when the name of the movement was changed from "Women's Liberation" to "Feminists" and that women settled for equality (Greer, 1999).

The consciousness-raising communications of early feminist activists have been instrumental in improving conditions for women and, equally important, have furthered understanding among women and society. Without their work and the work of more recent authors, women would not have gained the degree of self-determination they now enjoy. Those writers have laid the foundation from which today's women can proceed along the path of self-determination. Self-determination is an ongoing process to be initiated by the individual, to be monitored and changed by the individual, and to be maintained by the individual.

PAST EXPERIENCES AND FUTURE STEPS

This book—although attempting to raise women's awareness of themselves and their actions and responsibilities—will refrain from blaming anyone or any institution. In the case of Lori above, does the responsibility for her lack of interest in education and career rest with her mother, her grandmother, the school for not captivating her interest, the social agencies that provided incomes for her mother and grandmother? By placing responsibility outside the individual, we not only continue but we validate and perpetuate the individual's sense of helplessness and entitlement for reparation.

Logical connections between events and interpretations thereof will be used to demonstrate how self-determination can be obtained or how it was lost. By illuminating connections and pointing to available options, this book does not attempt to persuade the reader to behave in certain ways or to make certain decisions. Judgment of what is good or bad will be withheld. Issues of ideology, language, or cultural-social institutions will not be addressed as primary targets. Rather the purpose of this book is to increase the reader's awareness of reality and the options that are inherent in reality by focusing on women's actual experiences, a point convincingly made by Mary Beth Norton (1996) in the preface to her book *Liberty's Daughters*. Aside from theoretical, political, or social investigations, it is important to understand women's experiences from the basis of how women actually live their lives.

The women's actual experiences that are described in this book come from different walks of life. Women from the community who have volunteered to tell their stories and women who have been involved in psychotherapy face the same struggles, have similar abilities—if not opportunities—and can make changes within themselves and their circumstances. It is also to bring women together in spirit, mutual encouragement and motivation for self-determination instead of in competition and antagonism. Demonstrating that women in their wishes and goals are more similar than different helps to maintain a connectedness among women. Names and circumstances have been changed to avoid recognition of the individual. Where permission for disclosure was obtained, efforts to disguise the identity are less stringent; otherwise, the histories are composites of the women encountered in the process of this project.

TRANSITION: MORE OF THE SAME?

In the more than 2 decades of the modern women's movement women have made great strides. Issues of equality have been discussed repeatedly and, undoubtedly, significant progress toward equality has been achieved. But arguments over the proper place of women seem to continue not only in the general society, but also within individual women. Women worry about juggling and prioritizing their responsibilities as mothers, wives, daughters, employees, and—often last—responsibilities toward themselves. They worry about doing the right thing, making the right decisions, being everything to everybody else. In their efforts to improve themselves, women have become the targeted audience of the self-help book market. The American publishing industry and bookstores are offering unending supplies of advice ranging from improving relationships and becoming irresistible to significant others to handling just about every imaginable crisis (Simonds, 1992).

As pointed out by Carol Tavris (1992), women feel obliged to read the volumes directed toward them even though the promise of improvement seems to imply that they are not doing anything right. If women do not receive equal treatment, is it because they did not read the right book or misinterpreted its advice? If they become victimized, is it their own fault? Could it be that the self-help culture functions as another way of manipulating women into doing what they are told instead of determining for themselves what and how they want to be?

In her book *Rice Bowl Women* Dorothy Blair Shimer (1982) told the story of a beautiful, well-educated young girl living during the Ming Dynasty. Jade was the daughter of a well-to-do but socially not respectable man. Finding a proper husband for her was difficult. Finally, a penniless but ambitious student seemed to be the appropriate choice.

With his wife's money the student was able to buy all the necessary books and hire private tutors for intense daily studies. The young man passed his examinations in record time and soon obtained an elevated position in the government of a distant town. While traveling with Jade to his new destination, the young man decided to kill his wife, and he pushed her into the river to drown before continuing with his journey. Miraculously, Jade did not drown and was rescued by a couple traveling to the same destination as her husband. The couple adopted Jade as their daughter. As it turned out, Jade's new adoptive father was the new commissioner and Jade's husband was going to be one of his subordinates. Knowing the full story, the commissioner arranged for a marriage between Jade and her husband, now posing as a widower. Uninformed about the true history of his bride-to-be, the young man was overjoyed to become the son-in-law of his supervisor, a socially advantageous position for him. When the husband entered the bride's chambers, Jade's maids beat him with bamboo sticks until he collapsed. He was dragged before his bride who spat in his face and cursed him for what he had done to her. Finally, her adoptive father intervened and Jade resumed life with her husband. Marriage is predestined.

The purpose of telling this story here is to stimulate the readers' thoughts about themselves being in Jade's situation—how would they have responded? Given the time when the events supposedly occurred, perhaps Jade had no other choices. Her own values, as described in the story, dictated that she remain faithful to her husband for the rest of her life, no matter what he did to her. In her opinion, the true virtue of womanhood commanded her to stay with the man she was married to.

One could also think of "patient Griselda," the legendary wifely model in the Christian era. Griselda was married to a man of high rank who abused, neglected, and flaunted his adulteries before her. When he killed her babies she was not allowed to cry. After years of enduring his cruel treatment she was finally rewarded with his true love. She had passed all his tests and they could now live happily ever after. Apparently, Griselda was not afflicted with any resentment over the mistreatment (Walker, 1983).

Another reason for concluding the first chapter with these tales is that as we proceed through the book we may encounter the paths of women placed in similar circumstances—translated into the present time. Reading their stories, readers may be reminded of Jade's account or Griselda's legendary patience, whether the women portrayed in the different chapters of this book make decisions similar to or different from those made by Jade or Griselda. Readers may argue, "Surely, no woman today would stay with a man who had tried to kill her or her babies!" Some of the histories encountered in shelters for battered women give evidence to the contrary.

Responding to a crisis call on a Friday evening, a therapist met with a young couple in the emergency room of a local hospital. The police had escorted the couple to the hospital in response to the wife's call for help. In an argument her husband had beaten her in the face and chest and shoved her against the wall. As she hesitatingly reported her side of the encounter, the therapist fleetingly thought it was odd how her beautiful long hair covered almost the whole left side of her face. It was obvious that she was afraid of her husband. It was also obvious that this was not the first time that he had physically abused her.

From what the therapist gathered, the argument had started over the wife's having neglected to launder her husband's favorite shirt. He had planned a visit to his father's home in a neighboring state over the weekend and wanted to wear the shirt. Compared with the wife's expressed fear, her husband's emotional state now appeared oddly calm. He did not deny having hit her, but did not express remorse. He pushed his wife's sleeve up on her arm and almost with pride pointed to some recent scars on her forearm that looked as if someone had extinguished burning cigarettes on her skin. "This is what she gets when she does not obey me" was his comment. Scars like those on the wife's arm were also the reason for the wife's covered face.

After an hour of intervention work it was agreed upon that the husband would go on his trip as planned and the wife could pack enough items for herself and their two children to leave the house. The husband did not object and agreed to stay away from the house until Monday. Not trusting the husband's promise and his (under the circumstances) unusually calm mood, the therapist arranged for the wife and children to move into the local shelter for battered women. Another meeting with the wife was arranged for Sunday morning to plan the wife's action for the immediate future. By then the wife had decided to return to the home with her children and stay there. To the therapist's expressed concerns for her safety, the wife responded with, "We cannot live without our appliances and I can't move them out of the house before Monday morning." The wife's answer astonished the therapist who repeatedly pointed out the risk the family was taking by returning to the home. The wife, however, stated that her husband had never abused the children; she was the only one who had to endure his physical abuse and—she added—only if she did not obey his demands.

A follow-up call at the shelter later that Sunday revealed that the wife and children had left the shelter. The therapist called the home on Monday to inquire about the wife's well-being. The call was answered by her husband who calmly informed the therapist that everything was all right. He had returned from his trip as planned and did not seem surprised to find his family back in the home. When the therapist inquired about future plans, such as becoming involved in family therapy, the husband just laughed and added that life was continuing as usual. This had not been the first time that his wife had reacted so "foolishly." Then the therapist realized why the husband had been so calm and unconcerned during the crisis intervention. He knew that his wife would return home as she had done in the past.

Those of us who were involved with the early opening of shelters for battered women remember the frequent relocations of the shelters because some of the abusive husbands had managed to learn the location of the shelter and, therefore, protection for the women could not be maintained in the previous location.

Through the following chapters relevant theoretical explorations and research findings are presented as a logical basis for examination of conditions. All therapy sessions reported in the chapters are conducted within a cognitive-behavioral framework emphasizing challenges, options, decisions, and actions as significant steps in the overall process. The women's actual experiences illustrate paths that can be taken for a meaningful transition from past influences and present experiences to a future of self-determination for women of today and tomorrow.

SUMMARY

This chapter is meant to provide a very basic overview of the background issues that have been instrumental in shaping women's lives. Past efforts in pursuing equality are described briefly, and awareness- or consciousness-raising efforts of the feminist movement are gratefully acknowledged. However, the general focus of this book is on the individual woman and her situation. To understand the effects of sociocultural and -political influences on her life is only a first step. The following chapters illustrate how awareness leads to further steps of exploring options that are available to the individual woman and decisions about how to use these options to reach the desired goals.

CHAPTER TWO

Life as Usual

There are different ways of preserving the status quo, life as usual. Resignation and accepting situations, even though they are unpleasant, are one way. But there are others. Increasing the frequency and intensity of one's own familiar behaviors and expecting different results may ensure a similar stalemate. In general, people's behaviors fit into their overall lifestyle patterns. In the Adlerian sense, the lifestyle exemplifies the person's thoughts, feelings, and actions and weaves them into recurrent patterns characteristic of each individual person (Ashby, Kottman, & Rice, 1998).

PERSONALITY PRIORITIES

As a way of expanding understanding of the person's lifestyle, Kefir (1981) proposed the concept of personality priorities that function as avoidance strategies. Individuals have their own methods of moving away from a perceived traumatic event and gaining a sense of control over fear and chaos. The key to understanding an individual's personality pattern lies in knowing what the person wishes to avoid. For instance, the controller wishes to avoid humiliation. To avoid rejection is the goal of the pleaser, and the avoider wants to steer clear of stress. For the morally superior person, staying away from meaninglessness and anonymity is important. In order to measure personality priorities, Langenfeld and Main (1983) developed the Langenfeld Inventory of Personality Priorities, an instrument consisting of five subscales, tapping the characteristics of pleasing, achieving, outdoing, detaching, and avoiding.

Wanting to be accepted by others is the focus of the pleasing personality type. The needs of others are put before one's own needs, and people of this type have often developed a special talent, such as "mind reading" in order to make others happy. Striving for superiority without being competitive or critical of others is the main characteristic of the achieving personality type. Work and accomplishment rather than feelings and personal relationships are important considerations. The outdoing personality type also has striving for superiority as goal; however, this is being accomplished by outdoing others. People of this type have a desire to control others and to be "better" than other people. Striving for control of self is the focus of the detaching personality type. Pessimistic attitudes toward relationships, avoidance of risk taking and self-disclosure are prominent characteristics. Individuals of the avoiding personality type are easily hurt, emotionally expressive, and hypersensitive. They are unwilling to experience frustration or putting forth much effort.

Of course, most people do not fall neatly into one clear category; they may incorporate facets of several of the personality types. But it is helpful to remember the basic types when trying to understand the way people tend to cope with their situations.

AUTOBIOGRAPHICAL MEMORY, LIFE STORIES, AND NARRATIVE APPROACHES

More recently, an interest in life stories and narrative approaches has emerged as theorists, researchers, and clinicians are trying to understand human behavior, not in isolation but within the sociopsychological framework of the individual. Individuals' identities are representations of their life stories, complete with settings, characters, plots, and themes that McAdams (2001) proposed with his life story model of identity. Although biographical facts form their foundation, life stories extend beyond a mere report of facts as individuals selectively use particular aspects of their experience when they construct their stories to make them meaningful and assign sense to their lives within the social and cultural frame of their existence. The emphasis of the model rests on the integrative nature of stories, the manner that narratives can combine separate features and tendencies into a unifying and purpose-giving whole psychosocial accounts jointly constructed by the individual and the individual's culture. Thus, autobiographical stories reflect the individual's identity as well as the worlds in which the individual lives.

Introducing a framework to extend the study of autobiographical memory, Bluck and Habermas (2001) have combined the notions of life perspective and life span perspective. Life perspective represents how the individual strings together particular memories, whereas the life span perspective considers the chronological age and life context of individuals and how these factors influence abilities and motivations connected to the use of autobiographical memories. The following life stories demonstrate how individuals connect memories in different ways. Some start their reports with early memories and follow a chronological order, as seen by Anita and Jane's stories, whereas others, such as Julia and Helen below, begin their narrative with an event that ties to their current difficulties.

Julia: Anxiety as a Wake-Up Call

On a Saturday morning Julia, the mother of two young children, suddenly experienced difficulty breathing. Her heart was pounding and everything around her seemed fuzzy and out of focus. A noise in her head drowned out everything except the thumping sound of her rapidly beating heart. Julia's husband was out of town on business and she was afraid that she might be having a heart attack. She remembered experiencing similar attacks in the past month or so. But none of them had been as strong. Julia is only 30 years old and there is no history of heart disease in her family. She is in good physical shape, thanks to her regular aerobic exercises.

Two weeks later Julia had her first appointment with a psychotherapist. No medical evidence could be found to account for the frightening experience of that Saturday morning. Her family physician interpreted her symptoms to be characteristic of an anxiety attack and he suggested psychotherapy. Julia did not know what to expect. She was afraid to face the therapist, but she was even more afraid to experience another anxiety attack. Neither Julia nor her family could understand what was happening to her. She was married to a good man who worked hard to provide for the family. With their two healthy children they lived in a nice house in her small hometown. Julia's full-time job supplemented her husband's income.

Why would the anxiety strike on a Saturday? Julia usually looked forward to the weekends. During the week her life was hectic. She arose early every morning to get herself and the children ready. After breakfast on her way to work she dropped the children off at the baby-sitter's. At the end of the workday she was fighting traffic to pick up the children and get a few items from the store for dinner. Julia was grateful that her job was limited to regular hours. Her husband was not so fortunate, his job often kept him out longer. At times he had to work on Saturdays. After dinner, Julia put the children to bed and tried to read them a story. Little time was left for activities other than cleaning the dishes and preparing for the next day.

With the help of her therapist, Julia was able to recapture her thoughts and feelings on that particular Saturday morning. She remembered feeling disappointed when her husband announced the night before that he would have to work on Saturday. This had become more frequent lately. In addition to the disappointment, Julia remembered feeling trapped. For the whole day she had the full responsibility of caring for the children because she did not know how long Bob would work. While doing her household chores, Julia had pushed those thoughts and feelings aside. Julia liked her job. Her employers valued her work and understood that she had to take her vacation days without prior notice when one of the children was ill. That explained why Bob had vacation days that he could use by himself while Julia had no vacation time left.

Expressing her thoughts was difficult for Julia. Her method of dealing with frustration or disappointment was either to push it out of her memory or to swiftly turn around and criticize herself for wanting more than she had. Her own age felt insignificant to her. Although she was only 30 years old, she could pretty much predict how her life would be for the next 10 years. It would be a daily repetition of her current activities—not very exciting. Of course, there would be changes when the children got to be old enough to spend more time on their own interests. Perhaps then Julia could have time for herself and do some of the things she had wanted to do for years. Would she still be interested then, would she even remember what she had craved in the past? Compared with the needs of the family, her personal interests appeared insignificant, even selfish. She reminded herself that she was fortunate to have such a healthy family; wishing for more on her part was sheer greediness. Perhaps she was better off than she deserved. Thus, she added guilt feelings to frustration and disappointment without resolving any of them. Her anxiety attacks were the signals warning her that something in her life was not going right. These signals had become so strong that she could not ignore them anymore.

Looking at Julia's case in terms of personality priorities, it seems that she combined traits of the pleasing as well as avoiding types. Repeated themes in her life story were guilt and punishment. "How did I get this way?" Julia asked. Indeed, how and when was the foundation laid for her unhappiness that now expressed itself in immobilizing anxiety? There is no history of abuse to account for the anxiety. Julia's childhood was rather uneventful. Her mother did not work outside the house and was always there when the children returned home.

Julia's father was the disciplinarian and undisputed head of the family. Julia never felt close to him. If the children misbehaved during the day, their mother did not dispense punishment. Instead, she informed them that their father would administer the deserved punishment after his return from work. Julia reported that sometimes she or her siblings would forget the upcoming punishment and continue to play as if nothing had happened. By the time their father came home and was informed about their misdeeds, the children were surprised when suddenly the punishment descended upon them. In time they learned to remember, and Julia recalled how she often worried for the rest of the day if her mother had caught her in an unapproved activity.

With this bit of history we can see how Julia had learned in childhood to respond with worry and anxiety to uncomfortable or threatening situations. She also learned that punishment for indiscretions was inevitable. Furthermore, because children's memories regarding their behaviors are short, the delayed punishment carried an element of unpredictability.

Julia learned that power and decision-making resided in the domain of men. Women had the responsibility to take care of the home and children. Even though her mother was present at the time of the children's actual misbehaviors, she did not choose the nature of the punishment nor did she execute the punishment. Julia did not know whether her father actually wanted to discipline the children or whether her mother simply preferred to leave that responsibility to him. Although their mother was always available, she did not seem approachable or accessible for negotiations about "forgetting" the punishable behaviors. In retrospect, Julia wondered who had been the real disciplinarian—her father or her mother?

Julia had no doubts that her parents loved her, but they did not express positive emotions openly. The children usually knew when their behaviors were not acceptable, but they were never praised for having done things well. After graduation from high school Julia entered college. Her difficulty to focus on career goals led her to drop out in her first year, return home, and seek employment in an office. The values and beliefs formed in Julia's childhood had not prepared her for making decisions about her future. Nor did they help her in her relationships with men. She had learned that men had the power to make decisions that involve others, especially women. Men also seemed remote. To get along with men, one had to please and obey them. As could be expected, Julia's ill-fated relationships with men resulted in traumatic emotional consequences for her. Her belief in the effectiveness of punishment was again reinforced as she faced her penalties in those relationships.

Finally Julia met Bob, a sincere, quiet, hardworking young man. Although she was not passionately in love with him (by this time she did not allow herself to love any man), without knowing why, she felt comfortable with Bob. There was no doubt about who would make the decisions. Bob was goal-oriented and money-conscious. There were times when Julia was not sure that Bob really loved her because he was not outwardly affectionate. Though she may not have been aware of Bob's tender feelings for her, she soon learned to know when he was not happy. His way of dealing with disappointments was to withdraw into silence. Julia came to fear his silence and did everything she could think of to please him.

In therapy, Julia learned to recognize how her anxiety attacks were based on the patterns she had developed in childhood in response to the delayed punishment process practiced by her parents. Once she understood this and was able to remind herself that she responded according to old patterns in current situations, she experienced significant reduction in frequency and intensity of the felt anxiety. So far, clinically, treatment could be regarded as successful.

However, as the anxiety subsided, feelings of anger surfaced. Initially the anger was directed at her parents, but Julia realized that they had done the best they knew how. She was not a vindictive person, and blaming her parents now would not help her mature in her emotional responses; it would only impair her current relationship with them. Then she recognized that her anger was aimed at herself and at Bob. She was angry with him because he did not encourage her to consider her own needs. He did not support her in attempts to find her own gratification, to develop interests and activities that would lead to increased self-confidence. Bob not only refused to participate in her therapy sessions, but he resented the time and money spent on these sessions.

In an attempt to promote Bob's understanding for her situation, Julia bought and displayed self-help books, particularly those written by feminist authors. Some of the books were disappointing when she observed that the case histories used to describe women's struggle for identity, equality, and independence focused mainly on successful career women. Nobody seemed interested in the struggles of a woman who is "just working to supplement the man's income," she complained bitterly. She felt that because she did not have a glamorous job and did not earn "big" money, her struggles were of no interest to anyone. The moments of bitterness and self-pity gradually gave way to increased determination about changing her attitudes and behaviors.

Anita: Doing More of the Same and Expecting Different Results

Anita grew up in a small California town as the youngest of four siblings. With her curly, blond hair and big blue eyes her father considered her to be the prettiest of the children and called her his little princess. Because of the father's heavy drinking, the family's financial situation was unstable. Anita's father was moody and quick-tempered. His wife and children had come to fear his unpredictable verbally and physically violent outbursts. However, he never beat Anita. She remembered that her father often took her along when running errands or shopping. On those occasions he proudly presented her to the store owners and clerks. The people admired her and often had small gifts for her. At other times, her father's purchases turned out to be real bargains.

When Anita was 5 years old her father enrolled her in ballet lessons, although financially the family could ill afford it. He considered the lessons to be an investment because Anita's improved talents would be appreciated by her audience in the stores. Anita basked in the admiration of her public. She had more toys and prettier clothes than her older siblings, but she paid a price for it. Understandably, her siblings were envious of the special treatment she received, and they tried to punish her for it. Anita was never able to develop a close relationship with her siblings. Even her mother remained emotionally aloof in the way she interacted with her. Her father's attention not only prevented the natural bonding with the rest of her family members, it also resulted in her victimization when one of her older brothers sexually abused her. Anita thought her older sister knew about this but did not want to come to her rescue. When she tried to tell her mother, Anita was punished for making up such a lie just to get special attention.

Anita felt like a stranger in her family and adjusted to the admiration of strangers. When she was 10 years old she became a bit chubby. Her father remarked that she was becoming too fat for the ballet lessons and that the money could be put to better use. That ended her visits to the stores. She was no longer pretty enough to be on display.

As she ceased to be the "little princess", she learned the lesson that her beauty had been instrumental in having her father's protection and in receiving gifts and attention from others outside the family. This lesson marked the beginning of an eating disorder that she struggled with for several years.

In school, Anita's life seemed to duplicate her home life. She did not have to work hard. Her average intelligence and her good looks assured her kind considerations from many of her teachers. Just like at home, however, she had no close friends, especially not among the girls in her classes. As a result of her eating disorder, Anita had lost the excess weight and became popular with her male classmates. Because she did not have a circle of supportive friends, she yearned for someone who would protect her and take care of her. The star of the high school football team appeared like a good candidate for the job of protector. All the other girls envied her while she was dating him. She seemed to have resumed the special standing of her childhood. On one of their dates her boyfriend raped her. It is significant that Anita did not consider it rape—even though she had not consented to the sexual activities. She had come to believe that it was her price to pay for the attention she received from her male environment.

After losing her father's protection for the special place in the family, Anita felt insecure by herself. She had learned that she could not trust her mother or her older siblings. Even though her selection of a protector in high school had resulted in undesirable consequences, she was not willing to relinquish her search for other protectors. Blond and beautiful, she had no difficulty attracting men. As varied as the men in her line of boyfriends and lovers were, they had one thing in common—power. Whether it was physical, financial, or political power, Anita saw in each of these men a potential protector. Although she held a professional degree, she never considered herself a career woman or even a working woman. A wealthy businessman became her husband and official protector after she informed him about being pregnant by him. She gave birth to twin sons, and her future finally appeared safe and secure.

Anita was a good mother to her sons and a wonderful homemaker. Her husband spent time away from home on business trips. With the increase of her husband's trips, Anita felt bored and neglected. She longed for the excitement of being in the company of admiring males. A teenage girl in the neighborhood appeared to be acceptable as short-time baby-sitter when she went out with a mixed group of unattached females and males. Alcohol and marijuana were part of the group's social activities. When her husband discovered Anita's partying he divorced her and used his power to obtain full custody for their children by claiming that her substance abuse rendered her an unfit mother. Anita found herself without money, without a protector, and without her children, except for brief supervised visitations. In addition, her former husband was not only awarded custody of the children, but she was expected to pay child support to him from whatever salary she earned in future jobs.

What was Anita to do? She did what she thought worked best for her. Her personality structure included traits of an outdoing personality type. She wanted to be in control through others, especially men. In order to succeed she had to be better than others, mainly other women. After a brief period of employment she looked for a new protector. Her childhood experiences had demonstrated to her that powerful males were in a position to take care of less powerful females. She also craved the excitement of the male attention and admiration. Physical beauty and charm (or talents to entertain) were required attributes for female "trophy" status. Anita certainly possessed the beauty and charm to attract a wealthy or otherwise powerful man. What she had not considered in the past was that the powerful male can use the authority that comes with power to protect the female or he can employ that same power against her when the relationship is not of interest to him anymore. The decision to what end he will apply the control is his. By comparison, the power of beauty appears limited.

WHERE IS THE POWER IN DIVORCE CASES?

During divorce, power becomes more narrowly focused and one spouse may gain additional degrees of power. Emerging factors for increased power often favor the person who wants the divorce, especially if he or she has legitimate power or carries the moral or cultural perception of who should have the power. The individual may also benefit from "the shadow of the law," meaning a more favorable impact cast by the laws. With that the laws of divorce might cast a more favorable light on one partner regarding child support, alimony, or property division. The spouse who has a strong representative, such as a lawyer or other support people, and most significantly, the partner with the greater financial assets, has the advantage of power. Furthermore, Western society grants men greater power than women (Neumann, 1992).

In exploring important predictors of marital dissatisfaction and divorce, Sanchez and Gager (2000)—among other variables—considered the notion that decisions about divorce are more impacted by husbands' perceptions of marital dissatisfaction and their perceived relationship alternatives than by wives' dissatisfaction. Even though wives may feel dissatisfaction because of unfairness and disagreements, their greater fear about material costs of divorce lead them to suppress their dissatisfaction. Women who possess greater control over their own economic resources through their own careers, however, are expected to act on perceptions of inequality and dissatisfaction more readily. The results of the study indicated that, as expected, wives with traditional attitudes about marriage are less likely to divorce, whereas husbands subscribing to traditional attitudes are more likely to dissolve a marriage when they perceive dissatisfaction and relationship alternatives. The perception of dissatisfaction and awareness of options seem to foster an attitude of entitlement to a better relationship in traditional husbands. The implication here is that when both husbands and wives hold traditional attitudes, the wife's position is the more insecure. A situation that would describe Anita's case.

Anita is a devoted mother, and being separated from her sons is painful. She does not deserve the severe punishment that her former husband arranged for her. She thinks she has learned her lessons— but has she? So far she is doing more of what she did before, namely placing herself at the mercy of others, while expecting results different from those of the past.

Jane: Wanting to Be the Perfect Child

Growing up as one of twins can provide a framework for special attention for some individuals, but it can also create an environment of fierce competition for individualized attention and love. Jane's mother seemed to favor Jane's twin brother—at least, that is the way Jane remembers it. Her father was a quiet person who was gone a lot during the day, driving a vegetable truck. Her mother was critical and punishing. Jane was the frequent target of her mother's harsh physical punishments. Although Jane suffered the brunt of her mother's beatings, she did not turn against her brother, who got spared most of their mother's rage. Instead, Jane adopted an almost protective attitude toward her brother. Perhaps because of her mother's accusations that her brother's minor deformity was due to Jane's "crowding" him in the womb. Jane remembered her mother as being obsessed with her own beauty. She was proud of her little feet and hands and her curly hair.

Jane wanted to become a musician. She started piano, voice, diction, and dancing lessons when she was 4 years old. Her father, being interested in music himself, supported her training. In fact, he was proud of her accomplishments and took her along on some of his delivery trips in the neighborhood, where she sang for the people and collected pennies. She loved the applause because it gave her the acceptance she craved and did not get from her mother. Why wouldn't her mother love her? How would she have to be to earn her mother's love?

One day she saw a little girl visiting her grandparents who lived in Jane's neighborhood. From the interactions she observed between the little girl and her grandparents, Jane decided that this must be a much-loved child. This little girl should be her mother's daughter. She seemed to have what Jane did not have. Jane tried to become friends with the little girl and asked her to come to her house during her visits with her grandparents. A few weeks later the little girl was killed by a truck, possibly on her way to Jane's home. Jane felt as if it was her fault; it would not have happened if the girl had stayed at her grand-parent's house. Feelings of guilt were torturing her. To make up for the loss of the "perfect child," Jane became the Florence Nightingale of the playground, trying to redeem herself.

Jane's desire to please and to make up for her shortcomings result-ed in a chronically elevated level of anxiety, which interfered with her ability to maintain concentration on her studies. At the age of 17, medical complications made it impossible for her to sing. Not until she was in her 40s did her voice return after thyroid surgery. Her anxiety continued to impair her concentration and she dropped out of college. She moved to a big city, sharing a room in a women's lodge and started in her first office job. She did not like her job.

While still in college, she had met a young man in her drama class. He was interested in Irish playwrights and wrote very sensitive letters to Jane. Now that she had given up on her own goals she put her energies behind someone who had great dreams. They married when she was 21 years old. By then Jane's husband was in law school. He had hidden his drinking from her while they were dating. Jane at-tended church frequently, praying that she could become his salva-tion. She had given birth to three children, two daughters and one son. She did not work outside the home. Raising their three children and maintaining the home kept her busy. Her husband's parents paid his tuition as well as the family's rent and food bills. Although there was no money left over, her husband continued to drink and smoke expensive cigars.

After 11 years of marriage, Jane separated from her husband. He begged her to come back and have another child with him. He promised that he would stop drinking. Jane, still hoping that she could be instrumental in his salvation, returned and soon became pregnant with their fourth child, another boy. All during her pregnancy her husband continued to drink. Finally, her mother and aunt together managed to get Jane's husband out of the house. Jane found a low-paying job and got on welfare with the four children, ranging in age from 2 to 11 years.

In time, Jane remarried. Her second husband was also a lawyer whom she had met through her first husband. Although her second husband adopted her children, there were difficulties in adjustments of the new family. Her older son beat the youngest. He presented significant discipline problems in school and had to be placed in a home as a ward of the courts. Her youngest son became an alcoholic, with a drinking history that began at age 14 years. Her oldest daughter turned against Jane. The relationship to her children was strained; perhaps because she had never learned any mothering skills from her own mother. When Jane's mother died, her children managed to get a hold of Jane's inheritance without leaving a penny of it for her.

Jane is one of the women who volunteered her story for this book. Her children had been in counseling and Jane also participated in therapy for herself in addition to being involved in AA. In her 40s she briefly returned to college. She has carved out a place for herself but it is not an independent place. She belongs to a women's symphony society through which she derives satisfaction and pleasure. She is still living with her second husband in the same house that her first husband purchased. She is not happy about that—there are many painful memories—but she is accepting her environment and is trying to assert herself within it. She stopped trying to be anybody's salvation and refuses to accept the blame for her youngest son's alcoholism whenever he contacts her in his intoxicated state.

Anita's and Jane's histories contain similarities. Both were encouraged by their fathers to perform for small audiences and both cherished the admiration and attention that was bestowed upon them. As girls, neither was able to form a close relationship with the mother or any other female in their environment. Although Jane attempted to befriend another little girl, the girl's death prevented the development of an ongoing relationship and in addition imposed severe guilt feelings on Jane, which seemed to have been instrumental in her tendency to become a savior to others in her search for redemption. Neither woman could envision her future as an independent person, both relied on the presence of men for their livelihood—both paid a price for it.

Inge: Looking for the Perfect Other Half

Inge grew up in Europe as the older of two sisters. Her parents' marriage was not happy, and Inge's mother let the daughters know that she stayed in the marriage as a sacrifice to her children. Apparently, Inge was the reason for the marriage. Her mother had been pregnant with her and blamed her for her unhappiness. The younger daughter became their mother's favorite. Inge could not please her mother and she was often the target of her mother's harsh punishment.

Inge escaped the misery by marrying just before her 18th birthday with her father's permission. Eventually she and her husband left their native European country to start a new life in America. Several years and four children later, she admitted to herself that she was not happy in her marriage. She remained married and put her energies into raising her children and improving her professional career. Life was acceptable, though not exciting. Although married, her extraordinary beauty attracted a circle of male admirers. She managed to keep them interested but at a respectable distance. When she met David, the "love of her life," she divorced her husband. The divorce settlement left her with little more than joint custody of her children. Her husband had helped himself to most of the family's assets.

Believing that true love conquers all, Inge and David married after a brief intense courtship. A few weeks into the marriage problems surfaced. Inge demanded repeated reassurance from David that he would always be there for her. David, who never had children, had a difficult time adjusting to the new lifestyle. David spent time with his friends and Inge felt neglected. She thought that David had not followed through on some of his promises. When gentle reminders were unsuccessful she became angry. Because she was afraid that David would leave her if she complained, she kept quiet. But her anger built up to the point where she could not control it and she blurted out a whole list of grievances. David was shocked, he thought he had committed himself to the marriage and had done his best. Although his feelings were hurt, they made up and everything seemed fine for a while. However, Inge's anger flared up periodically. The intervals of bliss and happiness became increasingly shorter until David moved out. Inge felt abandoned and filed for divorce. David did not contest the divorce, and in less than six months the marriage was dissolved.

Inge and David still had strong feelings for each other. They started dating again and had wonderful times together but did not resolve any of their difficulties. Inge wanted to get married again but David refused to make such a commitment because basically nothing had changed. David's resistance again triggered Inge's anger. Following her latest anger outburst, Inge descended into a state of agitated depression. Following discharge from the hospital she was referred to outpatient therapy. Looking at Inge's story, her dependence on a man is not that obvious—certainly not to herself. In her first marriage, she spent time in pursuing her own goals, probably because she was not emotionally committed to her husband. Only when she met David and through their marital difficulties did her fear of abandonment surface.

Helen: The Angry Victim

Helen, a medium blonde, plain-looking woman in her early 30s, was referred to therapy because of debilitating anger and resentment that interfered with her daily functioning at work and in her social life and seemed to contribute to some of her physical difficulties. She attributed her anger to her divorce and her former husband. Helen had always been a hard worker. She was very frugal and managed to purchase a small house in the country. Soon after the wedding, her husband, George, quit his job. Helen was now the sole breadwinner. George explored different career options but did not exert himself unduly in his job search. Helen was tired when she returned from work, but the meal preparation and cleaning were tasks still waiting for her to be done. At the end of the day, she was exhausted and could not muster much energy or desire for sexual activities. Her rested young husband, on the other hand, possessed a healthy sex drive. After some initial times of compliance with his wishes, Helen fought her husband's forceful advances off when she felt too tired. George took his wounded pride and hurt feelings to other, more willing young women in the community.

When one of the women reported that she was pregnant by Helen's husband, Helen initiated divorce proceedings. The divorce swallowed whatever savings Helen had. She was barely able to keep her little house for herself. As she bitterly complained, she came out of the marriage much poorer than she had entered it. Her husband had taken advantage of her. She vowed that she would never let that happen again. Soon her anger received additional fuel from another source. Her father.

Helen grew up on a farm. Every family member worked hard. Helen and her older sister Nancy did not have much time for play or school work. When Helen was 12 years old her father started to force himself on her. She was afraid to stay alone in the house and asked her mother to assign her outside chores. But her mother insisted that at her age she was the one to stay in the house doing chores while at the same time keeping an eye on her younger sister. The older and stronger family members had to work in the fields. Without being able to pinpoint why, Helen knew she could not say more to her mother.

Besides visits when he could leave the field without causing suspicion, her father started his regular nighttime visits to her bedroom for intercourse. It was not every night. She learned to listen for and to dread her father's footsteps as he came up the stairs to where the children's bedrooms were. Her parents' bedroom was downstairs. Sometimes as she tensely anticipated her bedroom door to open, nothing happened. She held her breath and finally went to sleep, relieved. One night she thought she heard her father's steps continuing down the hall to her sister's room. She watched and listened for several weeks until she was certain that her father visited both his daughters on different nights. Away from the house, she talked to her sister and found out that for years Nancy also had been sexually abused by their father. It had started and progressed very much as it did with Helen. Helen asked whether Nancy had talked to their mother about it. Nancy, more timid than Helen, said she had tried but their mother had either not understood or not listened.

When Helen was almost 18 years old she started dating and the sexual abuse stopped. There were never any verbal interchanges between her and her father, except for his saying that "it was all right and she needed to obey." Around this time her older sister Nancy was getting ready to leave the home. She had found a job in another town. Before she left, Nancy and Helen discussed what to do about the safety of their youngest sister, Lisa. They were in a quandary: they knew their mother would not be of any help yet they thought Lisa was still too young to be told. They decided that Helen would confront their father and warn him that they would expose him if he tried to abuse Lisa. Her father firmly reminded her that he had stopped his sexual activities with her, and she believed him.

After Nancy's move everything seemed normal. But Helen could not forget their father's incestuous behavior and before she got married and moved into her little house, she took it upon herself to warn Lisa who was then about 16 years old. To Helen's surprise, Lisa did not respond as strongly to her warning as she had expected. After her divorce, Helen's father came to visit her in her house. He proceeded to make sexual advances, and when Helen refused, he stated that having been married she surely was used to having regular sexual intercourse. Now that she was deprived of it, he was there to help.

After the initial shock wore off, Helen decided to have another talk with Lisa and with her mother. Lisa was still living at home and had just graduated from high school. To everyone's surprise her parents had given their youngest daughter a car for her graduation.

Helen's mother said she would talk to the father about the alleged sexual abuse. The father denied the accusation, and Helen's mother said she believed her husband. She added that even if it had happened it was not a "big deal," indicating that she herself may have been a victim of sexual abuse when she was growing up. Helen talked again to Lisa who did not say much but had this strange smile on her face. Suddenly Helen knew how Lisa had gotten the shiny red car for her graduation. Helen's mother suggested that Helen not join them for the holiday meal at Christmas. The accusations that she had brought against her father had aroused tension in the family. Lisa was dating a nice boy from their community who would be a guest, and Helen's presence would interfere with the harmony of the family Christmas dinner.

Incidence of sexual abuse in rural areas may be equal to that in cities, but perpetrators are more protected in the country because of isolation. Thus they may be able to continue the abuse without interference from others (Foxhall, 2000). Helen's father sexually abused his daughters for years without interference from anyone because the mother did not want to acknowledge it overtly. When Helen wanted to bring it out into the open, she was banished from family meetings. Those who knew—her parents and her two sisters—turned against Helen and told her that they would never publicly admit that the abuse had occurred. Finally, Helen, being ostracized from her family, felt she also had to leave the family church and the community. In general, rural communities hold more difficulties for women than urban areas do. Due to the combination of fewer employment opportunities with fewer resources, such as child care or extended education facilities, rural women are more likely to have unpaid employment in family businesses and are more dependent on the few available resources—no matter what the conditions.

Ann: Love as Healing Power

Ann, the middle of five siblings, learned the importance of being financially independent as her parents struggled to provide for the family. Although there was love and caring in the home, it was difficult for Ann to gain the attention she wanted. She felt that her position in the birth order placed her at a disadvantage. She had an older brother and an older sister and a younger brother and a younger sister. Her parents put their pride into treating the children in an equal manner, but that did not diminish Ann's desire to be special in some way. She applied herself in school and made good grades, hoping her parents would give her special praise. But again, even her grades were in the middle when compared with those of the rest of her siblings. In fact, her parents seemed to consider this a sign of the children's healthy adjustment—they were all achieving equally well.

Ann prepared herself for financial independence by studying to be a nurse and later obtained a graduate degree in business administration. She did well professionally and found a promising position with a pharmaceutical company. She remained loyal to her siblings and the female friends she had made in college. Her social life was active, but her relationships with men were unremarkable. Although she wanted to get married and have a family, the right man just did not seem to come along. She was in her early 30s when she met a young man to whom she felt attracted. He was quiet and reserved and did not talk much about himself, except to say that he was divorced. He added that his former wife had lost interest in him and probably never loved him. He sounded depressed when he talked about it, so Ann did not press him for more details.

Their relationship progressed to the point where Robert asked Ann to marry him. Ann was happy; it had been worth waiting for the right man. Their values seemed compatible. Both wanted children and it seemed reasonable to start planning for the wedding. They would get married in Ann's church, and Ann's parents would provide for a small wedding reception. There were no disagreements about the guest list— everything seemed to proceed smoothly.

Following their engagement, Ann found out that Robert's first marriage had ended because of physical violence. One of Ann's friends had a cousin who knew Robert's first wife, and the friend felt obligated to tell Ann what little she knew about it. Ann couldn't believe what she heard, but she decided to discuss the information with Robert. He admitted that he had pushed his wife once. According to his report, he was so frustrated because his wife was only concerned with her career and did not care about him. She refused to settle down and have children. In his frustration he did not know what to do anymore. He pushed her only once and only to get away from her when she was standing in the doorway.

In Ann's mind his report was congruent with what Robert had told her previously about his first marriage. She hugged him and reassured him that she loved him and promised him that her love would help heal his old wounds. The wedding progressed as planned. Ann did not tell Robert that she had been offered a promotion to district manager. The promotion would have required a geographical move. Ann thought if she told him about the promotion, Robert would be reminded of his previous disappointment when his first wife placed her career before him. Two years later she found herself with a black eye after a "discussion" with Robert.

Ann's personality type contained facets of achieving traits; she tended to be competitive without being critical of others. Her desires for recognition did not result in a critical attitude toward her siblings. However, in wanting to be special, she was attempting to outdo Robert's first wife when she believed his explanations instead of obtaining additional information. This trait combined with the pleasing characteristics that emerged when she sacrificed her promotion in order not to hurt her husband's feelings proved to be damaging.

Cindy: The Goal to Have "Presence"

Cindy grew up as the youngest of three daughters. There was a considerable age gap between her and her two older sisters. Both of her sisters were beautiful; one had inherited their father's reddish blond hair and fair complexion and the other had their mother's dark hair with a reddish tint to it. Her skin was also fair and in striking contrast to her large brown eyes. Cindy described her own hair as "dishwater blond" and her eyes were of a grayish blue color. Cindy complained to her mother that her sisters apparently had depleted their parents' pool of beauty genes and not much was left for Cindy. Her mother's unsuccessful attempt to comfort her by saying, "plain girls make better wives" was not exactly what Cindy had wanted to hear. Except for the envy of her sisters' beauty, Cindy's childhood was unremarkable. Her grades in school were good and her behavior was satisfactory. Her college years were equally unremarkable. She graduated with a bachelor's degree in business, including a minor in psychology.

Cindy never stood out in any way. Her voice was soft and monotone. She spoke rather rapidly as if she were in a hurry to get it over with. Her clothes were congruent with the fashion of the time, but usually in subdued colors. Her dating experiences were about as unremarkable as the rest of her life had been so far. Her job did not hold much excitement, either. Cindy was intelligent, reliable, and performed well on her job, yet she was not given as much responsibility as her training qualified her for. She often felt like a glorified secretary.

One day Cindy saw an announcement in the newspaper about a series of seminars. The one with the title "Taking Control of Your Life" attracted her attention. The presenter was a local psychologist. When Cindy told the psychologist that her goal was to have "presence" instead of fading into the background as she had done most of her life, the psychologist suggested that Cindy participate in an ongoing group.

THE GROUP: INTRODUCTION

Tuesday evening marks the first meeting of the women's therapy group. Three young women sit around one end of the oval conference table that is situated in the center of the room. Four others occupy chairs along the sides of the table with empty seats between them. Another young woman hesitantly enters the room. She seems undecided where to place herself. Hushed voices and nervous laughter can be heard. It is the awkward atmosphere that is characteristic when strangers meet for the first time. Everybody seems relieved when the therapist appears, followed by two more women, who walk in the exaggerated quiet way that people adopt when they are embarrassed about being late.

The setting for the meeting is unusual, considering the central position occupied by the large, oval conference table. There are no additional chairs along the sides of the room; every participant is forced to choose a seat around the table. The arrangement was selected by the therapist, based on earlier experiments about the effectiveness of various seating arrangements on participants' involvement. At least in the early stages of a group experience, clients prefer a degree of protection that furniture like a table provides. They feel less exposed physically and find it easier to disclose on an emotional level while in the partial cover of the table. Also, the round or oval shape of a table functions to pull people together in discussions.

The therapist, after introducing herself, explains to the participants that they are in charge of confidentiality about the topics of discussion within the group. As every woman values confidential consideration of her personal issues, she is expected to extend that same respect to the other group members. Then the therapist invites group members to introduce themselves.

Jody, an attractive young woman, speaks first. She introduces herself as the mother of four children and the wife of a good, hardworking husband. Her high-pitched voice betrays the anxiety she feels when talking about herself. She nervously clenches and unclenches her hands, attempting to hide her fingernails that are bitten down to the quick. Her speech trails and stops in a hesitating way. As she perceives the questioning expressions on the faces of the other group members, she continues hesitantly, saying that she is trying to find out about herself and what she would want to do with her life besides raising her children. Almost apologizing she adds, "I know, having my wonderful family should be enough to fill my life, but I am restless, like I am missing something."

The astute observer understands that Jody is not used to making statements. Periods or exclamation marks do not exist in her language. Her sentences seem to end in question marks—even though they are not meant to be questions. Her speech betrays her low level of self-confidence. Major personality characteristics appear to be avoidance of conflict and a general lack of assertiveness.

Julia, a slim, young woman, nods her head toward Jody as she introduces herself as the mother of two healthy young children. She smiles and tries to reassure Jody when she says, "I thought, too, that having a good husband and children should be all I wanted in life. I have even been fortunate in my employment. I work in an office with very nice people. But I was restless—or rather anxious—and did not know why. My parents think I should be grateful for having such a wonderful family. As much as I love my children, there seems to be nothing for me personally."

Ann, a tall, young woman, continues in an angry-sounding voice. "I wished I had a family and a good husband. At least, I would be special to him and I wouldn't have to be here. I am divorced." Her voice indicates that she is not willing to say more about herself at this time. Her folded arms in front of her chest give her a defensive stance. Anita, a beautiful blonde, talks directly to Ann, "I understand your feelings; a family is important. I am the mother of twin boys. I lost them."

"Oh, I am so sorry, did they die?" Inge, a woman of dramatic beauty with short, black hair, looking like a model for successful female executives in her elegant business suit, inquires with sympathy. "I am the mother of four children. I don't know what I would do if one of them died." Anita seems to withdraw into herself as she answers, "No, they did not die. My ex-husband has custody of them. I guess that makes me a bad mother," she adds defiantly. For a moment silence looms heavily. Finally Inge comes to the rescue again. "I left my children's father for another man. I feel very guilty about it. Our marriage was not happy, but I should have stayed with him for the children's sake.

He never lets me forget it. He does not pay child support on a regular basis. When the children are with him he lets them do what they want, no discipline. I have to work twice as hard afterward and they don't like it. When anything goes wrong he blames me for it. My mother is on his side. I guess that makes me a bad mother, too."

A young woman with strawberry blond hair speaks next, "I am Liz, I am divorced, no children. I live on my own but would like to have a family. I have been dating several men, but nothing has really connected."

The next person to introduce herself is a plain-looking woman in her early 30s. She looks uncomfortable and seems determined to say as little as possible about herself. Her lips hardly move and she looks straight ahead without making eye contact with anyone as she introduces herself as Helen, a divorced woman without children. She turns her face to the young woman to her left, nodding and indicating that it is her turn to speak. Cindy, a small young woman, looks embarrassed as she says her name. She informs the group that she has no children, has never been married, and really does not have any "big problems." When she notices the questioning expressions on the faces of the other women, she adds in a murmur, "I seem to be invisible to others, nobody notices me and I don't want to live like that for the rest of my life." A silence follows her words. The therapist looks at the woman who had been quiet until now. She smiles at her and nods her head encouragingly.

Betty is the last one to speak. She is a bit older than the other women in the group. Her dark hair shows some gray streaks and her brown eyes reflect a mixture of sadness and anger. "I am the mother of two sons but they are grown. My husband and I worked hard all our lives and started a little business. In addition, I worked as a part-time bookkeeper. All the money we ever made either went into the business or toward the education of our sons. We never took a vacation. There was neither time nor money for it. Now that my sons are on their own, my husband took up with a younger woman and kicked me out. Instead of earning some of the fruits of our hard labor, I have to start all over. Although I am a partner in the business, it is not a 50–50 ownership and my ex-husband makes it very difficult for me to discuss the business with him. He wants me out of it with as little compensation as possible." With her voice and facial expression Betty gives the impression of an angry victim. Her facial expression is similar to Helen's.

The therapist thanked the members for their contributions and their listening to one another. She indicated that although talking about personal matters to people one has not known previously may be uncomfortable, all came here to explore and hopefully resolve some important issues in their lives. Therefore, it would be beneficial for each woman to prepare something of an agenda about topics to discuss and bring it to the next meeting. She suggested that members might want to use a notebook for their own questions as well as for taking notes during the group process.

Ending this first session, the therapist explained that the group process would follow a certain pattern. As members had been invited to think about issues they wanted to discuss, it would be helpful if they thought about these issues as challenges rather than problems. The therapist explained that the notion of "challenges" evokes the idea of a stimulating, provocative, or interesting task, inviting the person to engage in efforts that lead to the task's solution. The implication is that the person has the ability to manage the task. The word "problem," on the other hand, connotes a source of perplexity or distress, something that is difficult to handle. It may even reflect on the person as being "problematic" or incapable of coping. While the task may indeed be difficult, we want to assume that we are capable of working on resolving it.

Once the nature of the challenge has been defined, attention will be given to explorations of various options. When decisions have been made regarding which options to use, actions are the vehicle to bring about solutions to the challenge. The therapist summarized that important steps in the process are challenges, options, decisions, and actions—C-O-D-A. Jody, who had been the first of the group members to speak in this introductory session replied, "CODA, I remember that from my piano lessons, it is the end of a piece of music. I like that— at least, I won't forget it." The therapist, nodding her head in agreement, expressed her appreciation for Jody's perceptive analysis. "Yes, just like the concluding part of a musical or a literary work, these steps or components are formally distinct from the main structure of a person's life, but they serve to round out the balance within a person's world. At our next meeting we will start looking at the challenges that face us and exploring the options that may lead us to the fulfillment of our wishes and dreams."

GROUP PROCESS: INTRODUCTION

The first meeting of the group was characterized by the members' caution about what and how much to disclose of their backgrounds— as would be expected in settings such as this. Some of the women

ventured out a bit more with their introductions, whereas others remained less involved on the surface. The larger than usual group size
may have enabled some members to hold back with disclosing personal information. For the therapist, involvement of all group members
becomes a more difficult task with an increasing number of participants. At the end of the meeting, the therapist delineated guidelines
for the progression of the group process.

SUMMARY

This chapter described the lives of several women. Some have been
clients engaged in psychotherapy, others are women in the general
community who have volunteered to tell their stories. Regardless of
the sources of the stories, there are significant parallels. Influences
from the past have impacted the lives of these women in different
ways, and each has dealt with those influences in her particular manner. Some were able to resolve their difficulties independently or with
the help of friends, others have developed their new lifestyles within the
safe boundaries of a therapist's office, and some are still struggling.

The chapter closes with the introduction of a women's therapy group
participants. A few of the women were introduced earlier in this chapter, others appear for the first time in the group session. The group
members' struggles and their growth are traced through the following
chapters, illustrating how each of them arrives at a point of resolution
that is characteristic for her.

QUESTIONS FOR CONSIDERATION

As we have seen, there are parallels in Anita's, Jane's, and other wom-
en's histories, but Jane's story raises additional questions: What is the
attraction to be somebody's salvation? Is it power? Is it vanity? Is it
insurance against abandonment? What are the consequences if the
targeted person does not achieve deliverance? What is the savior's
fate—no salvation, no redemption?

Women's attraction to men of power: Is it biologically determined
because in the past the woman needed a powerful partner to protect
her and her children from predators?

RECOMMENDED READINGS

Neumann, D. (1992). How mediation can effectively address the male-female power imbalance in divorce. *Mediation Quarterly, 9,* 227–239.

> *Mediation in divorce cases may or may not be empowering women in the division of assets.*

CHAPTER THREE

Challenges: Searching for Meaning

T
he search for meaning or purpose or significance in life has occupied philosophers for centuries. Early philosophers asked the questions "What is the nature of being or existence?" or "What does it mean to be?" Their answers were "Existence is the attainment of possibilities" or stated differently, the actualization of human potentialities (Girvetz, Geiger, Hantz, & Morris, 1966).

MEANING: AN EXISTENTIAL QUESTION AND A PERSONAL QUESTION

Although, strictly speaking, "meaning," "significance," and "purpose" have slightly different connotations, they are used interchangeably in everyday usage relating to existential questions. According to Yalom (1980), a search for meaning indicates a search for coherence, whereas "purpose" implies intention and function. Significance is intertwined with a sense of personal power that helps individuals to integrate the self and in relations with others. Human beings need some sense of their own significance to exist (May, 1972). Albert Camus considered the question of life's meaning to be the most urgent question because people die or give up if life is empty or not worth living. To wake up with feelings of emptiness and aimlessness and to face days without meaning and a sense of direction leads to overwhelming boredom and sufferings that resemble depression or melancholia.

The literal meaning of the word "existence" is "to emerge, to stand out" and existentialism means centering on the existing person that is emerging or becoming. In psychology and psychotherapy, the existential approach maintains that we cannot leave will and decision to chance. Self-consciousness, people's awareness of their individual experiences, includes the element of decision (May, 1960).

What is the meaning of life? is a question about life in general and its meaning within the universe. The field of philosophy is a likely area to search for answers to this question. "What is the meaning or purpose of my life?" is a question that reflects the concern of individuals about functions and goals that apply to them individually. To find answers to questions of personal or individual meaning, the areas of peoples' search include cultural and social structures, religion, and history—among others.

INTERPRETATION OF EXPERIENCES

Individuals continuously search for and forge meanings and understandings about their particular purposes. How they learn to discern meaning and to construct and interpret their experiences develops from their own place within the company of others in their societies, within the limits of their unique individual histories and memories. Thus, people will generally agree with some of the roles their social environment has determined for them but will look in different places for their individual sense of purpose.

Anderson and Hayes (1996) developed the concept of a framework of life-ties, a set of related experiences and the perceptions evoked by these experiences. The authors explored how people shape and integrate their identities and self-worth within this framework of influential life-ties. They reported their findings to imply that for both women and men, self-worth is connected to achievement and work-related activities and that education is a critical component of self-esteem. According to the authors, among women, intimate relationships did not seem to be a primary source of self-esteem and self-definition. This finding appears to be incongruent with past and present observations; indeed, historical accounts report otherwise.

MEANING THROUGH MOTHERHOOD

Historically, women's life purpose has been defined primarily in the biosocial context of motherhood and secondarily as helpers and companions to men. Although less so now than in the past, women's answer for purpose and meaning is found in motherhood. Even late-nineteenth-century feminists, while considering women to be

morally superior to men, indicated that no woman was complete without the experience of motherhood (Langer, 1996). The message is
regrettable for two reasons: First, assigning superiority to any gender
serves to widen the already existing gap between men and women.
Second, it appears to tell women what their purpose should be without considering their privilege of self-determination, and it results in
unhappiness in those who are not able to achieve the 'fundamental
defining experience of motherhood.'

Giving birth to another human being has many meaningful facets.
For those who choose motherhood their role is expanded to that of
mother, carrying with it new responsibilities and new rewards. Children also may serve as an extension of the self, representing a kind of
immortality. In addition, the human infant is helpless when entering
this world. For any woman who wants to be needed, this is the purest
opportunity to fulfill the desire. At the same time, the new mother
may see herself as contributing not only to her family but also to the
world at large by raising healthy and well-adjusted children who can
serve society's future needs.

EXPECTATIONS ABOUT MOTHERHOOD

Laurie Wagner (1998) interviewed women concerning their expectations about motherhood. Many women expect that a child will make
them feel more womanly because they have been told so by others.
Other women experience difficulties and resentment when they realize that they have to trade in the carefree part of themselves for more
responsible behaviors. A few other women seem to compete with their
own mothers—or mothers-in-law—by promising themselves to be better mothers than they were. Still others regard motherhood as a transition from a state of selfishness to honoring home and family by
taking care of the family. It is noteworthy that prior to motherhood
many women mentioned selfishness and considering themselves as
having been a taker who needs to become a nurturer. If women had
not been conditioned to the nurturing role, would they have had
similar considerations or would they have continued with their carefree lifestyles free from doubts?

Perhaps the saddest situation was conveyed by this woman's statement: "Not being able to get pregnant really messes up your mind and
does a real number to your self-esteem" (Wagner, 1998, p. 55). She
went on to report her experiences as part of a group of couples that
were on the waiting list for adoptable babies. Apparently, the birth-

mothers were given pictures of all the hopeful couples and the birth-mothers were the ones to decide which couple would be the lucky one to receive a baby. Every time one of the couples was selected for a baby, the other couples felt rejected. Some couples faced rejection more than once. Intense competition developed among the couples.

INFERTILITY AND EMOTIONAL CONSEQUENCES

Certainly, the existence of children can enrich the lives of couples, and the desire for children can be a natural outgrowth of the love two people have for each other. Another question is, can their love sustain the absence of children. Gender differences in coping with infertility have been observed. Because women carry most of the burden of undergoing medical examinations and monitoring their menstrual cycles, women tend to assume more responsibility and often feelings of guilt about their childless state. Men in general demonstrate less emotional response compared with women and appear ready to agree with their wives in attributing the reasons for the infertility to them—even when the diagnosis was related to male rather than female factors (Gibson & Myers, 2000).

Domar and Dreher (1996) assessed a group of 338 women with infertility problems and a control group of 39 healthy women on several measures of depression. The infertile women showed significantly more depression than the control group. Individuals who stay focused on and ruminate about the causes of their depressing circumstances generally remain depressed for a longer period of time than those who shift their focus to other things, such as contemplating different goals. When people cannot achieve important goals in their life and are not able or willing to abandon them, the depression can lead to a situation of learned helplessness (Martin & Tesser, 1989).

INVESTMENTS IN INFERTILITY TREATMENT

A recent Canadian survey involving 65 heterosexual couples who had been seeking medical assistance for fertility difficulties showed that for 83% of them the value of having children was strongly reinforced in their families of origin (Daniluk, 2001). The age of the participants ranged from 26 years to 55 years with a mean of 37 years. On the average they had been trying to conceive for 7 years and had spent approximately 5 years in their attempts for medical assistance in producing a child. Following the lack of success of available treatment options, 55% of the couples had become parents through adoption, 14% were still registered with adoption agencies, and 14% decided to remain childless.

Interviews conducted to explore the couples' attitudes about their experiences of infertility treatments demonstrated that in all cases action to seek medical treatment was initiated by the female partners who held high expectations for successful treatment. When frustrations mounted after a period of time working with their family physicians, again, females were the ones to insist on referrals to fertility specialists. Although most of the couples had a basic understanding of the efforts required to participate in treatment, most of them were not prepared for the actual investment in time, money, and energy they had expanded in the pursuit of having a child. The participants described how they had experienced an emotional roller coaster month after month, year after year, until finally the realization set in that they were not going to be able to fulfill their dreams of having children. There was bitterness, anger, thoughts of unfairness; yet when asked if they would do it all over again if they had a chance—except for one couple—all replied that they would do it again. The couple that regretted their treatment search had completely exhausted their life savings on pursuing high-tech interventions such as in vitro fertilization and was now financially unable to qualify for adoption. In addition to describing the tremendous emotional turmoil that the participants struggled through, the findings of the survey showed that for making treatment decisions, husbands and wives were not equally invested in the pursuit of every available option.

SPOUSES' REACTIONS TO THE STRESS OF INFERTILITY

Domar and Dreher (1996) described the consequences of infertility on a young couple's happiness. Apparently, both husband and wife were almost obsessed with wanting to become parents. Nothing else in their life seemed to matter. Their whole sex life revolved around attempts to produce a baby. Faithfully recorded temperature charts showed the windows of opportunity for conception. Sexual activities during the specified times became a chore rather than a pleasure. When pregnancy did not occur after a year and a half of determined efforts, the young wife started to question whether her husband was the right person for her.

This story is not an isolated one. The records of clinics for treatment of sexual dysfunction include difficulties similar to those described above. The presenting problems are reported by the men as failure to obtain or sustain an erection. Although both partners appear for treatment after physical reasons for the infertility have been ruled out, it soon becomes the man's problem. Wives, who regard children as their life's fulfillment, diligently keep track of the opportune times and expect their partners to be able to engage in sexual intercourse at those times. For some men, the responsibility for guaranteed parenthood on demand at specific times of the month is too much to tolerate. Performance anxiety renders them incapable of achieving sufficient erections. For Henry, now in his 50s, the traumatic experience of repeated attempts to have sexual intercourse at the prescribed times, and the repeated failures, have left him with a lack of sexual desire. This condition has endured even after the couple adopted two children and the performance demand was reduced.

It is not surprising that some men resent the assignment to "baby machine." As one husband expressed his feelings, "When we got married I believed that my wife loved me for myself. Sure, I would like to have children, but if it does not happen, am I not worth keeping around?" Another man echoed similar sentiments, "We had a difficult time conceiving our first child. Lori, my wife, was determined to become a mother. She kept track of the times that were best for conception and told me right after I came home from work. I love her and wanted the best for us. We had sex whenever she decided. After our son was born her interest in sex diminished. She was always too tired. Now she wants another child and she expects me to perform just like before. I dread coming home; the pressure is too much. If we have another child, will her interest in sex decline again as it did before? I wonder what she thinks of me as a person."

Tim and Joan: Desired Motherhood and Performance Anxiety

Tim and Joan had difficulties conceiving. Joan always believed that motherhood is the highest level for a woman to aspire to—the ultimate fulfillment. Joan and Tim have a happy marriage and, until recently, had a satisfying sex life. Both agreed on wanting children. Tim's difficulty with achieving erections at this time came as a surprise for both of them. Joan thought that she might not be attractive enough anymore. Tim expressed his feelings by saying: "When it did not happen naturally it made sense to be more organized about it. I am glad Joan went through all the trouble of keeping those temperature charts. But when she tells me about the opportune time I feel I have to perform. Seeing her disappointment when it doesn't work is difficult for me to handle. Being a mother means so much to her. And now I am standing in the way of her reaching it. I would not want to deprive Joan of motherhood. I thought we might be able to adopt a child if she does not want to give up on me. I love her and want to make her happy."

By making conception more important than their feelings for each other, Tim and Joan had eliminated their previously experienced enjoyment in sexual activities and turned it into a demand and a chore. The responsibility for having erections at designated times in order to reach their goal left Tim with disabling anxiety. The spouses' strong feelings for each other helped them to consider alternatives, which could be expected to alleviate Tim's performance anxiety. When a goal is impossible to attain, people can move on by either abandoning it or by finding an appropriate substitute. By doing so, they search for new meanings in the process of reappraising their options and coping with the stress of the event (Park & Folkman, 1997).

The pain and stress are real for those who struggle under the baby-making mind-set. It is interesting—perhaps ironic—to read about comparisons of some aspects of sexual behaviors in developing and in Western countries (Osman & Al-Sawaf, 1995). It was the authors' opinion that in developing countries male sexual potency and fertility are highly valued attributes as they impact on rates of procreation. Cultural and social pressures, often based on myths or folklore, regulate socially sanctioned sexual behaviors. As consequence, males become highly anxious about their sexual potency regarding frequency and resulting pregnancies. In Western countries, due to the absence of stereotypical socially sanctioned sexual activities, the authors predicted a shift of concerns to emotional and pleasure-related factors. Anxieties in Western countries therefore would be expected to focus on desire and orgasm.

Jody: When Motherhood Is Not Enough

Jody, the attractive young mother of four children and one of the group members, saw motherhood as her life's purpose. Although she went to college and obtained an advanced degree, it was less for career purposes than for preparation as a well-educated mother for her children. She grew up as the oldest of four siblings. Her first marriage to a domineering husband was short-lived. His intelligence had attracted her, but when his intelligence turned into biting sarcasm her feelings cooled substantially. Her natural beauty and pleasant disposition attracted many male admirers. Despite her early experience with her husband, she always chose men for their intelligence. She married another intelligent and domineering man—fortunately, without the tendency for sarcasm. After 10 years of marriage, Jody came to the clinic with the presenting problem of lack of sexual desire.

Ther.: As you mentioned on the intake form, you have little interest in sexual activities. Is that a recent occurrence or is it of some duration?

Jody: With my husband it has been a problem for several years, although it was different in the beginning. Now most of the time I just let him have sex after he has complained for weeks. I don't think I really ever had a strong sex drive. At the beginning of relationships, it was more an excitement about the person I was with than real sexual desire. I always looked up to the men I dated. Their smartness was exciting and I wanted to please them. I was also afraid that they would leave me when they found out that I was not as intelligent as they thought.

Ther.: How did you feel in those relationships?

Jody: I was anxious; I couldn't relax.

Ther.: You couldn't relax enough to be yourself . . .

Jody: That's correct—of course, I don't even know what that is. I have played so many different roles just to be accepted. I wanted to be a mother, the best mother I could be. But I question even that now.

Ther.: Where do you think your doubts come from?

Jody: I think it comes from never doing anything big on my own. I know I can take care of children, now that I have four. But everything else I am unsure about. I have never done anything to prove myself. I always tried to anticipate how the men wanted me to be. I tried to do what they wanted before they even said it. There was no reason or time for me to find out how I wanted to be. Usually men were impressed with the degree of women's intuition I had. So I was praised for my anticipations.

Ther.: As you described your intuition, it seems to be more of a skill that you trained yourself in rather than an innate female trait. I remember reading about an experiment in which a psychologist placed men and women in work teams. Sometimes the assigned leader was a man, sometimes a woman. It was found that both men and women while in the follower position were sensitive to the leader's nonverbal cues. The experimenter suggested that "subordinate intuition" would be a more appropriate term than "women's intuition" because it is a skill developed by people for their own protection in interactions with a more powerful partner.

Jody: That is true! I have used my anticipation for my own protection. I thought if I did everything right, I would be safe in my little world. You are saying that while I was protecting myself I was acting in a subservient manner.

Ther.:   Sometimes there is a fine line between acting and protecting as there is between controlling and being controlled. It takes time and effort to achieve self-knowledge. Sometimes it is a painful journey and sometimes it can be an exciting adventure to discover ourselves with all the dreams, desires, and potentials. You could start thinking about it and then bring it up during our group work.

The interaction in this session reflected how Jody had lost sight of herself as an individual in her attempts to please those around her. The therapist's discussion of the experiment involving "subordinate intuition" (Snodgrass, 1985) helped Jody understand the dynamics of her own behaviors. Her response regarding her anticipation skills demonstrated her ability to differentiate between acting in her own safety and putting herself in the service of others.

Women who desperately want children but are denied motherhood suffer significant emotional pain. Even with children they deeply love and care for, there can still be a longing for personal meaning, as demonstrated by Julia and Jody.

MEANING THROUGH HUSBANDS

Nancy, a single woman in her late 30s, came to therapy because she was depressed. As she stated, her life was in a "rut." She was intelligent, had a good sense of humor and many talents. In earlier years, she had attempted to embark upon an artistic career. But she settled for a regular office job when her success was not sufficient to make a living. When asked why she did not use any of her talents for her own satisfaction, she answered that she was waiting for a husband. Whatever she did now, her life would be different with a husband. In her mind, her wedding day would be the beginning of her "real" life.

There was no prospect of a husband in her immediate future. Nancy was willing to put her life on "hold" until what she considered her "purpose" appeared on her doorsteps—no wonder she was depressed!

Inge: Dependency Expressed in Fear and Anger

Inge's background story was reported in chapter 2.

Ther.: The referral papers mention that you are trying to adjust to a recent divorce. How can I help you in this process?

Inge: I am still confused about the marriage and, the divorce and about David's behavior.

Ther.: What about David's behavior is confusing to you now? Can you describe it?

Inge: He calls me and tells me that he loves me, but when I ask him to come back to me and live with me and my children, he says he can't do that.

Ther.: How do you feel about David?

Inge: I still love him. I can't understand how he can say he loves me but does not want to live with me. If I love somebody, I want to be with him all the time. Why doesn't he just admit that he does not love me enough to be my husband? He just keeps me dangling.

Ther.: I don't know whether or not David loves you; but it seems to me that you are in charge of deciding whether you want to continue to dangle—as you call it—or whether you want to make a decision about the interactions with David.

Inge: Every time I hear his voice my hopes go up and then I'll be disappointed again.

Ther.: He calls you but he doesn't give you an explanation why he won't return, is that it?

Inge: Yes, and I keep searching my mind about what I did wrong to have the marriage disintegrate so fast. I think about it all day and it keeps me from sleeping at night.

Ther.: It sounds as if you are doing a lot of ruminating. Are you still using the medication you were given in the hospital? It should at least help with your sleep.

Inge: The medication helps, but sometimes I forget to take it because I am already so involved in my thoughts. You are right; I am ruminating. How can I get out of it?

Ther.:   You can investigate your thoughts as to whether they are congruent with reality, with what is really happening and whether or not they are conducive to your adjustment to the breakup of the relationship. We will work on that aspect a little later. Right now we need to focus on how to get yourself out of the ruminations. Are there any activities that will help you to distract yourself from the ruminating thoughts?

Inge: At the time I can't think of anything but walking or exercising, but the thoughts are still with me. I can't outrun them until I am physically exhausted and ready to collapse.

Ther.:   Ruminating thoughts are like a spiral, they go around and around. The spiral starts from the outside and winds up on the inside. With every turn the spiral gets tighter and tighter until the person is stuck in the center, unable to get out.

Inge: That's exactly how I feel! When I am in the center I get panicky. I feel like screaming but I can't make a sound.

Ther.:   Perhaps you could imagine yourself cutting through the spiral with a knife or scissors, cutting through your ruminating thoughts. When you become aware of those thoughts, it would be good if you could distract yourself before you get sucked deeper into the spiral. When you walk you could look at some flowers or a tree with an unusual shape. Focus on them in detail, to immerse yourself in the beauty and to distract yourself from those self-defeating thoughts. While distraction is not a substitute for problem resolution, it is a first step that you can use to avoid the rumination spiral.

Inge: I like to look at beautiful flowers, but what good is it if I can't share it with someone? I want David to hold my hand as we did on our walks together.

Ther.:   Are you saying that the flower is not beautiful enough by itself to hold your interest?

Inge: It does not mean anything to me unless David is with me.

Ther.:   Certainly, having a loved one with us when we admire a thing of beauty can turn the situation into a special and wonderful event. I agree with you on that. What happens when no one is around—does the beauty disappear? If we can only appreciate it in the presence of another person, wouldn't we become dependent on that person for all our enjoyment? When that person walks away or dies are we willing to give up all the enjoyable things around us?

Inge: I want to share it with David! I want him to be by my side.

Ther.: You said that without David the flower would be meaningless. You don't make it your own without him. What are things you can enjoy by yourself while he is not with you?

Inge: You are confusing me. Who cares about the meaning of a flower if David isn't with me!

Ther.: Yes, that may sound confusing. I tried to explain how we become dependent on others when we don't allow ourselves to enjoy things on our own.

Inge: I am sorry I got angry with you. I think I understand what you mean. I always considered myself to be independent, but maybe I am kidding myself.

Ther.: Being in love makes it easy to slide into some dependency on the loved person.

Inge: That is what happened to me. I can see it now. Much of my behavior while we were married was dependent on David. I did not assert myself because I was afraid he would not love me anymore if I did. But I did not like it and in my frustration I built up a lot of anger, which I finally blurted out. I felt I had to vent my anger or it would suffocate me.

Ther.: The way you described the situation, you suppressed some of your wants due to fear of abandonment. That fear put you in a position of emotional dependence. You did not feel like an equal partner in the relationship. You became angry with David—and perhaps with yourself. It's a vicious cycle, fear turning to anger and turning to fear again after an explosive expression of the anger. We will work on the fear-anger-fear cycle in our next session. For today, let's explore how you can distract yourself from the ruminating thoughts when they first appear in your mind.

Inge: Earlier when you were talking about the flower, did you mean that by not enjoying the flower by myself, I am only able to enjoy it through David because he gives it meaning for me? It is really not the flower I see but David's presence or absence? Is that how I become dependent on him because I want to experience everything with him?

Ther.: That is a very astute observation. You are learning fast. How can you put this learning into practice in your present situation?

Inge: I could go out and force myself to look at things for their own sake, although I probably will feel sad. I will need a lot of reminders to be able to focus on what I am looking at.

Ther.:   That is a good first step and, yes, you will probably feel sad.
         I like your idea of reminders—can you think of anything that
         would serve the purpose?
Inge: In my home country, we used to take pictures on many occa-
         sions. Recording events was a way of life. I could take my
         camera with me on my walks and the pictures will be my
         reminders that I can find enjoyable things on my own.
Ther.:   What an excellent idea! You have learned a lot today and I
         hope you will be sharing with the group what you learn.

In this first session, the client demonstrated her dependence on
David's actions. Rather than making her own decision whether or not
to cut off contact with David, she wanted him to tell her that he did
not love her anymore. Her dependence had been a significant factor
in their interactions but she had not acknowledged that to herself.
Her repetitive thought pattern became apparent as she persisted in
demanding that David's presence was required to give her environment meaning. The therapist's attempts to consider techniques to
distract herself from her depressive thoughts before she was caught up
in her endless ruminations elicited a demonstration of her quick anger. But Inge was able to recognize her anger in the session. The
therapist's gentle persistence led her toward a coping strategy for
immediate use, whereas the topics of her anger and dependency were
targeted for future sessions.

Additional concerns may arise from Inge's background. Her formative years were spent in a different culture, and those influences can
be expected to impact her thinking in many ways. Also, in her first
marriage—while living in America—the original cultural influences were
extended because she and her husband shared the same cultural background. Those concerns likely will become evident in future sessions.

THE GROUP: CHALLENGES AND MEANING

Observing in the first meeting that most members had introduced
themselves in regards to the roles they occupied in life, such as the
mother of their children or wife or former wife if being divorced, the
therapist had urged them to focus on what they wanted for themselves. As the members entered the room and seated themselves around
the table, their faces reflected various emotions—some seemed eager
to start, whereas others were still hesitant and perhaps undecided
about how to proceed.

Ther.: I had a call from Anita, she cannot be with us today. It is unfortunate to miss a meeting, especially so early in the group's existence when we are trying to get to know on another better. You came here with a purpose in mind. Perhaps the purpose is clearly formulated or perhaps it is a bit vague in your mind. What you want to have happen as a result of participating in this experience shall be our guiding light. You can think of it as a search for answers to why things are the way they are right now, or you can look at it as a challenge or an adventure, exploring what could be different in your lives. It is my hope that you choose the adventure approach. That does not mean that we will never look back for reasons, but it will be mostly for the purpose of learning from past experiences. Let's see what you consider your challenges to be.

Julia: (Appeared excited and eager to talk): I have a family and I love my children dearly. I also have a job in an interesting company. I enjoy the people I work with. But it is not enough, as I found out in therapy before I joined the group. I want something for myself. Actually, I have good news. I had taken this study course in preparation for going to college and my grades were excellent. When I told my boss about it, he encouraged me and said that the firm would probably help me financially if my studies were relevant to my work there. In fact, he thought there would be options for advancement with additional education. I am so excited about it.

Ther.: That is wonderful, Julia. I know you worked hard for this. How did your husband respond to your good news?

Julia: I haven't been able to tell him yet. He's been out of town. I did tell my mother though. She was not as encouraging. She reminded me that I had started college once before when it would have been easier for me, but I dropped out. Now with a family, how would I be able to handle it? I guess she is just worried that it will be a waste.

Ther.: The fact that your employer wants to support you in your plans is very encouraging. You have worked there for a number of years and they know your abilities. This could be the beginning of a new adventure for you, Julia. We are looking forward to hearing more about it as your plans develop. Allow yourself time for your explorations, some uninterrupted time with little distractions, so you can concentrate on your choices.

Jody: What you are saying reminds me of a couple of years ago when I thought I wanted to write or learn to paint. I wanted to take classes and the art teacher said we each needed to arrange a space for ourselves where we could concentrate, practice, and do our homework but would not have to put it away in between.

Ther.: A space that would not be used for anything else at the time, so you would not lose the continuity of your ideas?

Jody: Yes, she also said that if we had to pack and unpack our materials frequently, it would probably reduce our motivation.

Ther.: That seems like sound professional advice. Did you take the class?

Jody: No. I could not get a space for myself. We live in a four-bedroom house. My two daughters share one bedroom; they are about 5 years apart in age. Our twin boys each have their own rooms and then there is the master bedroom for my husband and myself. Besides the kitchen, dining, living, and family rooms, there is only one other room and that is my husband's study. He spends time in the evenings and on weekends there. My thought was that if the boys could share one room—like our daughters do—that would leave one room for me where I could practice artwork or writing.

Ann: That sounds reasonable to me. Your twin boys should be able to get along in the same room. Being of the same age, they would have many of the same toys and interests.

Jody: My husband did not think it was a good idea. In his opinion it is important for the twins to have space to develop their individual identities. He thought it was selfish of me to want a room for myself. He said "But, Honey, you have the whole house to yourself most of the day. What are you looking for? To take care of our family should give you all the happiness you want. We are your life—what more could any woman want?"

Ther.: How did you feel when he said that?

Jody: At first I felt angry. Why couldn't I have a small space just for myself? Then after talking to my mother about it I felt guilty. She agreed with my husband. He is a good man and a good provider and I should consider myself lucky to have this wonderful family. Later I talked to my friends, some said I should just insist on getting the space by moving my two sons in together. Others said I should have done that before asking my husband. Another friend said to take over our bedroom and make my husband sleep in his study. I didn't think any of the suggestions were a good way of handling the situ-

	ation. So I did nothing and started feeling like a victim, a victim of what?—my good husband? my children? my mother?
Ann:	Your friends were correct—you should have done something to get your own space. No wonder you feel like a victim. Even your mother is on his side—how could she?
Jody:	My mother is probably afraid that I will do something wrong and lose my husband. She worries that I will end up as she did, divorcing several times. After all, this is already my second marriage. It seems so unfair. I have a friend who calls herself a poet. Several of her short poems have been published in magazines, not a great deal but enough so that she can maintain her image as poet. She told me that when she got married, from the beginning she mapped out a space for herself, which she did not give up when she had children. Her husband did not even suggest she turn her study into a nursery or a bedroom for the children, and she has not published a poem or story in years.
Liz:	The difference may be that your friend had established herself in some way before she got married.
Ther.:	Liz, you are bringing up an interesting point. It seems that Jody's friend had identified herself as a writer or a poet before she got married and she did not change but rather asserted that image of herself. Whether or not she is writing a lot now is not the question for her. It is how she determines herself to be.
Inge:	I think we have a right to develop ourselves as we go along. Most of my career education occurred while I was married. Aren't we supposed to continue growing?
Ther.:	I certainly agree with you, Inge. (Turning to the group): Both Liz and Inge have raised valuable points, addressing the same issue, the issue of self-determination. For many women it would be advantageous to learn about themselves and what is important to them before they enter marriage—simply for the fact that once they are involved in the routines of raising children and running a household, often in addition to holding jobs, there is little time and energy left for such self-explorations. Julia's and Jody's lives are examples of this and they are not the only ones. Some women put their self-explorations deliberately on hold while they are waiting for the right man to come along because they believe that the future husband will determine what their lifestyle will be.

Jody: I have always been interested in art and literature, but I
          thought if I had any real talent it would have shown itself
          before now.

Liz: Did you think that without proven talent you would not be
          entitled to your own space?

Jody: You are probably correct, Liz. I may have thought I had to
          earn it.

Liz: When you look at it that way—what have your children done
          to earn their rooms?

Jody: That's a good point. We just take it for granted these days
          that children have their own rooms, but we don't think much
          about the wishes of their mothers.

Ann: My mother had a sewing room. With five kids there was al-
          ways something to mend and she did not want to mess up the
          family room. But come to think of it, her sewing room never
          looked messy. I wonder if that was her justification for having
          a space for herself.

Ther.:   This discussion about personal space demonstrates not only
          that it is important to us but it also shows that we act as if our
          beliefs are true. Jody's friend apparently believed that she
          was entitled to have a room for herself and acted accordingly,
          whereas Jody believed that her talents would not justify such
          a demand and she did not insist on having her own space.
          Rarely do we doubt our beliefs. If we believe it, it must be
          true; therefore, we act without challenging the belief.

Betty: When I was growing up, there was not much space for any of
          us, and in my marriage it was just natural that my husband
          and I shared a bedroom, the boys occupied one room, and
          there was a big family room.

Helen: My sisters and I all had our own small bedrooms upstairs,
          whereas my parents' bedroom was downstairs. Individual
          rooms can isolate you from your siblings. I can remember
          that my mother told us to go to bed and not waste time that
          we needed for sleeping. She said she could hear us walk
          along the hall when we tried to visit one another.

Ther.:   Helen, that is a different aspect, seeing individual rooms as
          serving an isolating function, something that we had not
          considered before. All of you have made important comments
          about whether or not women want, are entitled to, or have
          earned the right for personal space. It is an issue that every
          woman has to decide for herself rather than wait until it is
          given to her. (Turning to Jody): Jody, you could think about

whether you want to continue feeling like a victim or whether you want to become active in pursuing what you want. Your challenge is to find out what you want for yourself and how to get it. If you don't want to confront your husband because of the stress it may put on your family, start small. Walk through your house, room by room. Is there a corner that you can make your own? Perhaps a closet that is big enough to hold some of your materials? You may ask, "Why should I hide in a closet?" or you can say, "it's a beginning; I don't want to be a victim anymore. I'll start my journey now." (Turning to Ann): What do you see as your challenge, Ann?

Ann: I don't really know what my challenge is, except finding another man with whom to start a family. My track record is not impressive. I have not dated much and when I finally thought I had found the right person it turned out to be a disaster.

Ther.: Do you want to tell us more about it?

Ann: When I met Robert he seemed so quiet, serious, and sensitive. He did not talk much about his past except to mention an unhappy marriage. I felt sorry for him and thought I might be able to help him. I guess my nursing training is showing through. (Adding with a bitter laugh): I take care of the wounded. We dated for a while and I felt comfortable with him. I think I loved him because he let me take care of him, cheer him up. We decided to get married. Our engagement was brief and we were busy with wedding plans. Shortly before our wedding I found out that his previous wife had divorced him because he had beaten her. A friend of mine has a cousin who knew Robert's first wife, and my friend told me about it.

Liz: Did you ask Robert about it?

Ann: Yes, I confronted Robert. According to him, she was mean and put him down. He never seemed important to her. She did not care about him and his feelings. He admitted that he had pushed her once after she had provoked him. He could not take it anymore and lost control. I believed him; he seemed so sincere. Surely, he would not ever hit me; he would have no reason. I would never treat him badly—I loved him! I had not even told him that I had turned down a promotion to district manager because I did not want to hurt his feelings by letting him know that I had to give up something for him. So we married and for a while things seemed to go all right, though there were arguments when I had to work over-

	time. He did not want me to spend time away from home, except for regular working hours.
Liz:	(Listening intently to Ann): Didn't he ever have to work overtime?
Ann:	I never asked myself why he didn't have to work overtime. He never talked much about his job. I thought it was because he did not get paid very well. Anyway, one time we had a deadline to meet and my boss begged me to stay longer than usual. We worked very intensely for several hours and left the office together. My boss suggested we have a cup of coffee before going home, so we would not fall asleep while driving. When I came home, Robert was in a rage. I told him about the urgent assignment that had to be completed that day. He yelled at me that I was lying. He knew that I had not been at work because he had called my office. With that he slapped my face several times and the knuckles of his right hand hit my eye. I was paralyzed with shock and fear; instead of moving away, I just stood there. I never believed that this would happen to me, but it did! The next day I arrived at work with a black eye. I made up a story about an accident but I realized that I could not prevent my husband from beating me— even if I did not provoke him. Ironically, I remembered a book I had read a little while ago. It was an autobiography by Claire Bloom, the British actress. She wrote that when she married the writer Philip Roth she knew that he could turn his intelligence into biting sarcastic comments that were hurtful to others. She married him anyway, believing that he would not treat her that way—but he did, too.
Ther.:	What a sad experience to have your caring repaid in that way. You had a rude awakening. Actually, I know the book you mentioned. When I read it, like you, I was impressed by Claire Bloom's statement. We can all learn from it. Many of us think we can change people for the better if we only try hard enough, if we only love them more, if we only give more. But we are not that powerful. The other person has to want to change. Something would have to make it desirable for the other person to change.
Liz:	What would have made it desirable for Robert to change in the situation with Ann? It seems she did everything she could for him.
Ther.:	Yes, she did, Liz. We would hope that the possible loss of a loving and caring wife would be reason enough to change but it does not always work out that way.

Liz: Especially when we don't know the other person well enough. When I married my ex-husband, we had both just graduated from college. He was handsome and popular and all the girls were after him. It was a real challenge to get him to date me. During the first year of our marriage I realized that he was not as ambitious as I am. He never looked for better jobs than the one he had at the time, whereas I was always looking around to advance myself. We had several discussions about that. Although I had hoped he would change, his answer was always the same, "We have enough money to live on. I am comfortable where I am." But to me it was embarrassing when we attended Christmas parties with his colleagues or mine. Everybody seemed to get promoted except Donald. I lost respect for him and after some years I could not understand what I had ever seen in him. We finally divorced and, strangely enough, he remarried within the year. I often thought that he must have known her before and was just waiting for me to make the move. He never had much courage.

Ther.: Ambition seems to be important to you and it is good that you learned that about yourself. Donald did not share your ambition and, in turn, that cooled down your feelings for him.

Betty: But shouldn't we love the person for what he is and not for what he does? I want people to accept me the way I am. I never told my former husband that I would have liked it better if he had spent some money on us for a trip or for me to buy a new dress instead of putting it all into the business. That was the way he was and I accepted it.

Ther.: Betty, I agree with you, it would be great if we could love people unconditionally, the way they are. However, few of us have that capacity. We are human beings who, at times, have difficulty rising above our likes and dislikes. We may want to strive for the capacity to love unconditionally, but in the meantime, until we get there, it would be helpful to know as much about ourselves as possible, so that we make healthy decisions about the persons we want to spend our lives with.

Cindy: Betty, you said the other day that your husband left you for a younger woman. Is he as stingy with her as he was with you?

Betty: No, he is not, that's why I am so angry. We all went to the same church, and when her husband died suddenly, everybody tried to be nice to her and comfort her—myself included. When my husband sent her some flowers to cheer her up I was surprised because he never sent me flowers. But I thought he is a good Christian and he wanted to help. I actually was ashamed that I felt something like envy. Then he started fixing things on her property that she could not do herself. He did more and more for her and less and less for us. More recently I have seen her wear some nice jewelry. I could not help but think that it was bought with my money.

Cindy: So he is different now. Doesn't that indicate that we don't have to accept the person the way he is if we don't like the behavior? In a way, that reminds me of why I am here. Betty accepted her husband's behavior though she did not always like it. He took her for granted and took advantage of her good nature until he found another woman who seemed more special to him. Would he have left Betty if she had been special all along?

Betty: I think I understand what you are saying and you may be right. I never asked for any special considerations. I tried to be a good and reliable helpmate. I thought I was a partner in our marriage and in our business. I wished I had been as smart as you when I was your age, Cindy. But how does that relate to your reason for being here?

Cindy: At the previous meeting you all looked surprised when I said I did not want to be invisible for the rest of my life. You may have thought that this was not a big enough problem to come to a therapy group. What I meant was that I have never been special. My two beautiful older sisters always had all the attention. Even my mother could not make me feel special. Perhaps in order to receive attention, we have to feel special within ourselves. Perhaps if Betty had felt special, her husband would not have taken her for granted. Perhaps I am invisible because I don't feel special about myself. I want to have presence, so people will notice me.

Ann: I understand how you feel, Cindy. I am the middle child of five siblings. We had loving parents who tried very hard to treat us all equally—and they succeeded with it. I also wanted to be different in some ways, but even my grades in school were right in the middle of all our grades. My parents used to say how wonderful it was that we were all equally bright and talented. But secretly I wanted to be different. Although I am successful in my job, I am unremarkable when with my parents and siblings.

Ther.: I am glad that during today's discussion you were able to focus on yourselves, aside from your relationships with others. For some of you it may be the wish for personal space to explore your wishes, for others it is the desire to be special. This is a good beginning and we will continue with it at our next meeting.

GROUP PROCESS: CHALLENGES AND MEANING

This session started out on a high note when Julia reported her good news about getting support from her employer for returning to college. The discussion turned to women's search for fulfilling activities and the distractions from meaningful explorations that are inherent in many of the women's lives. Limitations of time and space can be discouraging hurdles in the search, as group member Jody revealed.

Whether or not Jody is entitled to her own space is not the question here. Perhaps if the couple had attended marriage counseling, this would have been an issue to focus on. The fact that Jody's husband considered it more important for the twin boys to have their individual rooms than for the daughters who were 5 years apart in age—which at that time in their lives seems almost like a generation—is difficult to reason with. Is it because females are not entitled to personal space or is it truly because of identity concerns related to twins? We don't have the answer and neither does Jody at this point. The issue here is what can Jody and other women like Jody do to learn about themselves, their needs, and aspirations? Another issue coming to the surface was the desire to be special in some way.

SUMMARY

This chapter has explored how individuals search for life's meaning and how to give purpose to their own experiences. For women this search is especially complicated. Cultural and social prescriptions significantly influence the quest. Should women conform to culturally prescribed paths to give their lives meaning? Should they seek to attain happiness and meaning through their relationships with others? Or can they search for something that is unique to them and fulfilling enough to give their life a purpose? Considerations of meaning and purpose are closely intertwined with aspects of sex-role identity development. The following chapter traces the development of sex-role identity and its significance in relation to motivational factors.

QUESTIONS FOR CONSIDERATION

Threats to the sustainability of human life in the future have become a topic for concern again recently. Global warming, the destruction of the ozone layer, exhaustion of agricultural land and fisheries are caused, we are warned, by the patterns of human overpopulation and overconsumption. To escape ecological disaster, urgent changes in human lifestyles, cultural practices, political and economical systems are necessary (Howard, 2000; McKenzie-Mohr, 2000; Oskamp, 2000; Stern, 2000; Winter, 2000). One of the key prerequisites of a sustainable society is population control; another is improved technological efficiency. Even though the world's rate of population growth has decreased, the overall world's population is still increasing by 80 million every year (see Oskamp).

Based on those considerations, is motherhood a right or a privilege to be earned? Are women entitled to have children in order to have a meaningful life, or do they have to earn the privilege through perhaps lowering overall consumption, reducing the number of children, or by working on increasing technological efficiency?

Physical violence, as encountered in Ann's case, should be regarded as a warning sign, like a red light. Should a woman terminate a relationship when the man reportedly has acted out violently in the past, even if he has not harmed her? Should she give him a second chance because he may have changed?

RECOMMENDED READING

Bohmer, C., & Ray, M. L. (1996). Notions of equity and fairness in the context of divorce: The role of mediation. *Mediation Quarterly, 14,* 37–52.
   The article describes some of the dynamics of mediation and questions the assumption of fairness in the process.
Wagner, L. (1998). *Expectations: Thirty women talk about becoming a mother.* San Francisco, CA: Chronicle Books.
   The book is an account of women's expectations about motherhood and their real-life experiences. Photographs by Anne Hamersky supplement the text.

CHAPTER FOUR

Sex-Role Identity and Motivational Forces

D ifferentiation between the sexes through assignment of different roles is found in all societies, though the standards for
males and females may differ from one society to another.
Societal institutions promote the development of different standards
and behavior patterns for boys and girls and provide experiences in
preparation for the roles they will assume as adult members of their
society. Parental influences function to monitor and maintain the sex-
role identification process.

Though most people would agree that childhood influences play a
significant role in people's development, prediction regarding which
experiences have the most lasting determining effect amounts to a
guessing game. Influences that have the greatest impact on our life
often are very subtle; indeed, most people are not aware of many of
the stimuli picked up from parents and other influential figures that
have shaped significant parts of their existence. Women's development is formed primarily through their mothers' modeling. Even for
women who disliked their mothers' behaviors and promised themselves to be completely different from them, the major influence on
their lives probably still stemmed from their mothers (Baker, 1991).

DEVELOPMENT OF SEX-ROLE IDENTITY

Katharine Milar (2000), in a recent article about the first generation
of women psychologists, described how Helen Bradford Thompson, as
the first psychologist to conduct experimental examination of the psychological characteristics of males and females, came to the conclu-

sion that it is not differences in average capacity or in type of mental activity that account for psychological differences of the sexes but the differences in the social influences that impact the developing individual from early infancy to adulthood. Thompson's dissertation was based on her research. Her dissertation was completed in 1900 and her findings were published in 1903; but psychologists like G. Stanley Hall, insisting that appropriate roles for women were those of wives and mothers, dismissed Thompson's research as "feministic."

In our society, little girls are still expected to learn many skills from their mothers, and they naturally spend more time with their mothers than do boys. Boys usually have their fathers as role models, and fathers spend the bulk of their time away from home—at work. Thus, boys much earlier than girls are allowed to spend their time and activities away from home and under less direct supervision and influence from either parent. Through the general translation of role models, girls are mainly exposed to maternal influences. The role of the father, and men in general, is often perceived through the consequences that the father's actions have on the mother's life and happiness. If the mother's position in the family is perceived as powerless and undesirable, a daughter may turn toward the father for guidance and may completely reject her own femininity.

Underlying those influences is the preference for sons over daughters by both parents, especially for the first child. The partiality for sons seems to be widespread and deeply rooted in many cultures. People's reactions to a young mother often show that they regard male babies as more desirable than female offspring. While complimenting the mother on having given birth to a boy, people at the same time communicate to the mother how she as a women is perceived of as being less valuable than if she herself had been a man (Baker, 1991). Sanford and Donovan (1984) cited a survey involving 1,500 married women and 375 of their husbands. Although many stated that they would like one child of each sex, twice as many women admitted that they preferred boys to girls. Their husbands favored boys to girls by four-to-one.

Discussing this topic in a recent conversation with a nurse clinician who works in a large obstetrics/gynecology clinic and who herself is the mother of three sons, the nurse clinician was reluctant to believe that mothers feel differently about giving birth to boys and girls. Intrigued by the statement, she, however, proceeded to question the patients at the clinic as well as her female friends. The overwhelming majority of the women confirmed that they felt more valued if they were mothers of boys. Such a powerful message is bound to have significant influences on the girls and women in our society.

ADOLESCENCE AND EMERGING ADULTHOOD

For most individuals, adolescence is considered to be the starting point of transforming and defining themselves, the time when identity formation occurs (Elder, 1975; Erikson, 1963; Kotre & Hall, 1990). During adolescence, individuals come to understand how episodes in one's life interconnect and become significant parts in overarching patterns. Individual stories are woven into the tapestry of their lives. The version of the tapestry may affect the kind of person the adolescent becomes in the future when individuals choose a course of action that is in agreement with what has already been written in the story (Bruner, 1987).

EMERGING ADULTHOOD AND SEX-ROLE IDENTITY

More recently the time from late teens through the 20s has been proposed as a period of emerging adulthood (Arnett, 2000). Emerging adulthood is thought to be different from adolescence and different from young adulthood because it is marked by relative independence from social roles and from normative expectations. It is a time of life in which few important decisions have been made and many different directions are still possible. According to Arnett (1998), individualistic qualities of character are the most important traits considered by emerging adults in their subjective sense of achieving adulthood. Accepting responsibility for one's self and making independent decisions are the two top characteristics for the transition to adulthood.

Similar to Arnett's proposed period of emerging adulthood that occupies the ages 18 through 25, Levinson (1978) determined that the ages 17 through 33 constitute the "novice phase" of development, in which the overriding task is to enter the adult life and construct a stable life. Levinson's statement was based on interviews with men at midlife describing their current situation and their earlier years. According to Levinson, the purpose of the study was to create a conception of development that could include biological, psychological, and social changes occurring in adult life. He decided not to include women in his sample. Therefore, the findings need to be regarded cautiously, even though *Newsweek* hailed the book as "the most ambitious account of the adult life cycle."

TIMING OF MARRIAGE AND PARENTHOOD

In industrialized societies, periods of emerging adulthood have surfaced through demographic changes in the timing of marriage and parenthood in recent decades (Arnett, 2000). Now the average age of marriage for women is 4 years higher than it was in the 1950s, and more women than before are marrying for the first time at age 40 or older (Coontz, 2000). For females there seems to be a link between their adolescent future aspirations and their expected role timing. Female adolescents with high aspirations for school and career consider the birth of their first children at a later age than do girls with pessimistic school and career aspirations (East, 1998). Postponement of marriage and parenthood until the late 20s would leave the period from late teens through early 20s accessible for explorations of different life directions. After reviewing the research available to support his theoretical proposal, the author suggested several issues for future research. The one we would be most interested in for the purpose of this book is the question of how the explorations of emerging adulthood are different for men and women and to what extent females are represented in any such explorations.

THE FEMALE EXPERIENCE OF EMERGING ADULTHOOD

How do females experience emerging adulthood? According to Pipher (1994), for females the period from preadolescence to adulthood does not constitute a smooth period of transition but rather a shift marked by the loss of precious traits such as curiosity, optimism, and resiliency to a condition of uncertainty, hesitancy, and concerns about what to do to please others.

The concerns about pleasing others for many women linger on through significant parts of their adulthood. For instance, female students at a university counseling center reported experiencing varying degrees of depression in connection with career-making decisions (Lucas, Skokowski, & Ancis, 2000). The students' ages ranged from 18 to 36 years. Relationships with others played a pivotal role in the dilemmas about their career decisions. Problems ranged from wanting to be the "perfect child" by continuing in a major area of study that they had lost interest in but knew that their parents wanted them to stay in, to parents' pressures to achieve, to difficulties setting limits with controlling boyfriends. These personal entanglements led to difficulties in concentration, which—in turn—exacerbated the women's difficulty in making sound decisions for themselves and in applying their skills and abilities to their studies.

THE CONTINUUM OF MOTIVATIONAL FORCES

The determinants of human actions cover a broad spectrum. Some people act out of curiosity, inspiration, or desire, whereas others operate on a more passive level, perhaps out of necessity or due to the prompting of others. People are moved to act by a variety of factors, from intrinsic desire to powerful external coercion. Between the two extremes of the continuum, various levels of motivational forces can be observed.

The contrast between internal motivation and external pressure has been the focus of studies concerned with motivation as a function of personality structure, as linked to cultural and socioeconomic background, and other domains of human experience. Factors determining motivation include energy, direction, persistence, and the definition of goals. Distinct types of motivation are thought to have specifiable consequences for learning, performance, personal experience, and well-being of individuals. By observing the forces that move individuals to act, self-determination theorists have attempted to identify distinct types of motivation and to outline a set of principles regarding how each type of motivation is developed and sustained, or forestalled and undermined (Ryan & Deci, 2000).

INTRINSIC MOTIVATION

The construct of intrinsic motivation is based on individuals' natural inclination toward spontaneous interest, exploration, assimilation, and mastery instrumental in cognitive and social development and leading to enjoyment and vitality throughout life (Csikszentmihalyi & Rathunde, 1993). Intrinsic motivational tendencies are found in many people, but supportive conditions are necessary to maintain the continued development of this inherent propensity. Whether individuals are proactive and involved or passive and alienated is considered to be largely a function of the social conditions in which they develop and exist (Ryan & Deci, 2000). The investigators' focus, while applying cognitive evaluation theory (CET), was directed toward the variability in intrinsic motivation. Based on those considerations, one would expect motivation to vary not only according to personality traits but also according to gender, because social conditions and environmental factors that are instrumental in facilitating or undermining the growth of intrinsic motivation have been different for males and females even within the same culture and the same socioeconomic environment.

Studies involving autonomy-supportive parents versus controlling parents have shown that children of autonomy-supportive parents demonstrated more intrinsic motivation than those of controlling parents (Grolnick, Deci, & Ryan, 1997). Intrinsic motivation thus seems to be linked to satisfaction of the needs for autonomy and competence. Ryan and Deci (2000) cautioned that the considerations regarding intrinsic motivation apply only to circumstances in which individuals are engaged in activities that are intrinsically interesting, have the appeal of challenge or novelty, or contain aesthetic value. Activities lacking such appeal are not felt to be intrinsically motivating and will be better explained within the context of extrinsic motivation.

EXTRINSIC MOTIVATION

People perform many activities and fulfill many responsibilities that are not inherently interesting but that are dictated by social pressures. Individuals' motivation for behaviors fostered by parents, mentors, or other significant models can range from unwillingness, to passive compliance, to active personal commitment—depending on the degree of individual internalization of the values connected to the requested activities. Internalization refers to a person's adopting and integrating a value as if it were the person's own. Although internalization and integration are central issues in childhood socialization, they continue in their relevance for the regulation of behavior throughout the life of individuals as they perform prescribed behaviors in many different circumstances. Thus, originally nonintrinsically motivated behaviors can eventually become self-determined as the social environment influences the process of internalization and integration.

Whereas intrinsic motivation refers to the performance of an activity for the inherent satisfaction of the activity itself, extrinsic motivation relates to the performance of an activity in order to attain some desirable outcome. Examples of extrinsic motivation can be seen in situations in which students do their homework because they understand the value of studying and doing homework in relation to their chosen career and their financial future. Students who do their homework because they are compliant with their parents' wishes also operate under the concept of extrinsic motivation but in compliance with an external regulation. Both types of students demonstrate intentional behavior, but they differ in the degree of autonomy. The students who do their homework because they realize its significance to their own future reflect instances of personal endorsement and thus are more likely to experience a feeling of choice.

Internalization of extrinsically motivated activities is also a function of perceived competence. Activities that are considered to be valued by relevant social groups are more likely to be adopted when the people feel efficacious regarding those activities. Feelings of autonomy also facilitate internalization of extrinsic motivation. When both aspects are satisfied, people feel competent and related.

WOMEN'S MOTIVATION: INTRINSIC OR EXTRINSIC?

For many women extrinsic motivation determines their actions. Females have been conditioned to value interpersonal relationships and approval from others. Rather than for the intrinsic value of achievement itself, women are thought to work for love, acceptance, and approval. But as was demonstrated in chapter 1, another, more subtle component of extrinsic motivation comes into play when we consider the significance of maternal influences that go beyond overt approval. Maternal work attitudes—may they be communicated verbally or through actual behavioral modeling—have a significant impact on daughters' career-related motivation.

The story of Tanya, one of the female volunteers for this book, serves as illustration here. Tanya remembers that she knew early on what she wanted to be. People were surprised when they asked the little girl about future plans, expecting her to say that she would be a "mother" or a "teacher" or a "nurse." Instead, unhesitatingly, Tanya responded with, "I'll be a lawyer when I grow up." Tanya's mother, whose short, unhappy marriage ended in widowhood, had to provide for herself and her daughter, working as laborer in a factory. To be certain, Tanya's mother complained about her hard life and the difficulties at work, as well as raising a child by herself. As she developed into a skilled worker, she earned the recognition and praise of her supervisors. Along with the strain and stress of the work, the mother also communicated her pride in being recommended for special tasks. And, equally important, Tanya's mother never failed to end her complaints with the statement that it was better to work for a living and have one's own money than to be dependent on a man.

Thus Tanya learned early to appreciate women's ability to become financially independent. At the same time she realized that hard manual labor would not be the most desirable way to achieve this goal. Despite difficulties that were outside of her control, she never lost sight of the goal to invest in her financial independence—even when she married.

THE ROLE OF ATTENTION IN COGNITIVE AND PERCEPTUAL PROCESSES

Motivation is a construct that is influenced by several different variables. The basic motivational process is dependent on cognitive and perceptual processes. Although the relationship between cognitive and motivational processes has been explored to some degree (Heath, Larrick, & Wu, 1999), the variable of attention has been largely neglected—except for studies concerned with attention deficit and research centering on information processing in people suffering from phobias and anxiety disorders (Arnkoff & Glass, 1989).

Deliberations about information processing and problem-solving or goal-setting activities discuss concepts such as cognition, memory, affect, and behavior but pass over attention—even though attention interacts significantly with all the other concepts. Attention has been described as the sharp edge of consciousness and the process of recognition in action. Many small flashes of recognition lend substance and focus to attention (McCrone, 1993). Incoming information is processed and structured by the person through encoding in conjunction with the knowledge the person has already stored about a given event.

Thus, encoding involves perceptual and integrative processes as the person attempts to ascribe meaning or understanding to events. Attentional aspects influence both perception and integration. If the individual attends to input that is irrelevant, misleading, or distorted, the perceptions of the event will be grossly inaccurate. If during integration processes the incoming information is matched to inappropriate stored knowledge, the person's decisions and behavior may miss the target. Without adequate attention to the environment, perceptions become less than accurate. Accepting inaccurate perceptions as "true" reflections of reality and acting on those perceptions significantly reduce control over the situation. Results may not always be disastrous, but the risk of harm due to misinterpretation of a potentially dangerous situation exists.

Another type of attention, self-focused attention, has been regarded as one of the moderator variables in psychological strategies for protecting one's self-concept (Campbell & Sedikides, 1999). Here, attention is directed inward and individuals who are in a state of self-focused attention are thought to become aware of the discrepancy between who they think they are (actual self), who they would want to be (ideal self), and who they think they should be (ought self). Self-focused attention has been considered to play an important function in assessing one's skills and talents as well as one's limitations. However, some investigators caution that the significance of self-focused attention is based on the assumption of perceptual accuracy on the part of the self-observer. The attention-accuracy link thus becomes the cornerstone for the perceptual accuracy hypothesis and, in turn, the beneficial function of self-focused attention, but there is no conclusive evidence to support the hypothesis. As argued by Silvia and Gendolla (2001), the process of introspection may not just simply record what is there but may change aspects of the self that are being examined. Considering those opinions and findings, we can accept the value of introspection as an awareness-increasing process with the caution that attention-accuracy links will be characterized by individual differences.

PURPOSE-RELATED ATTENTION SKILLS AND RESPONSE-RELATED ATTENTION SKILLS

Individuals' attentional focus or consciousness is a critical variable in learning, information processing, goal-setting, problem-solving, and decision-making for both men and women. However, there are indications that men and women exercise their attentional skills in different ways. Mary Catherine Bateson (1989) suggested that attentional characteristics are gender related insofar as men's way of attending is purpose related and focused more narrowly compared with women's way of attending. Women generally attend in responding and adapting ways and thereby their focus is more expansive. Bateson's premise for her statements was based on observations about interactions with her husband. In more than 20 years of marriage, her husband continued with his activities when she interrupted him, whereas she automatically discontinued her activities and responded to his interruptions.

While Bateson's observations do not mean that attention skills are genetically linked to gender, many would agree that women are trained through their roles in life to be able to attend to several different stimuli almost simultaneously. The sound of a crying baby in the house may interrupt the woman's attending to the family meal or the laundry. Similarly, it is the woman who answers most of the telephone calls for the family. No matter how many telephones there are in a given household, in the average home there is at least one in the kitchen.

Women are expected to attend and respond to many minor crises immediately. Over time, they have come to accept these demands on their attention and have adapted to them by not allowing themselves to focus intently on a given activity to the point of blocking out irrelevant noise or other distracting stimuli (Maass, 2000a). Although many believe that it is possible to pay attention to several events simultaneously, what actually happens is that the mind must shift back and forth between stimuli, causing attention to oscillate and thereby creating fatigue. One can cut down on random, energy-wasting shifts in attention by strengthening concentration. For many women who attempt to combine career and marriage, the lack of time periods for long-sustained, uninterrupted intense application of attention and concentration is a significant challenge.

Mary: A Shift in Attention Skills

Mary, a widowed mother of three grown children, reported how her golf game had improved with age. As a young wife and mother she had taken up golf as a leisure activity that she and her husband could enjoy together. Although she had cognitively comprehended the various aspects of the game and had nicely mastered the physical part of it, her performance had remained unremarkable. Several years after her husband had died and her children were grown, her golf game improved dramatically. Despite growing older, her performance improved. What accounted for the change? As she had adjusted to living by herself, her way of attending and focusing had shifted. Instead of attending to many different stimuli simultaneously in anticipation of her family's needs, she could now uninterruptedly focus on one thing at a time. She was able to tune out background noises and movements that were inconsequential to her own needs. Without being conscious of it, she had transferred her new way of attending to her golf game.

Losing one's spouse and waiting for children to move out of the house, is a high price to pay for the ability to focus attention intensely on one's activities. But Mary's experience demonstrated the possibility of changing long-established habits. Recognizing the potential for change can lead to planned shifts in attention wherein individuals can institute those shifts intentionally as needed. People are able to choose.

ATTENTION AND PARENTING

Working with single parents provided opportunities to observe how men and women approach their responsibilities as sole caregiver for their children in different ways (Maass & Neely, 2000). One obvious difference was that male single parents carried schedules or daily planners with them. Habits from the professional part of their lives helped them to schedule times required for child care activities and for completing chores.

One father who felt particularly overwhelmed when he suddenly assumed the sole responsibility for his two sons stated, "I would be lost if I did not write everything down. It scares me just to think that I might forget to pick up my boys from an activity because I had already committed myself to another task that required my full attention. The only way I can stay on top of things is to write everything into my daily planner." Slightly embarrassed he added, "I even developed a code to differentiate the type of appointments and activities that have to be attended to as scheduled from the ones that I could postpone or reschedule if I needed to. Actually, this developed out of my failure to make accurate estimates of how much time different activities consumed. By keeping a schedule of everything and checking it frequently, I am able to give my undivided attention to those projects that require it. Now I derive satisfaction from looking at my planner at the end of the day and realizing that I am in control of things."

On the other hand, women stated, "My life is basically the same hassle every day. There is no need to write down what I do. For doctors' appointments and things like that I paste notes on the refrigerator where I see them all the time." Undoubtedly, keeping reminders where they can be seen is good practice. Although they may not ever miss an appointment, the women do not have an accurate knowledge of the many activities they perform during the day. They usually do not have time assigned in which they are able to work on projects that require intense concentration. What is even more disturbing, they do not have the satisfaction as described by the single father above. At the end of the day the women may sink into bed exhausted without experiencing the positive feelings that come from knowing one has done well despite overwhelming demands and without the confidence of being able to conquer the challenges of another day. Motivation to confront new demands will be rather small under those circumstances.

MOTIVATION

SELF-CONFIDENCE AND SELF-EFFICACY IN MOTIVATION

Most people possess a mental representation of goals they want to attain. They also have a general idea of the likelihood of achieving those goals. There is a direct positive correlation between the degree of likelihood of attaining goals and the level of motivation with which the person will start and proceed along the path toward the target. The likelihood of achieving desired goals is a subjective variable that differs from person to person and changes as a function of the person's self-confidence. Self-confidence and high self-esteem are considered to be positive and desirable characteristics. But because they are not stable entities and vary according to different behavior dimensions, absolute levels of self-esteem are not the best predictors of a person's overall degree of self-enhancing behavior (Baumeister, 1997).

People's beliefs about their ability to reach desired goals will determine how much effort they will expand toward a certain goal. Although people may have reasonably correct estimates of the behaviors that will be required for the attainment of their goals, they may overestimate or underestimate the degree to which they possess the ability to perform these behaviors successfully. Thus, peoples' estimates of their self-efficacy influence their motivation. According to Bandura (1977), self-efficacy expectations stem from four sources: (a) the person's past accomplishments; (b) the observed actions of others; (c) the person's emotional arousal about the event; and (d) verbal persuasions from others. Women are considered to be far more vulnerable than men to persuasions from others when contemplating their self-efficacy expectations.

Self-efficacy expectations have a significant impact on career choices. Low career self-efficacy expectations constitute a psychological barrier to choice, performance, and persistence, especially for women because of the gender-role socialization process that women are submitted to (Sullivan & Mahalik, 2000). Low self-efficacy is seen not only to influence women's choice of a career, but also their performance in that career, and their persistence in the face of obstacles. Career-related self-efficacy explains how cognitive processes, developed through early learning experiences, influence later occupational behaviors (Lent & Hackett, 1987). Evaluating a group intervention for the enhancement of women's career development, Sullivan and Mahalik found that out of 61 women at a median age of 20 years who were enrolled in three universities in New England, 41% reported indecision about a major study path and 100% were undecided about career choices.

SELF-REGULATION AS MEDIATOR IN MOTIVATION

In attempts to advance motivationally based characteristics that predict the level or degree of human adaptation functioning, the notion of self-regulation received increasing coverage in the literature. The role of self-regulation has been described as the action-oriented mediator in the pursuit of personal goals with the goal construct being the key analytic unit (Karoly, 1999). The adaptive process of self-regulation is significant for how people respond to and manage transitional pressures rather than how they typically act. Utilizing their self-management strategies, people modulate their steady states, creating stability in the face of change. As internal representations of desired outcomes, people's goals provide the impetus for the continuing pursuit. Both conscious goal-guided self-regulation and nonconscious automated elements of the person's experiential-perceptual repertoire are employed. Self-regulatory processes are less content-driven than habits, more malleable than genetic predispositions, and more flexible than attitudes because their function is to convert the semantics of mental states into action.

Moretti and Higgins (1999) further expanded the concept by considering the role of own versus other standpoints in the function of self-regulation. One's own standpoint is the internal representation of one's own goals and values, whereas other standpoints take on the form of an inner audience, representing others' values and goals for the self. To make the roles of own and other standpoints comprehensible, the authors considered the concept of self-regulation within the framework of self-discrepancy theory. Individuals are thought to experience psychological discomfort when they perceive lack of congruence, or discrepancy, among the three domains of their self-representation. Thus, the self-representation consists of the actual self, the part that people believe they really are, the ideal self, the type of person they would wish to be, and the ought self, the kind of person they believe they should be. (This seems to be parallel to Campbell and Sedikides's (1999) notion of self-concept in the discussion of self-focused attention above.) When people observe discrepancies in their self-representations, they become motivated to self-regulate in order to achieve congruency and reduce psychological distress.

DEVELOPMENT OF SELF-REGULATORY ORIENTATION

Parents, as would be expected, play significant roles in the development of individual self-regulatory orientations. When parents socialize their children to value autonomy and individual initiative, the children are more likely to develop a self-regulatory style oriented toward their own self-guides than children who are socialized by their parents to regulate their behavior with respect to the inferred self-guides of significant others. Boys and girls may develop different standpoint orientations because of their distinct socialization experiences. As consequences of sex-typed socialization, girls are likely to construct a self in relation to others and develop self-regulation systems that correspond to standards that significant others hold for them. This relational self-regulatory style could be a function of the lower social status and power of women in our society, which serves to increase women's motivation to be sensitive to the perspectives that others who are in positions of control hold of them (Martin & Ruble, 1997).

Women's relational self-regulation may lead to reduction or elimination of opportunities to clearly identify and pursue their own goals. In turn, it robs them of experiencing themselves as successful and competent and may put them at risk for depression. For women, others' standpoints on the self play an important role in their self-regulation, but for men it is their own standpoint on the self that constitutes the significant standard of self-regulation. These individual differences in self-regulatory standards are related to socialization experiences rather than to sex differences per se (Moretti & Higgins, 1999).

DEVELOPMENT OF PERSONAL AUTHORITY

Usually, personal authority is observed more in men than in women because it requires behaviors that are consistent with the prevailing gender expectations for men, behaviors that are in opposition to the culturally defined norms for women (Rampage, 1991). Infants learn about personal authority through direct experience by exploring their environment. Behaviors, such as crying, crawling, and reaching are employed to obtain what is needed. In most cases, these behaviors get almost immediate responses from adults, usually the mother. With increasing age, the environmental responses contain feedback about the appropriateness or inappropriateness of children's behaviors. Messages given to little boys and girls are different. Boys are being reinforced for inventive and explorative behaviors, while girls are praised for docile, cooperative and caretaking behaviors. Parental modeling reinforces these messages. In most households, girls observe as their fathers express opinions and make decisions while their mothers demonstrate placating behaviors, agreeing with and deferring to the fathers' leads. Stories, movies, and television further strengthen the messages about personal authority for women and men.

SOCIAL INFLUENCES ON WOMEN'S LEVEL OF PERSONAL AUTHORITY

Women's greater vulnerability to environmental and social influences undoubtedly has an impact on their level of personal authority and therefore on motivation. The significance of past childhood influences has already been mentioned in connection with the formation of attitudes regarding employment. Long ago, Alfred Adler (1927) linked females' reduced self-esteem to early conditions in life. Pointing to research, Adler stated that daughters in families in which mothers were the sole breadwinners showed greater talents and abilities than girls in families where the mother's role was subordinate to the father's. According to Adler, girls lose self-confidence as they continually experience prejudices against women. The degree of dependence on social pressures is determined by childhood influences and consequently impacts individuals' psychological well-being. Compared with masculine traits, feminine traits are less valued by society, a fact women face every day of their lives. Not surprisingly, men are considered to have higher global self-esteem than women (Harter, 1993). .

The strongest childhood influences stem from the child's caretakers. As mentioned above, boys are given permission to explore at an earlier age than girls. While boys may take their freedom for granted without giving it much thought, girls become aware of the difference. How do girls interpret and respond to the overprotection? Some girls may learn to accept that the overprotection is justified because girls are usually physically weaker than boys of the same age. With time, they many find it normal not to go anywhere by themselves. They may even experience fears and anxiety when left alone. They may sense themselves to be fragile and in need of support and reassurance from others.

Other girls may rebel against their parents' overprotection and take off when they see a chance to escape for an adventure. Knowing that they will receive punishment from their caretakers after returning home, they may still seize opportunities to escape again as soon as they perceive an open door. What accounts for the difference in the girls' compliance or noncompliance with parental rules? Would we expect the noncompliant girls to have lower levels of self-esteem than the compliant girls because of the lack of parental approval that is expressed in repeated punishments? Apparently parents' influence is not as all-powerful as commonly expected. The recognition of less-than-absolute parental power includes some optimism: Parents do not have to assume full responsibility for their children's dissatisfaction in life, and children can learn that they have cognitive and behavioral choices even while under the rule of authoritarian parents.

Tanya: Determined Curiosity

Tanya, the young woman encountered earlier, identified with a childhood of noncompliance. Although not rebellious by nature, she was curious about the world around her. Her mother insisted that she stay within a certain radius from home at all times. Tanya regarded this radius as too narrow for her curiosity and secretly made use of the public transportation system available in her city. Although each time she returned unharmed from her little expeditions, her mother did not fail to dispense harsh physical punishment. Tanya knew that the probability of her mother not finding out about her excursions was negligible and the harsh beatings were almost a certainty, but she continued her explorations as frequently as she could. Tanya's mother believed that she had to increase the level of punishment to break down her daughter's resistance and gain her obedience. The fact that Tanya returned home unharmed from every one of her excursions would have implied that she was ready for them. Why was Tanya's mother so determined to stifle her daughter's independence and curiosity? Only much later in adulthood did Tanya answer the question for herself: Her mother was more concerned with her own peace of mind (not to have to worry about Tanya getting lost) than with her daughter's growth and independence.

ACHIEVEMENT

Although achievement is generally used as a single concept, it is the reflection of several characteristics. Potential is a prerequisite; however, without determination and effort, potential by itself can prove to be rather meaningless. Opportunity constitutes another important ingredient. It has been argued that opportunities for achievement are not readily available to women and that girls being more dependent on rewards stemming from interpersonal relationships work for approval rather than for the intrinsic value of achievement (Williams, 1983). The element of choice, then, adds another variable to the construct of achievement. What is the area of endeavor that the person wants to achieve in? During early school years there are no drastic differences between boys and girls in the ways that they can achieve. As girls grow older, there is often a shift or redefinition of aspirations. Puberty marks the onset of the shift. Physical attractiveness, social skills, and popularity become highly valued characteristics in combination with pressures to conform to feminine role definitions.

Adult achievement is considered around activities that are mostly performed by men. Female striving may be less obvious, especially if it entails striving for goals, such as being attractive, running a well-functioning household, or raising happy, healthy children. Clearly, these are significant achievements, but they attract less attention than being the president of a company, receiving the Nobel Prize, or being a football star. For their own satisfaction and happiness, women need to assume full responsibility for making their own choices, setting their own goals, and striving for the attainment of those goals on their own terms, independent of the opinions of others and independent of the support of social agencies or sociopolitical movements.

DEPENDENCY

It is generally believed that employed women are less dependent on their husbands and, compared with unemployed women, are better able to leave abusive relationships (Kalmuss & Straus, 1990). But a woman's employment may increase rather than decrease her risk of abuse if the husband is unemployed, because the husband's threatened masculine identity may lead to coercion and violence. Macmillan and Gartner (1999) found that the probability of a male partner controlling his spouse through coercion is greatest in couples in which the wife is employed and the husband is not. Why do the women stay with coercive or abusive partners? Is it because women feel power-less—even if they are not actually powerless?

Here are some answers from women themselves: "I love him," "He needs me," "It's not an everyday thing. It only happens when I come home from work tired and there are dirty dishes in the sink, the laundry needs to be done, and he tells me to hurry up with dinner so that he can watch the ball game. When I complain about that, he'll get frustrated and may shove me around," "He doesn't really mean it, it's just that he is so frustrated over not having a job," "I hope he'll change if he realizes how much it hurts me," "I don't think I could live by myself; I would be lonely," "You hear about women living by them-selves being a target for rapes and robberies; I would be scared being alone in the house," "He threatened to kill me if I ever leave him." These answers are not new and yet many women still use them as reasons for not getting out of an abusive relationship. Some of the women's concerns seem reasonable. Leaving the situation does not end the violence in all cases. A number of batterers continue to harass and harm the woman after she leaves (Walker, 1999). Shelters for battered women and the legal system provide much-needed help, but more work needs to be done by social agencies and by the women themselves.

The high occurrence of male violence against women makes it a social problem. Studies suggested that from 21 to 34% of women in the United States are physically assaulted by an intimate adult male partner (Browne, 1993). Except for women who cannot provide for themselves, the issue still remains that some women decide to stay in abusive relationships—even when they have the means to exit.

A less obvious form of abuse affecting women is that of emotional abuse. Many women are unaware of why they are depressed, why they are not motivated, why they have difficulty making decisions, and why they feel worthless and helpless. They often have been trained for years not to trust their own perceptions and decisions. Starting in childhood, by a process like brainwashing, these women have become used to and have internalized others' criticism. No matter how hard they try, they never quite measure up. Unfortunately, they have been prepared to attract and accommodate abusive people as they go through their lives (Engel, 1990). Convinced of their own worthlessness, the women hold on for dear life to the abusers, because if anything is worse than being worthless, it is being abandoned. The expected like-lihood of finding another companion seems very small for the woman with low self-esteem.

As long as women continue their basic orientation to others as a need for maintaining relationships because their own sense of personhood is defined mainly within relationships, threats of being disconnected from a relationship constitute threats of losing their place and identity in life (Miller, 1986). The dependency that results from such an orientation of self to others renders many women unable or unmotivated to choose behaviors that are in their own best interest. The fear and dependency aspects operate not only in physically and emotionally abusive relationships but also in sexual interactions, as mentioned earlier, when women expose themselves to the risk of HIV infection when they hesitate to insist on their partners' use of condoms (Amaro, 1995).

Issues in female socialization—as described above—may explain women's vulnerability to entrapment in abusive and subservient relationships. Stronger than the effects of the women's movement is the socialization factor that tends to make women defer to and become dependent on men, especially when the men occupy positions of authority. Women's difficulty of living at the center of their own lives has led to the recent phenomenon of bestowing a diagnosis of codependency upon them (Rampage, 1991). The very traits that are culturally prescribed as proper female behavior—to live in the service of others, such as husbands and children—are used to label women who demonstrate these behaviors as sick.

DEVELOPING WOMEN'S OWN PATTERN

Almost 50 years ago psychiatrist Clara Thompson (Green, 1964) cautioned women against believing that they must behave like men in order to succeed. She suggested that rather than to compete with men in a system created by men, it would be in women's best interest to develop their own pattern. Interpretation of this advice can be both encouraging as well as limiting. According to Carol Williams (2000), associate executive director of the American Psychological Association of Graduate Students, high-achieving women are not willing to accept resignation or sacrifice. Women create meaning and identity in the context of relationships. Therefore, women would do well to surround themselves with other strong women with whom they can share intellectual equality. Moreover, because the differences in self-regulatory standards are a consequence of socialization, as Moretti and Higgins (1999) maintain, these individual differences in self-regulation can be · assumed to be teachable. Women can learn to shift their focus from relational aspects to applying their own standpoint on self as standard in self-regulation. Once women become aware of and comprehend the underlying influences of socialization, they can begin to free themselves from their impact and train themselves to reach for personal authority with focus on their individual and combined achievements in order to avoid being tied up in crippling dependency.

THE GROUP: SEX-ROLE IDENTITY

Group members seemed to be more at ease as they entered the room and met one another with a smile and a few words of greeting. Some of the women were turning toward others in groups of three, whereas Helen and Anita did not gravitate toward any other woman and not toward each other. Helen sat with closed eyes as if she needed to rest.

Ther.:   (Looking at Anita): I am glad you could join us again today. We missed you.

Anita: I am sorry I missed the previous meeting. (Sounding evasive): I may have to stay away from time to time. Several things have come up that I need to attend to.

Ther.:   Julia, how did your husband respond to your good news?

Julia: He said he was glad for me but he was concerned how my attending college would impact on our family life and my duties as wife and mother. Who would supervise the children when I have to study—things like that. Naturally, he was not as excited as I about the prospect of my going to school. Nevertheless, I have begun the application process. If everything goes well, I could start this fall.

Ther.:   That sounds promising, we are all rooting for you. (Turning to Jody): Have you had an opportunity to look for your personal space, Jody?

Jody: Actually, when you mentioned a closet the other day, I thought of a walk-in closet at the end of the downstairs hallway. It is near the kitchen and could serve as a space for a freezer or other appliance or even being a pantry. There is a narrow window and a fluorescent light fixture on the ceiling. Over the years we put a lot of stuff in there that we did not know where to store. My plan is to go through the items and see what can be thrown away and what needs to be placed somewhere else. It will take a while because I have to work on it when I am alone in the house.

Cindy: Why couldn't your husband help you sorting out and moving the stuff in the closet?

Jody: Discussing my plans with Roger before completion does not appear to be a good idea, based on my past experience. He would still believe that as a woman I don't need space for myself. My children also should not be involved in it. I don't want to ask them to keep secrets from their father.

Ther.:   You don't want to burden your children with keeping secrets and you want to allow yourself to complete your plans on your own—that shows you have done a lot of thinking about it and decided to take on the whole responsibility by yourself.

Jody: Roger does not agree that I need to do other things besides taking care of our children and the house. There is always something to do. Whenever he sees spots on the faucets in the kitchen and bathrooms he points them out to me. Our water contains minerals, and when you touch the faucets with wet hands, it causes water spots.

Inge: It looks as if Jody's husband is a real problem. He should understand that he cannot treat his wife that way.

Ther.:   Yes Inge, it would be nice if Jody's husband would understand that this is not the best way to treat a wife. Who is going to convince him? So far, apparently, things are going the way he wants it. Why should he change his opinion?

Jody: (Face turning red, avoiding eye contact with anyone by looking at her hands in her lap, almost inaudibly states): Not everything is as he wants it. He complains that I am sexually unresponsive. I have no interest in sex. Especially after the twins were born—I became depressed. I could not face having sex, and my husband took me to a mental health center. Roger did most of the talking, and the therapist seemed to agree with him. He said I had postpartum depression and suggested medication to help me over the rough spots. He explained that my hormones were out of balance because of the pregnancy and childbirth. When I asked him why it had not happened after the birth of my first daughter, he said that probably the excitement over having my first baby carried me through the hormonal change until everything was normal again. Roger thought that made sense. Even my assertion that I love our twins just as much did not change their minds. I had a diagnosis and a supply of medication and was expected to "shape up."

Betty: Why didn't you ask for a female therapist? She may have
          been more understanding.
Jody: We were assigned to this therapist who scheduled me to see
          the psychiatrist who then gave me the prescription. It never
          occurred to me to ask for anyone else. Besides, the medica-
          tion seemed to help a bit. It leveled out my feelings.
Julia: Did the medication help your sexual interests? (Adding hes-
          itatingly) I have a problem with that too. Perhaps medication
          would be a solution for me.
Jody: No, my interest in sex did not increase. Actually, it got worse
          after my youngest daughter was born. I dread every time I
          have to have sex. I know I have to go along with it from time
          to time. I wait as long as I can. Usually, I go to bed early,
          pretending to be asleep when Roger comes to bed, or I stay
          up late, hoping that he will be asleep when I finally go to
          bed. When we do have sex, the best thing is that I will be safe
          for a couple of weeks. Sometimes during intercourse I catch
          myself thinking that I need to remember to wipe off the
          faucets if I go to the bathroom after having sex.
Ther.:   Jody, do you experience any pain with intercourse? If so, this
          needs to be checked with a medical expert.
Jody: No, I have no pain—just no interest. Sometimes the physical
          touch is irritating but it is not painful.
Ther.:   From what you said earlier it seems that even though it is not
          painful, you experience some relief when the sexual activity
          is over. I believe you said that you will be safe for a couple of
          weeks.
Jody: That's correct, that is about how long I can put it off and yes,
          I feel a sense of relief. But then over days the anxiety builds
          up again in anticipation of the next time.
Julia: That's exactly how I feel! I go through the same cycle of
          anxiety and relief.
Ther.:   Let's look at what is happening step by step. As you antici-
          pate having to be engaged in sexual activities, your anxiety
          builds day by day. It feels as if you are anticipating a dreadful
          event to occur. Then, when the day has finally come for you
          to have sex, you feel good—not because you enjoyed the
          activity, but because the dreadful event is over and you can
          relax for a few days. Julia and Jody, is that an accurate de-
          scription of what you experience?
Both: Absolutely!

Ther.: The accumulating anxiety over days as you anticipate the event serves to confirm that, indeed, it is a dreadful event that is awaiting you. Afterward, when you experience the relief, it again confirms that you were in a dreadful situation and it also functions to build up new anxiety. The underlying logic is "I would not have to feel relieved if it weren't dreadful; therefore, my feeling of relief confirms the badness or danger of the situation that I was in." This is the link that keeps some people paralyzed in phobias. There is the dreaded event that arouses the anxiety. When the person is able to avoid the event, relief is felt that makes the person dread the next occurrence of a similar event even more. If the person is not able to avoid the event and instead goes through with it, the experience of relief will again reinforce the fear. It is a vicious cycle that grows stronger and more debilitating with each repetition.

Jody: It seems either way, the anxiety grows. What should we do?

Ther.: Yes, the anxiety accumulates because the relief strengthens the belief that the person was or would have been in a dreadful or dangerous situation. Instead of indulging in "it feels so good when it's over," the person would do better to calmly examine the real danger and the underlying beliefs that make the event appear to be dangerous. Jody, I would also like to respond to your statement that sometimes physical touch becomes irritating. This could be because you feel tense as your anxiety increases. Touches that would otherwise be caressing can become irritating under those circumstances.

Anita: I don't understand why you dread having sex. Sex is one way we can get what we want. Men are powerful and they can demand sex or anything else. I must be different; I enjoy sex. I like the attention I get from men. I feel more important when I am with a man than with other women. It's like I am closer to the power with a man. It started with my father. He treated me different from my sisters and brothers. I was his little princess and I got things my siblings did not get. I learned that I had to be pretty and pleasing in order to get what I want. I don't have women friends, never did. In my marriage I took my husband for granted and became bored. That was my biggest mistake.

Helen: (Speaking slowly): Perhaps Anita is right. Men expect us to do what they want; otherwise we get nothing. My sister learned that faster than I did. My husband had affairs when I was too tired to feel sexy. He did not work and had plenty of time to rest and go out and play around. He did not help me so I would be less tired. I finally had to divorce him when he got another woman pregnant. It cost me most of the money I had saved but it cost him nothing. I'll never trust any man again as long as I live!

Ther.: That must have been very painful for you, Helen, and it is understandable that you have become bitter and don't trust men. Perhaps in the future you will have friendlier experiences. Would you like to tell us more about yourself?

Helen: I am not ready yet. I should not have spoken as I did. (Her jaw set firmly, her lips tightly shut—she looked like she would never speak again.)

Ther.: Certainly, we will respect your wishes. Whenever you are ready, we will listen. Some of you have shared personal matters. Here we are in a place where we can express our opinions without being punished but also without being punishing. Please remember that we all make judgments based on our own experiences and our own values. Those values and beliefs may not always be shared by others. The solutions we arrive at in our explorations should be congruent with the values of the person we assist at the moment. Let's see what we can learn about Jody's situation before we turn to other issues. Jody, does your husband know how you feel?

Jody: I don't think so, at least, not all of it.

Ther.: How do you feel about him, Jody? Did you feel this way when you first met him, when you married him? Has there been a change in your emotions over the years?

Jody: That is a tough question. I married him because Roger seemed so intelligent, so strong, stable, and dependable. He knew what he wanted and he was protective of me. I felt I could trust him.

Ther.: You thought you would find in Roger the stability you did not have in your childhood.

Jody: Yes, my childhood was very unstable. My mother married and divorced several times. My first husband had been unpredictable. When I met Roger I admired his confidence and the way he made decisions. When we planned our wedding I let him make most decisions because I could not rely on anything from my family. My brothers and sisters faced their own struggles, trying to get away from home as early as they could. It is strange there was no real emotional closeness between us siblings. I felt lucky that my husband stuck by me.

Liz: Jody, do you think that you didn't feel like an equal to your husband because of that?

Jody: Yes, it was his intelligence and his strength that attracted me to him and I did not realize that he was making all the decisions. It seemed so natural at first but I let it go on too long and now I resent it. But I don't know how to change it.

Inge: Jody, you are talking as if your husband's intelligence is to blame. Do you think that less intelligent men make better husbands? My first husband was smart but not ambitious and I left him because I fell in love with David, a very intelligent man who is also ambitious. David seems to know everything and he lets me know it. We had some bad arguments when I challenged him. He did not like it and left me. Are we then all doomed when we love intelligent men?

Ther.: One of the comforts we can derive from a group experience is that we have experiences in common. We can learn from one another as well as with each other. While Inge and Jody seemed to be attracted to intelligent men, Inge implied that there were arguments when she challenged David's intelligence. Jody indicated that her husband's decision-making behaviors became more pronounced over time. Perhaps if you had realized earlier how this would affect your lives and your feelings for your husbands, you could have prevented the development of the consequences you are struggling with now.

Liz: Are you saying that Jody's husband would not have become so domineering if Jody would not have let him be that way?

Ther.: We cannot prove that this would have occurred; but Jody seems to realize that she had a part in the development, that she refrained from making decisions when she had the opportunity to do so. It may have been out of recognizing her husband's importance or perhaps to avoid the responsibility for decisions that were not successful—whatever the reason, she stood back and let her husband act.

Jody: I think that is true. Although Roger would not have let me make every decision, I remember that early in our marriage I deferred decisions to him, thinking that I would not be to blame if I made a mistake. How can I turn that back?

Inge: You can tell your husband that it is time he treats you right.

Ann: What does all that have to do with Jody's lack of interest in sex?

Ther.: There may be a connection, Ann. As Jody told us, she could have been more assertive but she chose not to be responsible for the consequences of decisions. To avoid the responsibility, she let Roger take over more and more. The sad thing is that she was not happy with it and started to resent his growing authority until her feelings for him cooled to the point where she did not want to have physical contact with him anymore. In a way she may have traded her blamelessness for her love for Roger. It's a process that occurs over time, day by day—until it seems impossible to go back.

Inge: Wait a minute! You make it sound as if it is Jody's responsibility how her husband acts. Just because she does not want to make decisions does not mean he has to tell her how to live. He could still be as nice as he wanted to be. He does not have to be bossy.

Ther.: Of course, you are correct, Inge. People are responsible for their behaviors. But we do not live in a vacuum. In our interactions with others, we can, at times, have an influence on their behaviors. We also have the responsibility to see that we receive the treatment we want from others. If we believe somebody will treat us the way we want to be treated just because they chose to share our lives, that belief would need to be confronted with reality. Loving does not guarantee loveable behavior. Jody and Julia have accepted their husbands' authority, even though they may resent it. One of the challenges we face in this group could be redefining our sex-role identity and how it affects our motivation. Before we close for today I would like to remind us that Cindy and Ann mentioned in the previous session their wishes to be special. We did not get to it today but want to follow up on this issue. Most of us want to feel special, and that feeling can only come from within us. As we get to know ourselves better and find out about our talents and skills, we can learn to feel good about those parts in us. With the knowledge of what we can do and what we want, we can determine our paths and have presence among others.

Cindy: Where and when do we start?

Ther.: Right now you can start making an inventory about your skills and talents and where you want to apply them. And let's not discount previous experiences; even what looks like a mistake can serve as a learning experience if we regard it as such. In addition, as we consider our sex-role identity in connection with motivation, we can decide on a traditional path—giving in and giving up—or we can actively assume the responsibility for choosing what we want.

GROUP PROCESS: SEX-ROLE IDENTITY

Not all members have verbalized the challenges they want to consider during this group experience. But two of the members were able to start on a project and formulate the first steps toward resolution. Other challenges arose in the discussion and, again, some of those were experienced by several of the members. How the women's lack of happiness impacted on the levels of their sexual desire was a significant revelation. Although they consider strong men in leadership positions sexually attractive, caught in daily routines of being told what to do, the women's sexual interest wanes. As can be expected when different personalities come together, opinions vary and disagreements arise. Anita, with her statements about connections to powerful men, seemed to distance herself from the rest of the group. Was it done intentionally? Inge's behavior betrayed her difficulty handling frustrations. Her tendency to vent her frustrations in the group was reminiscent of a past incident in her individual session.

In an emotionally charged atmosphere such as a group therapy session, confrontations can be expected to occur. The skilled therapist will not avoid confrontations but will guide them to a point where the emotions do not overrule the content and the purpose of the meeting. Expression of negative feelings can alleviate the experienced distress if it leads to resolution of the underlying sources of distress. Whereas in situations where the expression of negative feelings takes on the form of ruminations without resolutions, the level of distress can actually become intensified (Kennedy-Moore & Watson, 2001).

SUMMARY

This chapter traced the development of sex-role identity as a determining force through the lives of women. As the process unfolds, many cultural, societal, and familial influences come to bear on the growing sense of personhood that each woman establishes for herself.

Various motivational forces come into play and intermingle in distinctive ways with developing aspects of women's sex-role identity. It is the unique reciprocal interaction of these variables that determines whether the woman's life is one of personal authority and achievement or one of dependency and unfulfilled potential.

QUESTIONS FOR CONSIDERATION

Women's self-determination—Is it the individual's responsibility or society's?

Should women place the importance of their own career goals above their husbands'?

RECOMMENDED READING

Arnett, J. J. (2000). Emerging adulthood: A theory of development from the late teens through the twenties. *American Psychologist, 55,* 469–480.
  Tracing individuals' development the author proposes a theory of emerging adulthood.
Ryan, R. M., & Deci, E. L. (2000). Self-determination theory and the facilitation of intrinsic motivation, social development, and well-being. *American Psychologist, 55,* 68–78.
  The authors identify different types of motivation and outline principles of development and maintenance for each type.

CHAPTER FIVE

Explorations and Discoveries

I f Socrates in his questioning about 'how are we to live?' found that the unexamined life is not worth living (Allen, 1985, p. 18), what is a life without explorations, explorations about what could be? As early as in the fourth century B.C. the concept of self-actualization was expressed when Aristotle postulated that the proper aim of each being or object is to come to fruition and to realize its own being.

SELF-ACTUALIZATION—REVISITED

This ancient concept has found its rebirth in the well-known term "self-actualization," introduced by Abraham Maslow (1968) in his comparisons of people who are motivated by growth needs and those motivated by basic needs. As healthy people have fulfilled their basic needs of safety, belonging, and self-esteem, their main motivational forces become trends toward self-actualization, such as actualization of potentials, capacities, and talents. Since then the term has become popular beyond the realm of psychology, making its way into the management of business and industry. Meanings of the term self-actualization have been translated into a fuller knowledge of the person's own intrinsic nature (see Maslow), and its image has been incorporated and integrated with the systematic creation of organizational dependency by management (Rose, 1990).

Maslow's concept centers on capacities, talents, and creative abilities that exist within people and self-actualizing people are considered to be less dependent, more autonomous and self-directed than people who are still in the process of actualizing or fulfilling basic needs.

Basic assumptions about these inherent capacities include the notion that it is possible to study and discover them and that they are not necessarily strong and overpowering like the instincts of animals. These inherent tendencies are often weak and subtle and easily defeated by habit, cultural pressure, and wrong attitudes toward them. Maslow raised the question: How can we encourage free development of these inherent capacities? Rather than to wait for the creative tendencies to surface on their own, active processes of exploration, of trying out different activities and behaviors as well as gently encouraging and nurturing the promises, options, and results is one answer to the question. Another view proposed that creativity requires a decision by the individual (Sternberg, 2001). Upon observing others and their attitudes in making creative decisions, individuals can decide to develop their own. Maslow's assumption that the person will become ill if the inherent essential core of these capacities is denied or suppressed implies a demand that people should dedicate themselves to actualize their inbuilt potential rather than leaving it to be a situation of choice.

The story of a talented young woman struggling with chemical dependency issues comes to mind here. The therapist attempted to help by focusing on the extraordinary talent of the client who, in turn, answered, "I am tired of hearing about my talent. It has become a burden. I did not ask God to give me the ability to paint. I should not have to do it when I don't feel like it!" One could argue that Maslow's assumption was correct because the young woman's chemical dependency was a reflection of impaired health; however, the purpose of this book is not to take sides in an argument but to focus on the choices individuals make.

INHERENT CAPACITIES

Of significance for our work are the assumptions that inherent capacities—despite their subtle nature—can be discovered with care and patience and can also be overshadowed and defeated by habits or outside forces. Consider the cultural pressure working on a little girl when she repeatedly receives dolls and domestic play items on her birthdays and other holidays. By its very repetition, the appearance of the dolls may stifle the blossoming of other creative activities in the girl. Or consider the following scenario: A supermarket chain on the East coast, as a promotional offer, gives customers the opportunity to select various art prints as their purchases reach a certain amount. A boy, about 5 years old, and his mother are observed as the mother encourages the boy to choose one of the available prints for his room. The gentle but vibrant colors in Van Gogh's well-known painting of the washerwomen at the foot of the bridge at Arles caught the little boy's eyes. He reached for it, his voice triumphantly saying, "This is the one I want." His mother removed the picture from his hands, substituting a print of a big locomotive and part of a train—all painted in dark brown, black, and gray colors. The mother explained that Van Gogh's painting was not appropriate for a boy's room. The little boy did not make a sound but the disappointment in his eyes spoke loud and clear—however, without impact on his mother.

Of course, that is not to say that either the girl or the boy would have become famous artists, the two scenarios merely demonstrate the potential power of cultural pressure and social attitudes on young, impressionable minds.

Louise: Defeated Capacities

The story of Louise, a single woman with a lifelong history of depression, contains similar elements of pressure. Louise grew up as the only child of a domineering, emotionally distant mother and a gentle but ineffective father. Louise recalled her mother as telling her frequently, "hurry up, Louise!" Louise interpreted this to mean that she was mentally slow. Their strained relationship continued through Louise's adulthood to shortly before her mother's death. Louise may have possessed a talent for music. In college it had been her wish to study music, but her mother insisted that she become a teacher. Louise did not enlist her father's support for her career choice. As she later said, "My father always seemed to suffer, I couldn't bring myself to add to his burden." Her emotional conflict became so intense that she was not able to conceive of the possibility to combine the study of music with the training as a teacher. She dropped out of college and returned home without achieving the security of a profession. Her self-confidence, not strong or stable to begin with due to her mother's dominance and lack of emotional warmth, plummeted even further. Career counseling may have been beneficial in Louise's situation, but—according to her recollection—it was not available when she was a young girl. The rest of her life was marked by hard physical labor, financial dependence on her mother for many years, and lasting deep depression for most of her life.

Whether or not her life would have been rewarded with a successful career in music if she had been strong enough to resist her mother's pressure is impossible to determine in retrospect. Whatever talents Louise possessed, they were overshadowed by other forces and were not sufficient to overpower the obstacles in her path to self-actualizing or even to recognize the fact that there were options for her.

EXPLORATIONS OF INTERESTS AND WOMEN'S VOCATIONAL CHOICES

As mentioned in chapter 1, for women, the process of career decision making is complex because of internal and external barriers and restrictions associated with women's career development. Aside from exploring interests and talents that will lead to certain careers, women have to consider the possibility of interruptions in their training and in the development of their careers if they plan to have a family. These factors could partially account for the fact that women remain underrepresented in many occupations, that they enter lower paying, lower status positions, that they are less likely to advance to higher positions, and that they underuse their skills and talents (Lyness & Thompson, 1997; Stroh, Brett, & Reilly, 1996). These factors could also explain women's hesitancy to act on satisfying their curiosity and exploring their dreams.

When female role models for balancing professional and personal life are unavailable, women may fear that their wishes and goals do not amount to more than fantasy. For female students within the field of psychology, mentoring programs have become a much-sought answer. Many female students are looking for role models to emulate, women in leadership roles who also have family responsibilities (Schlegel, 2000).

Ellen: Detours on the Way to Vocational Choice

For some women the existence of ambiguous role models can be confusing. Ellen, the youngest of four daughters, did not see any viable vocational choices for herself at the time her story began in chapter 1. She was a wonderful mother to her children and her talents and creativity centered on her household. Under her guidance, birthdays and little picnics turned into memorable feasts. Her imagination transformed simple foods into nutritious works of art. Ellen's friends encouraged her to sell her productions of sauces, salad dressings, condiments, and other items but because of the lack of any appropriate license she could only give away her creations. Ellen continued to drift from husband to husband until finally after leaving her fifth husband her restlessness brought her to vocational training as a dietary technician. During her training, she obtained a practicum-internship with a local restaurant chain where she was offered a permanent job after graduation. Remembering her mother's work-related responses when she was a young girl, Ellen was surprised over her own enthusiasm for her job. Her knowledge, creativity, and resourcefulness, combined with her friendly outgoing personality traits, resulted in steady professional advancements. Finally after many detours she had found her niche.

NONTRADITIONAL FEMALE STUDENTS

What other factors may play a role in women's explorations for change? A study involving 47 married women between the ages of 25 and 34 who were employed full-time and were enrolled in an evening program of a small liberal arts college revealed that enrolling in college was not mainly and solely determined by the women's motivation. The timing was a function of the state of their relationships and life events, such as postponing college until the children were older or they felt a reduction in family responsibilities, or even to avoid inconveniencing employers or coworkers (Mohney & Anderson, 1988). The barriers most often cited that had kept the women from enrolling in college at an earlier age were role demands, such as taking care of family of origin needs or extended family needs, as well as job demands.

Women who enter or reenter college have different experiences than traditional female or male students. Many reentry women underestimate their abilities even though they have developed valuable skills in organizing and time management through their homemaking, parenting, and volunteer activities. These skills are relevant and applicable to studying, but the women may not be aware of the transferability of those skills.

Marlene: Delayed Investment in Self

Marlene could be one of the women in Mohney and Anderson's study above. Her plans to study archaeology came to a premature end when she met Tom, a history and prelaw student, who envisioned a career in politics. Marlene agreed that an archaeologist wife would not be practical for Tom's career. She left college and obtained an office job to help pay for Tom's studies. They married while Tom was finishing law school. Marlene maintained part-time employment while raising their two sons. Years later, through her oldest son's studies, she developed an interest in architecture.

When she discovered Tom's involvement in an extramarital affair, her trust in Tom and her confidence in herself were shaken. Entering a brief period of counseling, she stated, "I have lived in a world that does not exist anymore. My family was my life. My jobs were good but did not mean much beyond the money I could contribute to my family. My husband's affair made me realize that I have nothing that is significant just for me." Upon her therapist's encouragement to explore current interests that could lead to a meaningful occupation, Marlene obtained information from a local college. Her old credits could not be applied toward current studies, but it was possible that she could test out on some of the core courses if her scores were high enough. Furthermore, the "General Studies" program seemed to be tailor-made for people like Marlene. Parts of her work history and life experiences could be applied toward college credits. when she told Tom about her prospects, he doubted that she would be able to test out of the core courses. Jokingly he added that her spelling skills did not seem to go beyond the letters, a, r, c, and h.

Marlene was not amused. She confided in her older sister, who advised her to put all her energies into working on her marriage to overcome the impact of Tom's affair instead of thinking about college. Marlene could not accept that Tom's involvement with other women should be all her responsibility. She decided to reenter college. Successful in her studies within a field still dominated by men, Marlene obtained her degree with high honors, accompanied by several job offers. Tom and Marlene's relationship has changed. Tom has gained new respect for his wife, confirming her statement: "By investing in myself I have done more for my marriage than I could have done otherwise."

FEMALE VOLUNTEERS

After years of marriage when the children have reached a certain age so that they become less and less time-demanding in their mothers' daily lives, women may search outside the home for activities that give them satisfaction. The field of volunteering offers a world of choices and opportunities to women. Volunteers work as hard as, if not harder, at what they are doing than their paid counterparts. They take their responsibilities every bit as serious as paid workers. But perhaps the fact that they are not paid for their services affords them an aspect of freedom. As volunteers, they may be more willing to try out something that seems interesting but for which they have no formal preparation than if they were to perform the same work for a salary. As volunteers, women also may be more likely to explore different types of activities, whereas in employment people are more inclined to follow a given path. Thus, detours can provide exciting side trips in the overall adventure.

Diane Rehm's (1999) story is a well-known example of such an adventure. During her participation in a course, designed to assist women in figuring out what to do with the rest of their lives, she was encouraged to try broadcasting, an area in which she had no training or experience. Despite her doubts regarding her own skills and despite her anxiety, Diane managed to get started in broadcasting, a medium that had fascinated her since childhood. From her first time on the air she was hooked and that excitement lasted for more than 25 years. Today, as host of the *Diane Rehm Show,* she is not a volunteer anymore but a much respected and admired professional broadcaster. Her explorations have led her to a place of excitement, satisfaction, and meaningful work activity—a place more stimulating than she could have imagined when she started out.

Women, involved in volunteer activities, are giving back to society and the community parts of the resources they have enjoyed. The reader will notice in chapter 12 that in the story of the "Draft-dodger's Bride" the mother of the main character was involved in volunteer work that eventually lead to a part-time job and, in turn, prompted her granddaughter to also donate her efforts and time in volunteer work. Thus, the philosophy of volunteering—while providing options for interesting and fulfilling activities—has become a family tradition for some.

EXPLORING VERSUS DRIFTING

Looking at a person's life in retrospect without the benefit of an autobiography, one cannot be certain if the path through the person's life followed a conscious exploration or if it was a case of drifting from one event to another like a journey through a shallow brook where rocks at different places determine turns in the flow of the water without active manipulation by the drifter. Sometimes it appears to be a combination of both.

Susan: The Storyteller

Occasionally, explorations need a little nudge from the outside to get started or to continue after a less than successful beginning, as happened with Susan, the single mother of three children (Maass & Neely, 2000). Like many mothers, she had made it a tradition to tell her children bedtime stories about once a week. It was a special treat for them. Although the stories usually began as popular fairy tales, they changed in their content and had very different endings from the well-known fairy tales. Susan did not record the stories. They would have been lost if it hadn't been for her children. One day while they were trying to entertain themselves at their grandmother's house, one of her sons started drawing cartoons. The grandmother became intrigued because the boy was obviously talented and the cartoons seemed to tell a story. With grandmother's encouragement the children helped Susan to remember the stories and write them down. The son's drawings were used for illustrations, emphasizing different parts of the stories. What had started as a Christmas project—producing little illustrated storybooks for friends and relatives—turned into a family business. The children nudged Susan's fantasy skills to continue with her stories. They recorded the stories while she spoke, her son continued to draw cartoons, and grandmother became the business manager, getting them published. Little by little, the younger children developed talents that fit into the family enterprise. Susan had never considered her storytelling talents significant enough to be known beyond the circle of her own family.

THE GROUP: EXPLORATIONS

The beginning of the fourth meeting was characterized by animated verbal interchanges among some of the women. Interactions in the previous meeting had brought more emotionally charged challenges to the surface than could be covered to completion in the session. Women's wish to be special and the lack of sexual desire are topics that several of the women have in common and need continuing discussion in following sessions.

Ther.:   In our previous meeting, we started out defining some of the challenges you want to tackle in your work here. In doing so, we uncovered another challenge that some of you face and that is the lack of sexual desire. This is not an isolated problem. As sex therapist, I see many women who have similar complaints. As we mentioned last week, an imbalance of hormones could be at the base of this, especially if you experienced a higher level of sexual interest in the past. This, of course, should be checked out with your gynecologist or a clinic that specializes in the treatment of sexual dysfunctions. Assuming that hormonal imbalance is not the cause, there is another aspect that we can address here and that is the change within you that occurred from your dating days to now. (Facing Julia and Jody): When you look back to that time of dating a young man, becoming interested in him enough to spend the rest of your life with—what were your thoughts and attitudes about sexual activity then? How did you feel when you were dating? What is the difference from then to now?

Julia: As a young girl I was in love like many of us. It was not a good choice. On the rebound I turned to another man. The outcome of that relationship was even more devastating than the first one. Then I met Ted. He was charming and exciting to be with, but he was also moody. My parents did not approve of him. He had these big dreams of what we would do with our life. We eloped and got married. Ted wanted us to go around the world, just starting somewhere, working for a while until we had enough money to go to the next place, stay for several months, and pick up and go again. When he talked about it, it sounded exciting. Then I found out I was pregnant and I told him we could not go on his planned journey. He said that if I loved him I would get an abortion. I could not handle that and told him no. He became very moody and finally took off by himself without telling me. One day when I came home he was gone. Several weeks later, I received a letter from him and a call from the police. In the letter he told me that he could not bear the thought that I did not love him enough to choose him over everything else in my life. There was no point for him to live anymore. From the police I learned that Ted had killed himself. That was his punishment for me. I miscarried; he might as well have lived— there was no baby to worry about or to compete with. Only later did I find out that he had been diagnosed with Bipolar Disorder or manic depression in the past, but he had not taken his medication as prescribed.

Jody: What a terribly sad story. How did you manage to go through all of that more or less on your own since your parents did not approve of Ted and probably not of the other two men, either, that you were involved with?

Julia: You are right, Jody, my parents did not approve of any of them and the experiences that I had with them proved my parents to be right. In their eyes, I lost all credibility to make decisions about my life. I returned home and lived with my parents. For a while I did not go out other than to go to work. I was afraid of the next mistake I would make. Finally, I met Bob. Dating him felt comfortable in a way but I was not excited. There was no romance. From what I had learned, excitement was bad for me and settling down into married life seemed the thing to do. My parents certainly approved of that. Sex is a duty rather than anything enjoyable, something I have to do to keep the peace.

Ther.:   You went through a lot of emotional upheaval at a young age. From the way you described it, relationships with men carried punishment for you. Misjudging their character or personality was very costly. It is not surprising that you don't find anything enjoyable in sexual activities. If you enjoyed it in your early relationships, you may have considered the price to be too high later on. How long can you go on considering sex to be a chore and performing the chore because it is your duty—that is the question confronting you now. Last time we talked about the way your negative anticipations and the feeling of relief may function to reinforce your dislike for sex.

Jody: I thought a lot about that discussion. For me it seems there was no time for anything, except feeding, diapering, and watching over the children after the twins were born. The cleaning and cooking had to be done while they were asleep. By the time Roger came home from work I was exhausted. In my tiredness his suggestions sounded like criticism, and his decisions, for which I had admired him in the past, seemed like orders and demands.

Ther.:   In a short period of time you transformed yourself from lover to loving wife, to loving mother, and finally to mother and overworked housekeeper. Your sensuality and sexual arousal capacity got lost in the transformation. When you were dating, you had much more time to think romantic thoughts, not only during the time you spent with Roger but at other times too. It is difficult to think sexual thoughts when you do the laundry, plan meals, run after your children, and feel hassled about all kinds of household chores. People don't switch instantly in their mind-sets from household slave to romantic lover. Changes like that take mental and physical preparation.

Jody: I never heard anything like this before. But it makes sense. I always considered myself more a romantic than a sexual being, and I blamed myself for losing interest when the romance turned into married life, thinking that I am a shallow person. In my experience, it seems that men easily fall into a routine with sex and leave out the romance part—or are we making it easy for them to drop the romance?

Ther.: That is a good question, Jody. You are implying that women, by performing their many daily activities and having little time left over for themselves, encourage their husbands to spend less time with lovemaking, even though the romance and playful part are extremely important for their own arousal? Consequently, without the romance and play, sex becomes just another dreaded chore to perform and finally leads to the "negative anticipation and relief when it's over" segment.

Helen: When you work all day at your job and do the housework at night, how much time and energy is left for romance? How can you help it when you are exhausted?

Betty: That's right. When you are worn out from a full day's work, there is not much energy left for sexual activities, let alone romantic settings. I never turned my ex-husband down, because I considered it to be a part of the marriage that I had to fulfill. I did not always enjoy it.

Anita: It takes a lot of time to enjoy sex and make sex enjoyable to your partner. It is a job in itself. I have to be rested to enjoy sex. I like to dress up in special clothes, wearing perfume, being as beautiful as I can be. The man's admiration and desire arouse me.

Inge: (Turning to Anita): I never thought I would agree with you on that Anita, but you are way ahead of us. With my first husband, I did not enjoy sexual activities. I was brought up very modest and we never left the lights on in our bedroom. With David it is so different. With him I have learned to be proud of my body, and as you said, seeing his desire for me is exciting. What is the difference? I guess my attitude about myself.

Ther.: As Inge said, it is a matter of attitude about oneself. Here is another part of life that we can explore. If marriage and sexual activities are to be part of our lives, it would serve us well to know what it takes to make it an enjoyable activity rather than a dreaded chore. Some of you may want to explore this aspect of life in more depth, perhaps in individual counseling. It deserves more attention than we can give it during our group experience. However, it would have been negligent and unrealistic not to address the issue, because it has caused some of you significant distress. Also, if you want to continue in the marriage, you may want to rethink how to improve your feelings for your husbands. For instance, what would be options that Jody can focus on to improve her relationship with her husband?

Betty: Thinking back on my own marriage and how desperately I had wanted to preserve the marriage, I would say for Jody to think about what would make her feel better toward her husband. She loved him enough to marry him, and there may still be some warm feelings left in her if she doesn't have to focus only on what she does not like about him. Although I don't mean to suggest she do what I did, just accept everything.

Ther.:   That is an excellent idea, Betty. Instead of continuing with the marriage as is, one of Jody's challenges is to improve her own feelings toward her husband by thinking what behaviors in her husband would make her feel more loving toward him. Are there any other options?

Liz: Once she knows what those behaviors are she could tell Roger how it makes her feel.

Ther.:   Great, these are good suggestions for options. Jody, I hope you have some ideas to consider.

Anita: If my ex-husband would take me back, I would go in a heart-beat. At least, I would be with my boys. I miss them terribly.

Helen: You said before that you are different. Why are you here if you feel so different from the rest of us?

Anita: I am here because it is part of my court deal. (She adds with a defiant laugh) I guess you could say I am serving time.

Ther.:   (Tension was rising to the point one could almost see it. If Anita had felt like an outsider before, after she had spoken, the gap between her and the other women widened even more.): Anita, I think we realize how hard the struggle is to get your children back and how lonely you feel in this situation, not knowing where to turn for help. We may not know how to assist you in the custody situation, but, with time, we hope you will feel closer to some of the women here.

Inge: I think I understand some of Anita's feelings. When she talked about not having female friends I suddenly realized that I don't have any woman friends. At first I thought it was because I grew up in Europe and had not had time to make friends here. But, of course, I have been here long enough to make friends. Perhaps it would have been easier if my first husband had been American. We both have a different cultural background and that may have kept us apart from others. Although when I think of it, even in Europe I did not have close friends when I was growing up. The other girls always seemed to be envious of me because of my looks.

Jody: You said you have four children—didn't that bring you together with other mothers?

Inge: No, not really, except for acquaintances on a superficial level, not really friends. Most of my efforts were spent in getting ahead in my career, because my husband was not ambitious and I wanted more for us. Through my work I always related more to men than to women. In fact, there were women who did not like me, but I advanced in spite of them. In the world of business, the influential people are men and we naturally try to do our best with them for our own benefit.

Ther.:   You have come to an important insight, Inge. The attention we want from men for whatever reason can isolate us from other women. As you said, you had your family and your work. That kept you busy enough so you did not miss the comfort of female companionship. In Anita's case, it seems that her father's early attention isolated her even from her own family, from her siblings as well as from her mother. This isolation prevented her from relating to other women until now.

Liz: I have female friends, but I get upset when they suddenly cancel an appointment we had scheduled some time ago because a man has just asked them for a date for the same time. What is worse, they expect you to understand and accept it because everybody knows it is more desirable to go out with a man. Women feel more important when they are with a man.

Ther.:   What is it that makes a woman feel more important with a man by her side than either being alone or with another woman? Is a man more important because he can bestow importance on us? Without a man—we are not important? And to think of it, women are telling themselves and other women that they are insignificant without men.

Cindy: It seems that a man's importance is all-pervasive. As Betty
          told us before, she accepted her husband's wishes as more
          important than her own. If she had known that the denial of
          her own wishes did not keep her marriage intact, her deci-
          sions might have been different in the past.

Ther.:   You are correct Cindy, Betty can still learn from her past
          experience. Our explorations will provide information and
          tools with which to forge our future.

Betty: This is mind-boggling! To think I lived my whole life wrong.
          All my beliefs that I thought were valid have not worked for
          me.

Julia: (Turning toward Betty with empathy in her voice and reflect-
          ed in her facial expression): Not all your beliefs are wrong,
          Betty. You believed in hard work, so do many of us and that
          is what has helped us to gain some independence. You raised
          two sons who are independent and productive. The beliefs
          that need modification are those that tell us to place the
          wishes of others in our lives before our own—the belief that
          our husbands are the ones to determine our lives and there-
          fore our husbands and our children are more important than
          we are. As we learned the other day, we act on our beliefs
          because we are convinced that they are right or true without
          doubting them—but they could be wrong for us. I am just
          starting to learn that and I have a head start in individual
          therapy. I still have a long way to go. I am trying to find out
          what I want to do—or what I can do, by going to college.

Betty: At least you see a beginning. I am glad for you.

Julia: Yes, it is a beginning. But I still don't know how to convince
          my husband or my parents that I can make sound decisions.
          Jody is in a similar situation. Your telling us about your life,
          Betty, is helping us to consider our own wishes earlier than you
          did. I can only hope that we can help you in some way, too.

Betty: That was the nicest thing anyone ever said to me. I will always
          remember you for that, Julia.

Ther.:   Your statements are very helpful, Julia. We have an opportu-
          nity to explore and learn a lot from and with one another.
          There is another aspect of exploration that we might as well
          consider now. Are there any wishes or thoughts you may have
          had as you were growing up about how your life would be or
          what you would want to do? For instance, like Amelia Ear-
          hart, the first woman pilot to cross the Atlantic and Pacific

oceans, as a young girl watched the planes take off at the airport and vowed that she would become a pilot some day. Or the actress Claire Bloom, as you read in her book, Ann, knew early on that she wanted to become an actress.

Ann: That reminds me of another book I read recently. It was a biography about Agnes de Mille, who always wanted to be a dancer even though her body did not appear designed for it. With fierce determination and hard work she managed to become a prominent dancer, choreographer, and writer in a world that was mostly occupied and directed by men. It was her opinion that if women were happily involved in creative work, they would be better wives and mothers. However, I was disappointed when I read that she also believed no matter what a woman achieved, her life was not complete without husband and child (Easton, 1996).

Jody: I thought having children was the most important thing in my life—but even that does not make me completely happy. There is something empty, something missing, and I don't know what it is or where to find it. It makes me feel anxious all the time.

Ther.: What do you think might be missing? What are your thoughts connected with that?

Jody: There was a time when I thought I wanted to be a writer. One of my college professors thought I had talent and encouraged me to continue. One semester there was a workshop with a visiting author. She told us about her decision to become a writer and how difficult it had been for her to become recognized. I remember her statement about being unable to write after she had declared that she was going to be a writer. Her acknowledgement had become a source of stress that she could not overcome for a long time.

Ther.: Do you think that the author was afraid of her own intentions once they were known?

Jody: Yes, it was like making a promise that you don't know you can fulfill. The author's story has haunted me. I remember thinking that if I were to become a mother, I could write and nobody would expect me to produce any great literary works. Children would naturally be more important than anything else. (After some silence): I wonder if I used becoming a mother as justification for my existence so I wouldn't have to worry if I have what it takes to be a writer?

Ther.:   Jody, that is a significant question, one that takes time and
         courage to explore. Just asking the question took courage.
         Whatever the answer will be, you could start now to discover
         your talents.
Jody: It is a troublesome question that I could only ask in a safe
         environment. I have used similar reasoning when I thought
         about the possibility of painting or music. I have all these
         little talents.
Ther.:   I am glad you feel safe enough here to explore about your-
         self. We don't know how 'little' your talents are, but there are
         ways to find out.
Jody: I wonder what else I will find out about myself.
Ther.:   We share your curiosity about discovering things about your-
         self. Ann, you seem to be reading a lot of books about wom-
         en. I am glad you are sharing your information with us. The
         story of Agnes de Mille is a stimulating example. Of course,
         we only hear about the ones who became famous. Many of us
         have had—or still have—dreams and wishes like that, but we
         may not have expressed them, even to ourselves. Please write
         down what you remember, it may be grandiose or it may
         seem unremarkable. It may be as short or as long as you
         think appropriate. I will keep your writings confidential until
         you are ready to disclose them.

GROUP PROCESS: EXPLORATIONS

By outlining the significant aspects of the group approach in earlier
meetings, the therapist had established the atmosphere of a journey
of discovery, where every member was invited to explore alternatives
that would be acceptable to them instead of what others might expect
from them. By the same token, others may not be willing to fulfill our
expectations unless there is a good reason for it, such as a benefit to
them.

To develop an environment of support among the women, the therapist emphasized similarities in thoughts and beliefs that some of the
women shared as well as parallels in their backgrounds. Lack of sexual
desire was a significant ongoing concern for several group members.
Continuing the discussion about it early in the session made it possible to reach a point of closure on this topic. Other common themes
were women's attraction to intelligent and powerful men as well as

women's desire to be accepted, to be protected, and to be admired—
often to the point were they become isolated from other women.
Anita's and Inge's lives appeared focused mainly on their relationships
with men to the exclusion of establishing or maintaining friendships
with other women.

It was remarkable that the group member, Ann, remembered parts
of a book written by the British actress Claire Bloom (1996), as it
became meaningful to her own life and explained some of her own
behavior. In Bloom's own words: "He had shown me, and not for the
first time, that he would do things only his way, and do them as and
when he wished" (p. 151). The part that was particularly relevant to
Ann seemed to be: "I noticed the warning signals; but of course the
situation would be different with me. So most women imagine it
will be with them, as they enter a new and challenging relationship" (p. 146). Describing her experiences after she had neglected
those warning signals, Claire Bloom explained: "The answer is that
I was intimidated: Philip always gained the upper hand in an argument, and with his razor-sharp wit could easily say something amus-
ing and cutting to make my position appear futile and humiliating"
(p. 147). Those statements reflect some of the costs that women
may pay when they become infatuated with men of superior intelligence.

Important concepts previously introduced by the therapist, such as
people act as if their beliefs are true and their perceptions are accurate, made an impact on some of the group members. The assignment
for members to verbalize wishes or dreams that they may have had in
the past was meant to guide the women toward thinking about themselves independent of others and also to become aware of additional
options that may exist for them.

SUMMARY

This chapter dealt with women's explorations in various areas. From
concerns of self-actualization to discovery of inherent capacities, interests, and talents that may lead to women's vocational choices, the
stories of women in everyday life situations were used for illustration.
The process of exploration can occur in a determined and planned
manner or it can be initiated through accidental happenings. The
second half of the chapter continued to trace the development in the
explorations of members of a women's therapy group.

QUESTIONS FOR CONSIDERATION

How do women transform themselves from lovers to wives and mothers, misplacing the lovers? How can they prevent losing the lover in themselves?

As a female reader of this book, how would you respond if you had a date with a female friend and the friend called you to cancel the date because she had an offer to go out with a man at the same time of your date?

RECOMMENDED READING

Mohney, C., & Anderson, W. (1988). The effect of life events and relationships on adult women's decisions to enroll in college. *Journal of Counseling and Development, 66,* 271–274.

This survey article describes how women experience difficulties in their personal lives that impinge on their adjustment to their college attendance.

Williams, C. (2000). Desperately seeking female mentors [Education]. *Monitor on Psychology, 31,* 37.

The article introduces the notion of female mentorship for the benefit of female graduate students in their search for accomplishment.

CHAPTER SIX

Development of Personal Significance

M axwell Maltz (1973) considered twentieth-century man's great-est enemy a sense of emptiness. Many people go through their days with a feeling of aimlessness, lacking a sense of meaning or significance. They may blame facts, such as not being married, not having children, or not being highly successful in their chosen careers, for this feeling of emptiness. Yet the reasons do not lie in circumstances, they lie within the person, and they may have devel-oped in childhood. The growing child attempts to find out his or her personal worth when incorporating the perception of parents' assess-ment of the child. If the child feels unappreciated or not loved by the parents, he or she will likely believe they are not being lovable or worthwhile.

CHILDHOOD INFLUENCES CRUCIAL TO THE DEVELOPMENT OF PERSONAL SIGNIFICANCE

When Erik Erikson (1963) talked about an "inner institution," such as the ego, safeguarding the order within individuals on which the outer order or environment depends, he meant a lasting ego identity that, beginning with the infant's age, cannot be completed without assur-ance of fulfillment of the dominant image of adulthood. The amount of trust that the infant develops depends on a combination of sensitive care and a firm sense of personal trustworthiness that is demonstrated by the primary caregiver. Thus the basis for the child's sense of iden-tity is formed, leading to a sense of being oneself and becoming what others trust one will become.

ATTACHMENT THEORY

Proponents of attachment theory similarly stated that in order for the individual to reach a secure stage where the person does not worry about abandonment but feels comfortable depending on others when needed, the individual has formed in childhood representational models of attachment figures as being available and responsive to attachment-related signals (Bowlby, 1988). Additionally, a representational model of the self as lovable and worthy of care is important for secure adult attachment. A secure attachment also seems to encourage a tendency to explore. The child can venture out, knowing there will be a safe haven upon return.

The positive experience when turning to others for help is thought to foster children's capacity for secure attachment in adulthood and healthy adjustment in romantic attachments. Individuals who feel lovable—reflecting a positive representation of the self—are unlikely to express behaviors that are destructive to a healthy romantic relationship, such as seeking endless reassurance from the partner, demanding excessive closeness, or refusing closeness to prevent feeling abandoned later on (Cassidy, 2000).

The literature on attachment issues has focused on children who have been exposed to inconsistently available attachment figures and who became more clingy and showed less tendency to explore their environment, toys, and others. There is a similarity of characteristics displayed by ambivalent adults and ambivalent infants and children. Although ambivalent adults look for emotional closeness in relationships, they do not find it satisfying (Hazan & Shaver, 1987). Similarly, ambivalent children seek physical closeness to the parent but do not find it satisfying. Just as ambivalent infants are upset when separated from their mothers in strange situations (Ainsworth, Blehar, Waters, & Wall, 1978), so are ambivalent adults particularly upset by relationship breakups (Feeney & Noller, 1992).

Models that are developed during early attachment relationships can influence an individual's behavior in a romantic relationship that elicits rejection or withdrawal from the current partner. Thus, the current attachment environment becomes a product of the current treatment as well as of the early experiences that are contributing to bring forth the treatment. Attachment theory suggests that people's behavior in adult romantic relationships is influenced, at least in part, by early caregiving experiences (Fraley & Shaver, 2000). Attachment, sex, and caregiving aspects are involved in romantic love-relationships, but in the early stages of the relationship the sexual part is considered to be more intensely involved than the other two parts.

INDIVIDUAL DIFFERENCES

As a basis for organizing observed individual differences in the ways adults feel and behave in romantic relationships, Ainsworth and colleagues (1978) devised a scheme identifying secure, anxious-ambivalent, and avoidant attachment styles. In turn, Bartholomew and Horowitz (1991) expanded the scheme to a four-category attachment system by distinguishing between two different avoidance patterns—a fearful-avoidance pattern that is adopted by individuals who want to prevent being hurt or rejected by others and a dismissing-avoidant pattern that is used by people who want to maintain a defensive sense of self-reliance and independence.

Among the core hypotheses that are central to attachment theory and describe the past history, consequences, and nature of secure attachment are the *sensitivity hypothesis,* the *competence hypothesis,* and the *secure base hypothesis* (Rothbaum, Weisz, Pott, Miyake, & Morelli, 2000). In their criticism of attachment theory's failure to consider in depth the influences of cultural differences, the authors questioned the universality of the theory's basic tenets. In their comparisons between Japanese and American conceptions of certain childrearing characteristics, they pointed out, for instance, that a mother's tendency to overemphasize caregiving and to prioritize the child's needs over her own is promoting the child's dependency and insecure attachment—thereby qualifying for an instance of insensitive caregiving in American thought. However, indulgence of the child's dependency and complete devotion of oneself to the child constitute the main ingredients of sensitive caregiving in Japanese mothers' conceptions. These considerations are certainly interesting; however, an exploration of the cultural differences that led to the criticism surpasses the scope of this book.

Briefly stated, the sensitivity hypothesis refers to the ability of the primary caregiver to respond in sensitive ways to the child's signals. The competence hypothesis makes a connection between the security of the child's attachment and later social competence. Secure children show a tendency to be less dependent and better able to regulate their emotional states. They are more likely than insecure children to form close and stable relationships. The secure base hypothesis relates to feelings of being protected and comforted that will encourage the child to explore the environment, as mentioned earlier.

OTHER PARENTAL INFLUENCES

General parenting styles have important influences on the psychological well-being of children and adolescents. Comparisons of children raised in authoritative homes and those exposed to authoritarian parenting styles or raised in indulgent or neglectful homes have shown that children from authoritative backgrounds score higher on measures of social development, self-perceptions, competence, and general mental health than their peers (Maccoby & Martin, 1983). As part of a larger investigation of psychological development and schooling during adolescence, Gray and Steinberg (1999) evaluated data from a two-part self-report questionnaire obtained from approximately 10,000 students, 14 to 18 years old. Some of the questionnaire items were chosen to correspond with scope of authoritative parenting along the dimensions of acceptance-involvement, behavioral supervision and strictness, and psychological autonomy granting (the opposite of psychological control). The results indicated that psychosocial development and internal distress were more strongly related to both psychological autonomy granting and acceptance-involvement than to behavioral control, whereas behavior problems were more strongly associated with behavioral control than with psychological autonomy granting. Academic competence showed significant correlations with all three parenting variables.

Comparing the influences of inter-parental consistency versus interparental inconsistency on their high school student offspring's academic competence, psychosocial development and internalized stress, Fletcher, Steinberg, and Sellers (1999) analyzed data obtained from sets of mothers and fathers classified as authoritative, authoritarian, indulgent, or indifferent. The findings indicated that adolescents with one authoritative parent showed greater academic competence than did peers with parents who were consistent but nonauthoritative. Adolescents with one authoritative and one nonauthoritative parent demonstrated greater concurrent internalized distress than those from consistent homes. Thus, where the adolescent's emotional distress is concerned, the interparental inconsistency reflected by a combination of an authoritative and a nonauthoritative parent has the greatest impact. In relation to academic competence, interparental inconsistency is less significant in relating to the adolescent's performance than the presence of at least one authoritative parent.

GENETIC AND ENVIRONMENTAL INFLUENCES

For several decades, studies have been designed and conducted to determine the degree of influence of parental socialization versus the impact of inherited and other dispositional factors upon individuals' adjustment in adolescence and adulthood. The task of sorting out hereditary and environmental influences is complicated by the fact that genetic factors and environmental factors are correlated rather than independent. Individuals who are genetically closely related usually have similar parental environments. Siblings growing up with the same parents generally live in the same milieu. But children's temperamental characteristics elicit differential responses from parents, thereby opening interaction paths that may put the child at risk or protect them from developing behavior problems. Some studies indicated that well-functioning parents can even buffer children who are at risk genetically. The type of parenting can function as environmental triggers that elicit genetic vulnerabilities or strengths.

INFLUENCES OF GENDER-BASED ASSUMPTIONS

The influences that shape children's development are far more complex than nature versus nurture considerations of the past (Collins, Maccoby, Steinberg, Hetherington, & Bornstein, 2000). When children's temperamental characteristics are thought to evoke different parental responses, children's gender characteristics also elicit different parental responses. The parental responses, in turn, may function to instill gender-based assumptions in the children—thus further complicating the issue. The reader may remember the story of Jane in chapter 2. As she related, she and her twin brother received very differential treatment from their mother. Another young woman, Irene, who will be introduced in chapter 7, was aware that her parents expected her older brother to go to college for professional training, but they had no such career expectations of Irene. When she attended vocational school her parents seemed pleased.

Ruth: College Education for Boys Only

Even stronger gender-based expectations impacted the life of a young divorced mother of two children (Maass & Neely, 2000). Ruth, the only girl among three siblings, revealed in therapy how her mother had applied different gender-related assumptions and expectations regarding the future of her three children. The mother's main focus of attention was on her two sons. Ruth felt that her mother trained her to be the family servant by relegating a large share of the household chores to her. Although she received good grades in school and wanted to go to college, Ruth's mother made it clear that there would be no money available for her education. In fact, her mother collected the money Ruth earned with summer jobs and after graduation from high school to help pay for her brothers' college tuition. Living in a small town without public transportation and very little resources, Ruth felt stuck. Her only act of rebellion was to get married. At least now her mother had no access to Ruth's earnings. Shortly after the birth of her second child, her husband, a truck driver, abandoned her, leaving her dependent on the welfare system and occasional food packages from her mother in exchange for performing chores.

What brought Ruth to therapy was the debilitating anger she experienced at her mother's treatment of Ruth and her two children, especially the treatment of her daughter. Ruth's challenge in therapy was to resolve her inner conflict about her mother's treatment and to explore options for her own future. She decided on an option that made it possible for her to attend college as well as graduate school and to achieve a professional life for herself. Her journey took her from the situation of "welfare mother" to a position of sufficient strength to shape her own destiny and make an impact on the community she chose to live in.

Would Jane and Irene have embarked on paths more richly filled with personal significance if they had received the same treatment or encouragement as their brothers? Would Ruth's professional life have been even more successful had she been allowed to pursue a college education as a young girl? These are interesting questions, but the answers remain unverified, constituting not more than hypothetical approaches at increasing awareness about how various factors may exert long-lasting influences by the ways they determine the development of our sense of personal significance.

THEORETICAL CONSIDERATIONS APPLIED TO CASE HISTORIES

Consideration of theoretical approaches about the reasons why individuals develop along certain paths can be helpful—at least in part—in providing answers. The application of theoretical considerations can be useful in explaining individuals' current psychological status and behaviors. Indeed, they can be beneficial in increasing a person's awareness as to why certain emotions, beliefs, and behaviors may occur. However, one needs to be cognizant of the fact that these explanations are based on assumptions. Because we are not able to go back in history and observe the actual situations that may have laid the foundations for the development of the phenomena we observe today, our elucidations constitute working hypotheses—at best.

If the capacity for secure attachment in adulthood is based on positive experiences in childhood where the child has been successful in attempts to turn for help or care—as suggested by attachment theory (Cassidy, 2000), Ruth as described above and Julia introduced in chapter 2 did not achieve secure emotional attachment. Although Julia's parents were overtly available, they were not accessible when support was needed. Julia's early relationships with men proved traumatic for her, and even in her marriage she did not find emotional closeness or the sense of being lovable. Similarly, the group member, Anita, in her intense focus on how to be desired and appreciated by men without giving significant attention to her own identity and independence, could be interpreted as a consequence of lack of secure base attachment in childhood when intimate mother-daughter bonding was prevented by the father's selfish attention to the child. Liz, another group member, growing up in the shadow of a dying sibling, felt a lack of attention and emotional security from her parents who were preoccupied with the greater needs of a terminally ill child. Although Inge's mother repeatedly expressed the sacrifices she made on behalf of her daughters, Inge was keenly aware of her mother's emotional aloofness toward her and the preference her mother had for her younger sister. Inge's fear of abandonment and extreme need for reassurance can be traced back to her childhood experiences.

As was pointed out in chapter 3, parents' influence is significant but not necessarily the all-powerful determining factor for eternal shaping of their offspring. Some persist in their dreams even if they are at variance with their parents' dictates. For instance, Tanya, the young woman who volunteered her story, was fully aware of her mother's demand that Tanya not leave the neighborhood. She was also aware of the punishment that every act of disobedience would bring; yet she persisted in exploring her environment.

THE GROUP: PERSONAL SIGNIFICANCE

For this meeting, Ann had chosen a seat between Liz and Cindy, with Julia sitting next to Cindy. The four of them were involved in conversation. Two of the remaining three seats were occupied by Inge and Anita, which left the seat between them at the head of the table vacant for the therapist.

Ther.:   I am glad everybody made it to today's meeting. We had an emotionally charged session last week and I am curious what challenges you want to tackle today after we have gone over Jody's options. Jody, have you been able to identify behaviors in your husband that would elicit warm feelings and behaviors that leave you disappointed?

Jody: I remember Betty's comments about what behaviors I like and I made an effort to tell Roger whenever he did something I appreciated. He seemed a bit surprised, probably because I haven't said anything nice to him for a long time. On the list about the things that irritate me, the water spots are at the top.

Ther.:   What are your thoughts connected with the water spots? Can you identify them?

Jody: I see every little spot as sucking and gluing me to the house. There is no end to it.

Ther.:   It sounds as if the water spots turn your house into a prison in your mind. What other thoughts may be connected to the water spots?

Jody: Roger is using them to keep me imprisoned.

Ther.:   Aren't you also thinking that he should not do that? (After Jody nods her head): Our thoughts have a lot to do with our emotions and if you believe the thoughts that he keeps you imprisoned, you would not feel loving toward Roger. How would you know whether or not the belief was based on the truth? Whether or not Roger really wants to keep you tied to the house? Also, when you focus on Roger and what he should not do, you are less likely to think about how you can affect changes that you can live with more happily.

Jody: I never asked him why the spots are important to him. I just kept wiping them off.

Ther.:   Because . . .

Jody: I wanted to be a good wife and I don't want to cause confrontations.

Ther.:   But as you told us you could not be a loving wife. In your mind, by whose standards are you supposed to be a good wife and what are the standards?

Jody: I guess my husband's standards?

Ther.: Jody, when you think about it, before you married your husband did you discuss with him what kind of a wife he wanted
and how you wanted to be as wife?

Jody: No, we did not discuss anything like that. We agreed that I
should stay home while our children are small and we talked
about the kind of house we wanted, but no details about me
as wife.

Inge: I wonder if some of my problems with David did not come
out of our different ideas about how we would function as
husband and wife. I had been married before, so I thought I
knew how to be a wife. But I wanted David to be a completely
different husband than my ex-husband was.

Ther.: Inge, you made an excellent observation. You are also touch-
ing on another aspect of the same issue. You were a wife
before, but to a different man. If we accept the husbands'
definitions of a good wife, would we become different wives
with every new marriage? Apparently, none of you discussed
with your husbands what would make a good wife, but you
acted as if you knew what your husbands' standards for a
good wife are. Then you tried to follow those assumptions
without checking them out. Our discussion seems to center
around the question "Who determines how the wife should
be?" After you make that decision you can look at criteria for
the good wife. There is another point in what Jody said. She
dislikes confrontations. I wonder how many women do not
assert themselves in order to avoid confrontations.

Betty: Avoiding confrontations is a serious issue with me. My relationship with my sons needs mending but I am hesitant to
interact with them. They don't want to be with me because
my anger toward their father poisons our relationship. They
don't want to take sides; he is still their father. Part of my
anger is due to fear. All my life I have been afraid of people
who were angry with me and I tried to avoid making anybody
mad. Inside I become angry, too, but I have tried to swallow
my anger silently to avoid confrontations. My ex-husband
knows that and he is using it against me. He has a way of
putting me on the spot on the telephone.

Ther.: How does he do that?

Betty: He usually calls when I am busy. When I tell him I have no
time, he says it will only take a few minutes and then he
rattles off whatever he wanted to say and adds something like
"That was all. See, it didn't take long at all." Before I can ask

any questions he hangs up. I have tried to call right back to ask my questions but his wife answered the phone and told me he just went out the door. I get scared when I hear his voice on the phone. I start shaking and my voice quivers. Everybody can hear that I am nervous and afraid. They take advantage of that.

Ann: Betty, I would never have expected you to become intimidated like that. You seem much more forceful.

Betty: Sometimes my anger makes me sound stronger than I am.

Ann: He is trying to control you. You don't have to listen to him. Who pays for the telephone? You do, right? Hang up when you feel uncomfortable. You can send him a note or if you call back and his wife answers, instruct them to leave a message on your answering machine or to send you the message by mail or fax.

Ther.: As Ann said, it is your telephone and your decision when you want to talk. You may conceive of a two-level approach, one to deal with your ex-husband and the other with your sons. As you gain more control over your communications with your ex-husband, you may feel less like a victim and find it easier to leave out the anger from interactions with your sons. Also, as you feel less like a victim, you may be able to handle confrontations when they come.

Betty: I see what you mean. Ann's advice sounds workable. The other day I called my oldest son. He was very cold and did not want to talk. This was one of my calmer moments. I remained friendly and told him that for a while I would not contact him until my life was more settled. However, he certainly could call me if he wished to. Thinking back on it, I realize that I was able to remain calm because I had prepared myself for the call and I felt in control of my part of the interaction.

Ther.: Betty, that is valuable information. Generally, we do better when we are prepared. It makes sense to practice behaviors that we know work for us. Instead of fearfully avoiding confrontations at all costs, we can prepare ourselves how to handle them. (To the group): As you heard, Betty's ex-husband may be using his knowledge of her fear of confrontations to manipulate her. Instead of protecting ourselves by avoiding confrontations, we make ourselves vulnerable to be manipulated by others.

Inge: I wonder what makes us afraid of confrontations. At work, I never have problems with that. My job includes performance evaluations and even terminations of employees. In my personal life with David I was always holding back expressing displeasure or disagreement until I just could not keep it in any longer and blurt it out in anger. Why can I handle it in one setting but not in the other?

Ann: At work it is part of the job and we get paid for it. Therefore, it is acceptable and we have time to prepare for the confrontation. Also, there are no strong emotions involved. In our personal life, we are supposed to be the peacemakers. My mother used to say, "It is the woman's task to structure a harmonious atmosphere in the house."

Julia: I don't know what I am more afraid of—my husband's anger or his silence. I guess they are both confrontations in a way.

Ther.: That is a good observation, Julia, both instances can amount to confrontations. Silences can be just as intimidating when you are afraid of them. With silences others can attempt to control you by cutting you off. You can accept the silence as meaning that the other person's point in the discussion is valid and not subject to change, or you can look at silence as being just that—silence.

Julia: Why am I afraid? Why is Betty afraid? Why do we act out of fear so much?

Ther.: Julia, you are asking an important question. If you tried to answer the question "What am I afraid of?"—What would your answer be?

Julia: That my husband would not like me anymore; he might even leave me.

Ther.: The fear of abandonment—is that what lurks behind the dislike of confrontations? Fear turns people into slaves or victims in some cases. The fear that comes from believing that we cannot make it on our own. Except for Cindy, you all have lost a husband either through divorce or death and you all made it on your own. Do you really need to hold on to that fear? Or is there another component to the fear?

Anita: It says something about us; that we are not beautiful enough, not smart enough, not entertaining enough, not good enough to keep around.

Betty: Anita is correct. When our marriage fails we feel judged as not measuring up. How come we don't turn that around to men? Because women are not important enough to be judges? As we discussed the other day, the notion that men are more important than women is all-pervasive.

Ther.:   Betty, that is the underlying problem. We give away the power over ourselves because we don't consider ourselves important enough to determine how we want to be.

Jody: I think most of the time we are not even aware of what we are doing to ourselves. I have always been a great admirer of Maria Callas, the opera star. Of course, everybody knew that she had a long affair with Aristotle Onassis. When he left her to marry Jacqueline Kennedy I was furious. How could he betray her like that? Then I read a story about them in a magazine. Apparently, Callas had been pregnant and she was writing to Onassis that she was expecting their child. She corrected herself to say 'our son' because she would not insult Onassis by giving him a daughter. I clearly remember that she used the word 'insult.' I was stunned, then sad. I can't bear listening to her records anymore.

Ther.:   That is indeed a sad story, Jody. I had not been aware of the details in the Callas-Onassis story. How demeaning to herself that note was. Thank you for telling us about this. We can learn from it. We have options to define or redefine ourselves. We can define what a good wife is or what type of person we want to be. If we don't use those options, we are making the same mistake that Callas did. (Turning to Cindy): Cindy, you haven't said a word today. Are we neglecting issues you would want to discuss?

Cindy: I feel out of place. I don't even have an ex-husband, let alone a current one. I may never have to worry about what makes a good wife or how to remain married.

Ann: We are not just talking about being good wives, Cindy. We are talking about making changes in our lives. The other day you said you feel invisible and you wanted to have presence. So do I. Within my family I am unremarkable, just one of five kids. I want to feel special.

Liz: (Cutting in impulsively): When you read my homework about describing ourselves and our wishes, you'll see how much I have craved attention, how much I wanted to be special—at least, to my parents! I didn't get it. I think we could all do with a lesson on how to become remarkable or special or have presence.

Inge: I agree with Liz. I get attention mostly from men because of my looks. I don't deny that and I enjoy it, but I still don't feel special. My mother always reminded me to be modest. I still have trouble accepting compliments and even more trouble asking for things. Every time we visited relatives, my mother took me aside and instructed me "Don't ask for anything, wait until it is offered to you! When it is offered always share it with your sister. Don't keep anything just for yourself."

Ther.:   The lesson is that we have options to redefine ourselves and to change those aspects of our behaviors that do not work for us. (After a brief pause the therapist turns to Cindy): Cindy, when you described yourself as being invisible and wanting to have "presence," these are vague terms that make it difficult to work with. Can you define your goals in more specific terms?

Cindy: I would like people to seek my company because I am interesting and they admire me. I know that sounds conceited and even narcissistic. I would like people to ask my opinion instead of assuming that I don't have anything important to contribute.

Ther.:   That's good, Cindy; we can work with that. Do you know any people who have those qualities and who receive attention or admiration from others?

Cindy: I can think of a few people at work who come close.

Ther.:   Good, you can observe them. What is it in their behavior that makes people respond favorably to? See if you can identify the qualities that seem to bring them the attention of others. For instance, how do these individuals greet others? How do they listen? How do they speak, move, or smile? In addition to observing the responses of others to those individuals, notice what you like about them, what attracts you to them? Then try some of those behaviors on yourself; see how it works for you.

Cindy: You mean I should imitate them?

Ther.:   Not the whole person, just what you think works for them and might also work for you.

Ann: What about our personalities? Aren't they fixed?

Ther.:   Yes, many of our personality characteristics are relatively stable—but they are not birth defects. (Group members are laughing.) We are talking about behaviors that we might want to change, not whole persons.

Cindy: Wouldn't I just be putting on an act?

Ther.:   It may feel like that at first. As you continue practicing the behavior, with time you could let it become part of you. You can look at it as modeling. When you observe a person who behaves in ways you admire, you can use that as an example to model yourself after. As I said earlier, select characteristics you like, not the whole person.

Betty: Can you give us an example? Perhaps I can profit from that.

Ther.:   Let's assume that Cindy studies a particular person to whom people are drawn and talk to. Let's also assume that Cindy finds out that it is not the person's wisdom they seek, because she very seldom gives advice. It is the way the person *listens* that makes people seek her out. On the basis of that discovery, Cindy decides to observe and study the behaviors that make the person such a well-liked listener. It could be the way the person turns her body toward the speaker, or the calm and continuous eye contact, the way she nods her head that seems to encourage the speaker to continue, perhaps an occasional smile—all these minute details could come together to create a sought-after listener.

Betty: I wonder if that is why people don't talk to me . . .

Ther.:   What do you mean Betty?

Betty: I am usually tense when people talk to me. I am always afraid that I don't understand what they are trying to tell me or that I will forget some important detail. That fear makes me nervous, and I bet people can tell. Do you think I could learn skills like that?

Ther.:   I don't see why not. As you said earlier, you want to change your approach in communicating with your ex-husband and your sons. Listening is a part of communication. As I explained in our first session, we are here because of certain challenges in our life and we want to explore what options are available to us. Learning new skills is certainly an option.

Helen: I am having difficulties knowing where to begin. I came here because I am angry and depressed. My physician said that my feelings could have something to do with the worsening of my physical symptoms.

Ther.:   Helen, you told us that your former husband took advantage of you. We don't know much else about you. Could it be that the nature of your challenge has not been sufficiently defined and therefore the range of options is not easily apparent? What is it you are hoping to achieve by being with us?

Helen: I want to feel better. I know that is not specific enough. People have said I have a "victim mentality." They are correct I have been a victim for a long time. I did not want to talk about it here because I thought I had talked enough when I was in therapy before. For several years, as I was growing up I was sexually abused by my father. I was not the only one but everybody in my family denied it.

Ther.: I can see why our discussions may not have appeared relevant to you. In the process of facing challenges, exploring options and the promises they hold for resolution, we were trying to identify concrete situations and future expectations. You are looking at events that happened in the past over which you have no control. Your unhappiness is more pervasive and abstract. Therefore, it is difficult to define what the challenge would be. Related to the future, what might be your challenge?

Helen: Stop seeing myself as a victim? (Her voice hesitating): Or is that too abstract?

Ther.: Well, let's see what we can do with that. How would your life be if you did not consider yourself a victim? What would you do? How would you plan for the future? What activities would you wish to pursue? Where would you go? What kind of people would you like to be with? Those are questions to think about when attempting to define the challenge in practical terms.

Helen: (Appears stunned, but answers after a moment): The answer is the same for all the questions: 'I don't know.' Beyond my move away from home I have not planned for anything. I go to work and occasionally I go to a movie. It is as if I am suspended in time. I exist without direction. Before I left, I remember learning some sign language and using it in our church, but I have not done that since the move.

Ther.: What preceded your move must have been traumatic events, even more traumatic than the statement 'sexual abuse' conveys. It sounds as if you may have been emotionally numb for some time, except for the anger.

Helen: Yes, the sexual abuse was bad enough, but I was able to deal with it in some way until I learned that I was not the only victim. I wanted to warn my younger sister, but it was too late. What was worse is that my mother must have known all the years when it was going on. She did not protect us. When I talked to her about it she called me a liar. My bad marriage did not make things any better. My whole family turned against me, even my sisters denied that the abuse ever happened. My mother excluded me from family gatherings. That's when I realized that I had to move away. (Helen is crying and covering her face with her hands. The group members look at her, not knowing what to do or say. The therapist motions them to remain quiet. After a few minutes, Helen raises her face but without looking at anybody): I guess I did not move far enough away.

Ther.: Helen, you moved, but you took your memories with you. If you moved to the end of the world, that would not be far enough as long as you carry this burden with you. I am not saying you should forget what happened—you couldn't. What happened to you was horrible. You survived a terrible ordeal. But surviving is not enough as you have shown. By merely surviving and keeping your memories alive, you continue to be the victim. When we are helpless in a situation we feel like a victim. As Betty pointed out earlier, she felt like a victim because she thought she was vulnerable and taken advantage of by her former husband.

Helen: How can I not feel like a victim when I have been a victim?

Ther.: You were a victim in the past and you cannot make the past undone. By keeping your memories alive, you give those who have already hurt you so much the power to continue hurting you. With all that pain in your past, wouldn't you deserve to make your future life as happy as you possibly can? You could start by relegating your memories to the past, by shedding the victim role, and by focusing on what might be out there for you to enjoy. Perhaps thinking about answers to the questions I mentioned earlier could serve as a beginning for your new life.

Helen: I don't know how to be happy and I don't want to. I have not cried for many years. I was afraid of it. I have bottled up my feelings except for the anger, as you noticed.

Ther.: What about crying made you afraid?

Helen: I thought I would never be able to stop if I started crying. I would not be able to control it. I would just be a dissolving quivering mess—a total collapse.

Ther.: You cried and you stopped crying. You did not dissolve. Now you know that you are in control. (After a brief pause, turning to the group): Feelings are a very important part of us. If we deny their existence in our awareness, we lose valuable information about ourselves and about life around us. Feelings, when interpreted carefully, function as signals about what is going on within us and around us. (Turning back to Helen): I wonder why you allowed yourself to feel the emotion of anger? What did it do for you?

Helen: It made me feel strong. It kept me from forgetting what had been done to me; and it kept me from becoming vulnerable ever again. It keeps me from expecting anything good to happen. It keeps me from being disappointed.

Ther.: You make it sound as if anger serves as protection.

Betty: (Breaking in): Well it is! Even Ann thought I was more forceful when I was angry. It keeps people at a distance. They don't mess with you when you are angry.

Ann: But from what you were saying earlier, it did not help you to cover your fear and anxiety about your ex-husband when he tried to intimidate you.

Ther.: When we talk about emotions, most of us want to think of love and happiness, but for many anger seems to be the predominant feeling. Anger is a powerful force in feeling and acting and is often regarded as a motivator. When do we experience anger? Usually when things don't go our way, when we perceive a violation of our rights and when we feel helpless in obtaining what is rightly ours or in preventing hurt and damage inflicted upon us by others. The degree or intensity of the anger is often correlated with the degree of helplessness experienced in the situation. Anger is closely related to other negative emotions, such as hate or depression, and to thoughts regarding behaviors, such as retaliation or revenge (Maass & Neely, 2000).

Ann: Don't we have a right to be angry and isn't it natural to think of revenge when somebody hurt you?

Ther.: Indeed, you have a right to be angry and thinking of revenge seems only too natural. But what are the consequences when you act on the anger? How does the anger help? Perhaps you could give us an example when you acted out of anger. Do you remember an incident that would fit here?

Ann: Right now I can't think of anything that involves revenge. But I was angry last Saturday. It was at my parents' house. We were all together for my youngest sister's birthday. The day before I had my annual performance evaluation, and my boss told me how much he valued my work. Of course, I was proud and could hardly wait to tell my parents. As my sister was opening her presents I mentioned the evaluation. My father said that was really nice and my mother added how wonderful it was that all five of us have been so successful in our lives. I felt instant anger and blurted out that it would be even more wonderful if I could be special in some way just once.

Ther.:   What happened then?

Ann: Everybody got quiet and looked at me. My sister said, "I didn't know you resented my birthday." Of course, I didn't resent her birthday and I told her so. Then my mother started crying and got up from the table. She went into the kitchen. My father looked at me sternly and told me to apologize to my mother. I did and drove home.

Ther.:   How did you feel on the way home?

Ann: Terrible. I took a bath and went to bed, but I could not sleep. I thought about calling my parents but I did not have the courage.

Ther.:   You have told us how you felt about being one out of five equally talented and wonderful siblings. We did not have the opportunity yet to work on this in detail. Let's see what we can do now. From the suddenness of your response, we could assume that in the past you have gone through similar thought processes regarding this issue.

Ann: They should treat me as an individual person, not as one of many. I can't count how many times I thought that.

Ther.:   With repeated thoughts like those in many situations, you have actually formed the belief that your parents should behave differently. But they did not and you had no control over their behavior. You felt helpless in achieving what you thought was your right and you acted as if your beliefs are correct.

Ann: That is true. There was also a moment of sadness and I felt tears coming up. Perhaps the sadness was part of the helplessness. Like Helen, I didn't want to cry. I didn't want to make a scene. But that's what I ended up doing anyway—just with anger, not with tears. My mother's tears were much more powerful than my outburst of anger. So, in addition to feeling being wronged, I acted wrong and had to apologize.

Ther.:   That was a painful lesson, Ann. Thank you for sharing it with us. In retrospect, how would you have liked to handle the situation?

Ann: Certainly not the way I did! I can't really think of a better way, except to keep my mouth shut.

Liz: (Interrupting): But shouldn't her parents be told how their behavior makes her feel? Parents sometimes have no idea how they hurt their children. How often I wanted to scream at my mother, "Look at me, I am hurting too, not just my sister!"

Ann: Did you ever do it?

Liz: No, I did not dare. How could I compete for affection or attention with my sister who was dying? I felt like a monster at times and I felt helpless and angry and guilty.

Ther.:   Helen, Ann, and Liz—you are all hurting over things that occurred over time, things you were helpless to change. The more helpless you felt, the angrier you became. Helen and Liz did not express their anger toward the people they thought responsible for it. Helen was also afraid to express her sadness, fear, and grief—her general unhappiness—through crying, because she was scared of falling apart. It is the fear of intense feelings that often prompts people to avoid the experience or expression of those feelings. The effort spent in avoiding the expression of strong emotions prevents them from learning to tolerate them and to realize that they are not going to be swallowed up or dissolved by their feelings. Ann acted on her anger and regretted it later. Just like in Helen's case, the anger keeps you from shedding the victim stance. It keeps the wrongdoings of the past alive and active in you. Rehashing the same angry thoughts and feelings repeatedly, without coming to a resolution, functions to reinforce and emphasize the anger and with that the victim stance.

Ann: I don't want to lose my family, although right now I feel like moving to the end of the world. I am ashamed to face them after my outburst. What can I do?

Jody: You could write them a letter, explaining how you felt all those years. But you realize that they were doing what they thought their best in treating you all equally. You could add that you are working on changing your feelings about this issue.

Ann: That is a good idea, Jody. I think I will write to them. I don't know that I want to tell them that I am in a therapy group to work on it. They may worry that their treatment has maimed me for life.

Ther.:   That seems like a valid and sensitive consideration. (After a
         brief pause): We have several loose ends: Jody is continuing
         with her explorations of options for modifying her feelings.
         Cindy, Ann, and Liz may think of ways to establish their per-
         sonal significance. Julia is working on her options as she is
         preparing herself for college. Anita, you have been quiet to-
         day. I hope you will share your thoughts with us next time.
         Also, those of you who have not written your stories—please
         do so. And another concern we did not get to explore in
         detail: Where do our ideas about the importance of women
         and men come from? Please think about that. Just a remind-
         er about today's discussion: The topic of anger has been rel-
         evant for several of you. Remember the correlation of anger
         and helplessness and how unprocessed anger can prolong
         the victim stance. We also talked about being special or hav-
         ing significance—to achieve personal significance is our indi-
         vidual responsibility.

GROUP PROCESS: PERSONAL SIGNIFICANCE

This session dealt with topics that several of the women could relate
to. First of all, what are the standards for a good wife and who sets
those standards—the woman, the husband? Another part of the discussion centered on women's tendency to avoid confrontations, even
to the point where they make themselves vulnerable to manipulation.
Some of the women's challenges were stated in vague terms and the
therapist encouraged them to define them in more specific and manageable ways. Lessons that can be learned from people we admire—
even negative lessons, such as Maria Callas's sad experience (Gage,
2000), constituted another important part of the discussion.

Finally, Helen, who had not actively participated in disclosing her
goals for change, related significant background information. It was
imperative to help Helen leave the victim stage behind and start on
her way to planning the future, independent of the past. Even though
the group members may have wanted to comfort Helen, the comforting behavior actually could have served to reinforce Helen's role of
victim. Also, in retrospect, it was important that Helen's crying was not
interrupted by any comforting behaviors. For Helen it was crucial to
learn that she was in control of her crying. She could stop it. As

pointed out by the therapist, the fear of involuntary expressions of emotions can be a stumbling block to learning to tolerate the feelings and to resolve the underlying source of the distress (Baumeister & Exline, 2000).

It is also noteworthy that the therapist stated to Helen, "With all that pain in your past, wouldn't you deserve to *make* your future life as happy as you possibly can?" The therapist conveyed the notion that the client could actively do something to be happier—not that the victimization and pain entitled Helen to future happiness. This distinction is important because as tragic as victimization is when it occurs, it does not carry with it entitlements for future better conditions. Unfortunately, some people who had been victimized in the past expect retribution from others around them. This expectation not only prompts them to prolong the victim stance, but it also alienates others who initially expressed their sympathy.

SUMMARY

This chapter addressed the concern of how people own a sense of their significance and how this sense of significance or identity develops. As a theoretical developmental approach, attachment theory with its concepts and hypotheses was explored as one path to individuals' sense of personal significance. Other parental influences as well as genetic and environmental influences were examined.

Continuation of the group process demonstrated how various members approached their challenges and search for personal significance. The interactions within the group process concluded the chapter.

QUESTIONS FOR CONSIDERATION

How do we establish criteria for what makes a good wife?

Should the group member, Ann, have told her parents how she felt about their treatment of her and her siblings much earlier when it started to bother her? How should she have communicated her wishes for being treated as unique rather than an equal among five?

RECOMMENDED READING

Rothbaum, F., Weisz, J., Pott, M., Miyake, K., & Morelli, G. (2000). Attachment and culture: Security in the United States and Japan. *American Psychologist, 55,* 1093–1104.

The authors give an overview of the different hypotheses proposed within attachment theory and compare the validity of some of the hypotheses in the United States and in Japan.

CHAPTER SEVEN

Options, Goals, and Decisions

No matter how positive or how negative a person's environment is, it is less crucial than the individual's choice about how to respond to that environment (Samenow, 1989). The more options are at the individual's disposal, the more freedom of responding is contained in the situation or environment. Some individuals welcome the idea of many choices, whereas others may feel overwhelmed by the task of choosing.

FREEDOM OF CHOICE VERSUS FREEDOM FROM CHOICE

Exploring and choosing among options may feel like invitations to determine their future to those who want to be in charge; others work hard to ignore the existence of options. Individuals who deny the existence of options—when indeed there are several available—and resist consideration of alternative actions, place themselves in a condition of helplessness that is self-imposed instead of stemming from environmental forces. Acting in the manner of self-imposed helplessness, the individual repeatedly experiences failure to reach desired goals or to remove the presence of an undesired condition, resulting in a conviction of hopelessness and finally in capitulation. Such a process leads to a condition of what Martin Seligman (1975) called "learned helplessness." Because we choose everything we do—including our feelings (Glasser, 1998) and including doing nothing, the state of learned helplessness is thus one of the options that can be chosen by the individual.

Why do the "resisters" choose to place themselves in the condition of learned helplessness, while others excitedly embrace the opportunity to explore alternatives and select what they consider to be the best option? One reason is that options bring with them conditions for decisions. When faced with several attractive options some individuals cannot bring themselves to choose one, thereby losing the advantages of all of them. Others are confronted with options that all appear to be negative. Their difficulty may be to determine which one is the lesser evil. They may decide to flip a coin or to do nothing (Lipson & Perkins, 1990).

Being faced with mutually exclusive options introduces another dilemma. By selecting one, the remaining options become, at least for the moment, useless or superfluous—all the more important it is to the decision maker that the absolute best option is chosen. Anything less than the perfect decision in this selection process will come back to haunt the person. Therefore, it is not necessarily the act of choosing that is disturbing or even debilitating, but the demand that it will be guaranteed that the chosen option indeed constitutes the perfect solution. Insisting on making the perfect choice, without the possibility of having to accept responsibility for making a wrong decision, often renders individuals paralyzed and unable to move in any direction. By refusing to actively select an option, they passively make the decision to accept whatever develops in a given situation, a strategy that rarely delivers the best choice. Thus, avoidance of postdecisional regret becomes a higher priority than the sense of freedom and satisfaction that could come from having the opportunity to choose (Maass & Neely, 2000).

THE MYTH OF A MANDATORY CHOICE BETWEEN CAREER AND MARRIAGE

Many successful career women report having difficulty being equally successful in their personal lives (Levine-Shneidman & Levine, 1985). Apparently men can have it all, but it is not as easy for women. When career women complain about having to choose between successful careers on the one hand or marriage and motherhood on the other, what are they saying and believing? Another informational item regarding women's career decisions that initially is overlooked may become relevant in situations in which a marriage ends in divorce. Whether a wife's career decision is a purely personal one, or one made for the benefit of the family, poses an interesting question in some contemporary divorce cases. Some lawyers and judges recommended that women's career sacrifices while being part of a family unit should be taken into account in determining appropriate compensation. On the other hand, many mediators and some lawyers argued that if a wife had chosen a low-paid profession so she would be able to devote time to the children of the marriage while her husband was engaged in a time-consuming and lucrative career, the wife was fully responsible for her career choice and did not need to be compensated (Bohmer & Ray, 1996). Thus, a woman selecting a career that will enable her to also be a fully nurturing parent, may later be penalized for not having chosen a more lucrative career if the marriage should end in divorce.

DEFINING OPTIONS CORRECTLY

Is the choice really between career and family? Does it mean that a woman who does not embark upon a career will experience a blissful marriage and happy family life? Of course not, most people would say and reality confirms that response. For many of the women who discard the option of training for a professional career, the issue is what will they do if their husbands leave them or if they wanted to leave the marriage? With no profession to fall back on, a life in poverty is the consequence for many of them.

When women exclaim that because of their careers they feel they are handicapped in relationships with men (Levine-Shneidman & Levine, 1985) are they projecting that their career success with all its rewards has affected their ability to have intimate relationships? What is wrong with this projection? There is no evidence that financial dependence and weaker self-images lead to improved ability to form intimate relationships. Nor is there evidence that submissiveness and serfdom facilitate intimacy building more than do autonomy and freedom.

The situation of options would be more correctly defined as one of choosing between a deferential versus an autonomous lifestyle. The selection of a husband would be a function of the lifestyle and thus a choice between a man with traditional attitudes, who in his authoritarian philosophy occupies the position of power and a man subscribing to egalitarian values. Various combinations of the factors range from being mutually exclusive to workable to favorable in the process of building intimate relationships. Describing the matrix in oversimplified terms, spouses with a combination of authoritarian and submissive-deferential attitudes would form many of the "blissful" unions of the past. From an authoritarian-authoritarian combination, one could expect a rather volatile relationship. In reality, most people fall somewhere along these continua rather than occupying the extreme endpoints. The ideal combination would be one in which both partners hold egalitarian values; both are autonomous but also cooperative in their attempts to support the other.

Attitude assessment prior to committing to intimate relationships could serve a valuable function, and indeed, in premarital counseling, personality inventories are often used to assess the compatibility of the two prospective spouses. However, the point of the discussion here is not primarily the compatibility of individuals involved in intimate relationships but the need for clear and accurate definitions of the variables involved in decision-making. Choices in career and mate selection involve separate although not completely independent variables.

SELECTING THE MOST FAVORABLE OPTION

Selecting the most favorable option in a given situation requires time and patience to collect available information about the options, to estimate the possible outcomes, and to select the choice that looks the best—without insisting on a guarantee that it actually will be the best. The more extensive the information collection process is the better are the chances that it will indeed be a good choice. While realistically weighing probable outcomes and keeping track of the goal, there may be chances for creating additional options, or synthesizing options.

Consider, for instance, the person who thinks about traveling from Kansas City to San Francisco. There are different paths to get from one point to the other based on different criteria to be determined by the traveler. The criterion of fastest travel may lead to the most direct route or one where the majority of the way follows interstate freeways. Air travel is another option for satisfying the criterion of speed. The requirement for the most scenic route will most likely result in a different path. Wanting to visit historical sights along the way would lead to yet another trail. The person who wants to avoid the stress of choosing among all the options probably can still be found sitting in Kansas City.

The process of eliminating choices due to reasons described above is not difficult to observe and understand. Less obvious is the method of reducing options by rebelling against suggestions from others and doing the exact opposite of what was recommended by others, just for the sake of rebellion, called the "rebel without a cause" syndrome. In cases like this—as clinicians—we usually focus more on the element of resistance than on the elimination of options that occurs in these situations, but in reality the elimination of at least one option is very much in evidence.

GOALS PROVIDING DIRECTION AND PURPOSE

Engaging in explorations of options and decision-making skills without specific goals may make for entertaining activities—like playing games among friends—but overall it would be rather meaningless. Normally, goals reach beyond experiencing the pleasure of counting choices and feeling good or powerful about it or the desire for reduced stress through refusing to make decisions. Goals bestow direction to the exploration of options and purpose to the decision-making process. They prevent us from wandering around aimlessly. The successful journey will include actions that are aimed at goals and the actions will terminate in reflections and representations of those goals. Declaring goals for ourselves, preferably on paper or other records, can start a powerful psychological and emotional process that will help us gain awareness of what we can accomplish (Beattie, 1987). Goals that cannot be reached because they are unachievable, can teach us to become more realistic in the overall goal-setting process. After the initial disappointment has subsided, energies can be applied to a fact-finding exploration regarding the reasons for the lack of attainment of particular goals.

FACTORS FACILITATING OR PREVENTING GOAL ATTAINMENT

Unrecorded goals are easily lost, forgotten, or changed in content and thereby are rendered useless. To be achievable, goals need to be clearly defined. Vague goals don't let us know when we have arrived. Even if they are achieved in a vague sense, the person is deprived of the positive feeling that accompanies the accomplishment of having reached a carefully selected objective. More often than not, setting vague or undefined goals is a sure way not to be successful. People may blame predetermination or fate for not reaching the target. "It was not meant to be" is often heard in rationalizing unsuccessful efforts.

Another means of avoiding to reach goals is by setting more or larger goals than can be accomplished. The goal-setting literature includes reports on goal difficulty that might persuade some individuals to set unrealistically large or difficult goals. In 192 studies where participants did not know the objective probabilities of the task solution, apparently 91% demonstrated that higher goals produced better performance (Locke & Latham, 1991). People, however, are not the same with regard to effort and ability. For individuals with low ability or low effort, the cost of reaching the goal may appear rather high to them. A rise in goal difficulty may be discouraging enough to them to decide not to increase their level of effort. On the other hand, those individuals who experience lower costs with their efforts may find it easier to increase their performance with a shift in goal parameters (Heath, Larrick, & Wu, 1999). People also respond differently to the perceived distance from the goal. If they see the goal as too distant in the future or too far away, progress may be too small to motivate them to even start. Thus, some people who have set unrealistic goals or goals that are poorly defined and communicated may regard themselves as ambitious and complain that their ambitions are misunderstood or thwarted by those around them when, in effect, their communication concerning their efforts and targets was poorly articulated.

To be manageable, goals need to be realistic in number, content, and size. They need to be well-defined and specific. There may be a need to rank or prioritize goals, as to which one is the most important to pursue. For instance, a woman deciding to have a rewarding career and a family may pursue the career goal first and then look for a husband who's values and attitudes are congruent with her career wishes.

In cases of poorly defined goals, it is possible to have opposing or mutually exclusive goals without being aware of their opposing nature. Thus, a young woman may find career and financial independence interesting concepts but deep down may want to have somebody to depend on in case her career efforts don't succeed. At times the wish translates into fear that can be expressed as "If I am independent and self-sufficient I will always have to be self-sufficient and nobody will help me if I need it. Therefore, I better continue being dependent on others." Hence, opposing goals may combine to a situation of ambition and passivity without fulfillment of any wants. While passive, the person can still entertain expectations of being discovered for some grandiose position or scheme. This type of extravagant expectation in the face of passivity resembles the magical thinking of early childhood when one dreams of becoming a princess upon the awakening kiss from Prince Charming (Krueger, 1990).

ARE TODAY'S GIRLS DIFFERENT FROM THEIR MOTHERS AND GRANDMOTHERS?

Females today have more options to choose from and more goals to determine than ever before. Traveling the country for 2 years and studying what passions today's girls are pursuing, three daughters of Pulitzer Prize–winning writer John McPhee have found that for girls today the sky is the limit (McPhee, J., McPhee, L., & McPhee, M., 2000). Young females now are not aware of glass ceilings. Their way of thinking has changed. But have the "glass ceilings" disappeared for all females or just for some? There are girls who see themselves as feminists and those for whom the word *feminism* represents a slur, a label to be avoided. The authors explained that many of the girls did not clearly understand the history of the feminist movement and its achievements. They assume different interpretations about feminists.

The authors talked about young girls' imagination as it would be expressed in music, writing, painting, and other artistic activities. There is the account of a girl who started writing sonnets at the age of 7, when she was inspired by observing a total eclipse of the sun or the 13-year-old who had been painting since the age of two, driven by a power that she does not quite comprehend. There is the girl who has been playing the piano and composing short pieces of music since the age of 4. She has played at the New York City's Symphony and has been on *Good Morning America*. There is also the 13-year-old girl whose paintings sell for as much as $200,000, and her works are exhibited in galleries in New York, Los Angeles, and Paris. She has been featured in *Vogue* and on the *Oprah Winfrey Show*. There is the 13-year-old girl who started to write, a novel and always knew that she wanted to be a writer—even before she was able to write and there are young poets and performers. These stories are about especially gifted children, child prodigies that have existed before in history. They are not necessarily evidence of a dramatic change in girls' thinking. Clearly, these are not ordinary girls.

There is the account of the young woman who is engaged in brain-tumor research and is determined to become a neurosurgeon and the girl who joined the U.S. Naval Academy in Annapolis to find out if life in the navy was for her. Other girls excel in various sports, and cheerleaders are not neglected in the report. Whereas once female cheerleaders were considered to be performing mainly for the aggrandizement of the all-male ball teams, now the girls consider their activities as a dangerous sport because of its physical challenges. They are varsity cheerleaders, participating in national cheerleading competitions. Some, in addition, are involved in Christian squads that cheer for God. Indeed, some churches advertise cheerleading classes to young girls in the community.

The determination and energy these young girls display in the pursuit of their goals and ambitions are truly admirable and worthy of encouragement. That they are not aware of glass ceilings and other discriminations does not mean they don't exist anymore. The girls may simply not have encountered these restrictions yet. Or as in the case of the feminist movement mentioned above, they have not fully comprehended the concept—as mentioned by the authors—or the girls have not sufficiently studied the recent history. Another point for concern is that these wonderfully goal-oriented girls and young women have not come to the critical decision point yet, the point that is illuminated by the story of the female volunteer below.

Irene: Unrealistic Demands and Changing Directions

Irene, one of the women who volunteered to tell her history, expected to be able to confirm the opinion of the authors mentioned above. As she related her story, she was one of three siblings, right in between an older brother and a younger sister. Their parents worked hard to provide a better life for their children. Although both parents worked, her mother's job was not career oriented, whereas her father was a professional engineer. There was no doubt that Irene's brother would attend college. His choice was to become a chemical engineer, a choice their parents strongly approved of. For Irene, her parents did not have any definite career expectations. They encouraged her to obtain skills that she could use to earn money before marriage and if need be during marriage, very much as her mother had done. In high school, Irene did not follow the college tract. She liked her bookkeeping classes. Through a vocational school she obtained the equivalent of an associates degree with concentration in bookkeeping and office procedures. After graduation she found an entry-level position with a local law firm. Her parents were pleased. Her younger sister wanted to become a teacher. She started college but dropped out in her second year to get married.

Irene enjoyed her job and had an active social life. After a few years she advanced to assistant office manager. One of the interns, law students placed at the law firm during the summer, became interested in Irene. They started to date and eventually got married. Irene continued to work full-time because her husband, Leonard, had another year or more to complete his studies. After Leonard passed the bar examinations they planned on having a family.

With the birth of her first child, a girl, Irene stopped working. Little Irene soon had a sister. The two girls were less than 2 years apart in age. The family seemed happy. Irene's husband advanced in the law firm to junior partner, and Irene was busy raising her daughters. She took them to museums, concerts, ballets, and the theater. The younger one seemed to have inherited her father's musical talent. Her piano teacher told the parents that she showed great promise. Little Irene was pretty and a good student but showed no extraordinary talents.

Shortly after little Irene's 11th birthday, her younger sister was killed in an automobile accident. It was a devastating blow to the family. Each family member coped with it differently. Irene spent more time and attention on her older daughter because she worried that her daughter would feel neglected with excessive mourning over the younger one. Little Irene tried to cope by pleasing her parents more than before, as if she wanted to make up for the loss they had experienced. Leonard started to spend more time at the office. He worked longer hours than before to avoid coming home at a time when his younger daughter would have been practicing the piano if she had been alive. Part of his increased office hours he spent with a young female lawyer who had just started with the firm. He became her mentor until mentorship strayed into their personal and sexual life.

During the divorce settlement, Irene's husband suggested that they sell the house the family had been living in, buy a smaller house, large enough to accommodate Irene and her daughter, and put the leftover money into a college trust fund for their daughter. In addition, he would pay child support as appropriate. The proposal sounded fair to Irene. It was only later that she understood that her husband had meant that her half of the money that was left after the sale of the old and the purchase of the new house would be placed in the college fund. He took his half of the money with him. When she realized that her daughter's college fund was much smaller than she had expected and actually came out of her portion of the family assets, she understandably became angry; however, the agreement had already been signed and executed.

Although bitter about the unfair treatment, Irene tried to spare her daughter detailed knowledge of the divorce settlement. She wanted her daughter to be able to carry on her relationship with her father without influence from her. Little Irene spent every other weekend with her father and his new wife and the baby boy who arrived a few months after the wedding. During her visits she would often spend time baby-sitting her half-brother. Fortunately, her father did not take advantage of her but paid her as he would pay a regular baby-sitter.

Irene encouraged her daughter to develop her intellectual abilities, concentrate on her studies, and prepare herself for an independent lifestyle in the manner her father and stepmother were enjoying. Although it was painful for Irene, she hoped that her daughter would observe the difference in status between her mother and her stepmother and would take the achievements of the stepmother as guidance for her future professional development. Irene seemed to be successful in her attempts. Little Irene became part of a group of highly independent young women. They excelled in their studies, made independent plans for their hobby activities, and exercised great caution in the selection of young men they deigned to date. They were all high achievers in their high school and early college years and planned to embark upon great professional careers. When they talked about marriage it was in terms of partnership. They would be equals to their husbands, they would not be "managed" by their husbands. Little Irene had changed her name to "Renée" because it sounded more sophisticated. They had a special little ceremony for that on her 20th birthday.

Irene, who had returned to work and was taking classes toward becoming a certified public accountant, was pleased with her daughter's development. Although one or two of the girls seemed a bit militant about their gender attitudes, Irene considered this to be still better than the submissive attitudes she remembered having in her own late-teenage-to-young-adult years. In fact, Irene thought that Renée could have been a great role model for her own mother. She was proud of her daughter. In discussions with friends and coworkers, Irene often remarked how the world had changed. Young girls of today were making their mark. They looked toward autonomy as a given. They were able to strive and achieve like any man could. They were not willing to accept gender-based limits or restrictions in their careers or their personal lives.

About a year and a half before her graduation from college, Renée talked less about her female friends, her grades dropped, and she appeared less excited about her college activities. She appeared quieter and seemed to have difficulty concentrating. Irene inquired about her daughter's well-being. Renée answered that she had a lot to think about but did not offer any further explanations. Finally she dropped the bomb: Renée was going to drop out of college to get married. She had taken a liking to one of her male classmates and shifted her attention from involvement with her female friends to dating this young man. He had a promising job offer she said and he was leaving college without graduating. He wanted Renée to go with him. They would get married. Irene thought it inappropriate that the young man planned to take Renée with him without meeting and discussing it with Renée's parents. She arranged counseling for Renée, thinking that an objective professional would be better able to guide her in her decision making than an emotionally involved mother would—although Irene assured her daughter that she would be there for her to help her and to discuss options and alternatives.

Renée did not change her mind. What about her career, her independence, the dreams she and her friends had talked about—her mother asked. Renée was in love, she answered, and she wanted to be with the man she loved. Also, Renée was pregnant. Termination of the pregnancy was out of the question for Renée, so was giving the baby up for adoption. She left college in her third year without completing it, got married, and moved away with her husband. Renée's parents arranged for a small wedding. The rest of the money from the college trust fund was given to her with the understanding that there would be no more financial help from her father. Her father blamed Irene for the change in their daughter's life decisions.

Irene wondered how deep and significant the observed changes in young girls' attitudes really are. She did not keep track of her daughter's former friends and how their lives proceeded. Did they also settle for a future of marriage and motherhood without the rewards of their own professional achievements? Or were they able to follow their own paths, investing in their autonomy and self-determination? Had she been too lenient with Renée? Was she overprotective when she did not tell her about the unfair divorce settlement? Irene did not find the answers to those questions, but she continued to work on her own independence. Completing the studies for the certified public accountant added another option to her professional life. She could continue to work for employers or she could start her own consulting business. On the personal level, she stayed in frequent contact with her daughter and she entered into another romantic relationship. But never again would she surrender her autonomy—was her promise to herself.

Several years later, Renée disclosed to her mother what had contributed to her change in direction. The young girls in her group of friends transferring from high school to college had taken an 'oath of sisterhood' that demanded that the girls were to excel in their academic studies to the point where they all had higher grades than the young men in their classes. Renée had encountered some difficulties in her science classes and she could not maintain an "A" average. She felt ashamed and guilty for letting her friends down. Without confiding in anyone, she decided it would be less embarrassing to change directions than to fail at the declared goal. The young man's interest in her seemed to be the solution to her dilemma. Being married and pregnant, nobody would expect her to place her career first. The need for competition and the fear of coming in second were removed.

The struggle Renée experienced in her chosen isolation must have been tremendous. The counseling had not been effective in assisting her to choose realistic career goals because Renée had not been any more open with the counselor than she had been with her mother. Irene decided to observe her daughter for any signs of returning desires for a career. She would be there to help her daughter set more realistic goals. The story of Irene's daughter is not an isolated one; Jody, one of the group members, had employed a similar line of reasoning as Renée did.

THE GROUP: OPTIONS AND GOALS

Helen was the first of the group members to enter the room. She chose a seat in the center of one of the long sides of the table. She was facing the open door—on purpose. Her long hair, which was usually combed back straight and fastened in the back of her head, was cut and now framed her face in short, soft waves. She also had applied some makeup, which made her face look more animated and softer. As group members filed into the room they could not miss Helen's new look and complimented her admiringly. When Betty entered she and Helen exchanged one look and started to laugh. Betty also had decided to start this period of her life with a new hairdo and less gray in her hair. Although being just superficial changes, their new hairstyles symbolized a beginning as well as a similarity in the two women's thinking.

Anita was the last to enter the room. She complimented Helen and Betty on their new looks. Anita wore a colorful kerchief around her neck and a necklace of black and red beads. She sat down, unfastened her kerchief and handed it to Helen, saying, "This matches your dress better than mine." Looking at Betty, she took off her necklace and let it slide over Betty's head. She leaned back, looked first at Betty then at Helen, nodding her head, pleased with the effects she had created. While Helen and Betty thanked Anita, the other women applauded, as the therapist entered. Ann reported to the therapist what had just transpired.

Anita: This is probably the first time that I ever did anything for
          another woman spontaneously, without thinking about possi-

ble benefits to me. It has not changed my way of thinking about preferring the company of men to being with women. (Looking at the therapist slightly defiantly): But when you mentioned that my father's behavior isolated me from the rest of my family and from other women, I started thinking about that. None of my siblings liked me, and although my mother was not the mushy type, she seemed to interact with my siblings in a warmer way than she did with me. I always thought she distrusted me because I was closer to my father. Even when my father stopped treating me like a princess, my mother still did not show me any warmth. I am wondering if she actually hated me. Perhaps that is why she did not protect me when my brother sexually abused me.

Helen: You were abused too? How awful! I would never have thought that something like that happened to you. You don't act like a victim—as I did. I saw myself as "damaged goods" and I am sure it influenced me in the choice of a husband.

Anita: No, I did not consider myself a victim, just not smart enough. Later I was raped by my boyfriend, although at the time I did not regard it as rape. It was the price I paid for dating the most popular boy in high school. I learned to think of sex as power in exchange for what I wanted. I know you think that is terrible but I think it is fair. (Again looking at the therapist): I have to think some more about my isolation from other women. I had thought that the only worthwhile protection came from men and that women had nothing to offer me. They would just be competition.

Ther.: You have done a lot of thinking, Anita. Your spontaneous gifts to Betty and Helen show a generosity that you may not have known you had. I am sure Betty and Helen will treasure your gifts and so do the rest of us. Yes, there is competition among women—as there is among men, but it is of a different kind. Women generally are competitive about their looks because they think that is one of the first aspects women are assessed for by men. Unfortunately, that is often true. All the more charitable on your part to present Betty and Helen with items that are meant to enhance their attractiveness. (Turning to Helen): It is good to see how you are thinking about leaving the victim stance, Helen.

Ann: Wow! Anita, that was a wonderful thing to do.

Anita: Not really, a kerchief and necklace were too much to wear at the same time anyway.

Inge: She is doing the same thing I do! Anita can't accept a compliment from another woman about her niceness.

Anita: (Blushing): Perhaps you are right. I may have to learn that. (Looking around questioningly): Where is Julia?

Ther.:   Unfortunately, Julia will not be with us today. We have talked about the challenges we face and the options that we are exploring here. The challenges are not only situations that confront us now; challenges also include goals for the future that we may define for ourselves. Without goals, options are meaningless if they do not lead to something. The goals may include behaviors, feelings, attitudes, whatever we want to accomplish for ourselves. This group can be a great training ground for experimenting with new attitudes and new behaviors. Before we do that let's look at some of our old attitudes that could be replaced. You all have some attitudes about women's importance.

Ann: I told you, I grew up as the middle of five children. The interesting thing is—and I never thought about it before— although my parents were proud to treat us children the same way, at the dinner table my mother always served my father first and gave him the best pieces of meat or vegetables. She never served herself first, though she did get her meal before the rest was equally divided into five portions for us. You would think if she believed that everybody was equal, she would at least have served herself first every other day. The equality she attempted to instill in us children she did not claim for herself.

Ther.:   Your parents may have wanted you to feel that you are loved equally by them but did not think about how they role-modeled gender differences. I wonder if that influenced your behavior toward your former husband. Didn't you tell us that you kept the fact from him that you had turned down a job promotion in order not to hurt his feelings?

Ann: Yes, I did not mention that to him. At the time I thought I decided to be quiet about it because his ex-wife had been more interested in her career than in him. But now that you mention it, it could have been a combination of the two. Another thought just popped into my head: Although my friend had warned me about Roger's violent behavior, I chose to believe Roger, thinking his former wife was a mean person. I judged her unseen. Was it because she was a woman and therefore had to be at fault?

Ther.: That is a very interesting thought, Ann, and it's difficult to know for sure. It is understandable that you wanted to believe and trust the man you were going to marry. Naturally, you wanted to trust him more than someone you did not know. Perhaps you could have obtained more information through your friend and her source before going ahead with the wedding. There is another aspect though. You mentioned how desperately you wanted to be special. Perhaps trusting and loving this person who had been hurt before gave you an opportunity to be special in the love you could show him.

Ann: Oh, that is true, I remember thinking that I would be a special person to him because of my love for him. My love would be great enough to take his pain away. This is extremely complicated—all the different aspects that could have combined and influenced my decision.

Ther.: It is complicated, you are right. The motivating forces of our behaviors are indeed complicated. That's why it is so important to know all we can about ourselves. The more we know ourselves the better are we able to make decisions that are in our best interests. To know how our thought processes are shaped is valuable information. Without it we cannot truly become autonomous.

Jody: What you say is scary to me. Most of my behaviors come out of what I think other people expect me to do. I want so desperately to be accepted and liked. I also avoid confrontations at all cost—as we talked about it the other day. (She spoke in her usual rapid way with her voice trailing off at the end of the sentence.)

Ther.: Jody, where do you think this need to be liked by everybody comes from? Who may have taught you that?

Jody: I think it must have been my mother. My father left her when I was quite young. My younger brother and sister were babies at the time. My mother worked as a nurse. She got married and divorced several times after she and my father split up. There was no steady male influence while I was growing up. My mother used to say that as a single mother, she had to be especially nice to people because she needed their help. We moved a lot and she had to find new people who could baby-sit for us. If a baby-sitter quit, my mother would say that we had not been nice enough. It was important that we pleased the baby-sitters. None of us wanted to be the culprit who made the baby-sitters quit, so we competed for their affection. To this day my mother tells me to please my husband because my children need the stable environment that he can provide. I have some female friends, but again, I do what they want me to do, which often causes trouble with my husband because he does not approve of them. In order to avoid confrontation I make up stupid little lies, acting as if I had not been with my friends. Then I get tripped up in my own lies—and for what?

Ther.: Jody, it sounds like you are afraid of being abandoned and to avoid that you try to please everybody. That causes a lot of stress, how can you ever relax?

Jody: You probably have seen my fingernails. I try to hide them; they look so bad.

Ther: Yes, I have noticed your fingers. What would be the challenge you want to work on regarding your need to please everybody?

Jody: To find out what I want to do for myself and not be afraid of people not liking me.

Ther.: And how would you go about doing that?

Jody: When friends ask me to do something not to agree quickly but to ask myself if that is what I really want. I have taken some small steps. The hardest thing is not to respond quickly just to be off the hook for the moment. I have tried to imagine that I have a zipper on my mouth. When I hear a request, I imagine that I am closing the zipper. It's really funny because a few times I have actually put my hand to the right corner of my mouth. I always close the zipper from right to left. (Group members join in with Jody's laughter as she demonstrates 'zipping up her mouth.') I am not always successful, but I keep practicing. (For the first time Jody's voice was not trailing off at the end.)

Ther.: That's a fantastic idea! I am glad you shared this with us, Jody. Coming up with a humorous solution is very effective because you derive enjoyment out of your imaginary action. What about the fear of being left or abandoned?

Jody: Looking at that realistically, I have moved to so many places, left so many people and people have left me and I have survived. It is more important that I like myself because I take me along wherever I go.

Inge: I think it's great how Jody identified where her need to please came from. It helps me to focus on my own attitudes. Similarly to Ann's family, at meal times my mother always served my father first with the best selections. Then she filled our plates before she put the smallest piece of meat on her own plate. But there was a ritual: One piece of meat was left on the serving plate. She always asked my father if he wanted it. Sometimes he let her give it to him. At other times he would leave it. If we kids did not take it, she would finally eat it herself. I observed her frown if I took it. When my younger sister took it there was no frown. Although she was unhappy, she served my father hand and foot. She always made it a point that her husband and her children came first before she could ever think about herself. I thought that was the European way to do it and I started a similar ritual with my ex-husband until I went to work and had to cut down on my "slave work." Like Jody, I was too tired to enjoy sex; it was just another chore. With David I learned to enjoy sex—but that's another story. Although American, David was not as much help around the house as I would have liked. Working full-time and taking care of my four children and the house, I could have used more help. Remembering my mother though, I kept quiet and did what was necessary until I became angry and threw a fit.

Liz: Could you have hired a housekeeper or cleaning person? That's what I did when my ex-husband did not share in the housework.

Inge: I tried, but David absolutely did not approve of the expense and did not think it was necessary. I did not want to cause a confrontation.

Ther.: There is that word again. It's almost as if the avoidance of confrontation has determined women's lives. While we are talking about it, please make a note to think about what are the worst consequences of being in a confrontation, as you would see it. If the consequence is the possibility of being abandoned, like Jody mentioned, let's work on this in future sessions.

Betty: Listening to your opinions is quite an education for me. If I had ever thought of having someone to help with the house-work, both my mother and my husband would have thought I lost my mind. My parents worked hard and the same was expected of me. Yet my ex-husband's new wife has a cleaning woman. (Turning to the therapist): Of course, those are thoughts that keep me engulfed in anger and I better not dwell on them. I have made progress how I approach people. With my new hairstyle I decided to smile more.

Ther.:   Betty, it is great that you are becoming aware of how your thoughts lead to certain attitudes and subsequently to feelings and how painful some of those thought-feeling connections are. Your new hairstyle definitely calls for smiles. As we have discussed before, feeling important or special has to come from within ourselves, but with our behaviors we give out signals to those around us. Some of those signals communicate our ambivalence or uncertainty about ourselves. When a woman is not well defined within herself, those around her may attempt to mold her according to their plans and wishes.

Jody: Are you saying that we should know what we want to do and to be like before we ever enter a serious relationship?

Ther.:   It would not hurt. The more you know about yourself and the more interests you have explored, the more grounded you are in yourself. With a new romantic relationship it is so easy to lose track of yourself as you become engulfed in the relationship.

Jody: The very thing I admired in Roger I lacked in myself; but I thought I would get it through him.

Ann: Your comment about knowing oneself before entering into a serious relationship makes sense. When I just think back of the complicated combination of my attitudes and needs that may have set me up for marrying a physically violent man, it scares me. The painful confrontation with my family that I told you about is another reason to pay more attention to my own attitudes and beliefs. I better learn fast because I have met a young man who seems very nice and who asked me for a date.

Liz: Great! We may be in for an interesting turn of events. I am dying to hear more about the mysterious young man.

Ann: I am sure that I will have a need to talk about him, depending on how things develop. He is a physician but is involved in research. He is very intelligent. He has a PhD in addition to his medical degree.

Ther.:   It looks as if everybody will be waiting for your next report, Ann.

Betty: I would like to tell you about a new option, which hopefully will add some interesting aspect to my life.

Ther.:   Please, Betty, tell us about it.

Betty: Now that I am less angry and more outgoing, I have made it a point to be friendly to people, as I said earlier. My attitude makes a difference in how I approach people. I have been talking to people that I meet in my apartment complex. Several times I met the same neighbor in the elevator. Her name is Nancy and she runs a small travel agency. One Sunday afternoon we decided to meet for coffee. She talked about her business and mentioned that she needed someone to do her books on a part-time basis because some of the things she can do herself. I offered her my help and we came to an agreement that would be beneficial for both of us.

Ther.: That sounds as if it could be a good start for becoming independent in your own little business, as you had mentioned an interest in that earlier.

Betty: Yes, that in itself will be nice. (Adding in an excited voice): But there is more to it. Every other year Nancy organizes a trip abroad for a group of professional women who years ago met as an art study group at the museum. Some of them have moved away since then, but they still get together for their trips. They select a town or country that they want to explore for a week or 10 days. These are all art-related trips. Through her travel agency, Nancy is arranging and correlating their complete trips. Some of them may bring a friend or spouse along and add another side-trip or extension. Nancy handles that, too. She was a member of the original study group and goes on the main trips with them. While there, she functions as their tour guide. She knows what they want to see. It is a special group and they receive special attention.

Jody: That sounds like a neat group. Are you going to become a member?

Betty: Even better, Nancy told me that she could use someone to help with the local arrangements and lend a hand with the travelers. She can't pay for an assistant and she can't take anyone away from her office during the time of the trip. She offered to share her room with me free of charge if I want to help her. I would have to pay for my airfare, public transportation there, food, and extras during the trip. Other ground transportation, such as renting a bus for the group, would be free for me. Admission to museums and galleries would also be paid for me because I would be acting as Nancy's assistant while there. I would have a chance to see and learn a lot. Nancy will discuss it with the group to see how they feel about having another person around. She does not foresee any difficulties, but these ladies are a bit spoiled by her special attention.

Ther.:   That would be a great opportunity. We will be eagerly await-
          ing the good news. Nancy would have a wonderful helper in
          you and the ladies would be in good hands. You will have
          plenty of opportunities to smile. (Turning to the group after
          a brief pause): To expedite learning about ourselves I think
          we want to look at what you wrote about your wishes or sig-
          nificant experiences as you were growing up. But before that
          I need to make an announcement. I told you earlier today
          that Julia will not be with us. Sadly, it is not just for today. I
          did not want to tell you before because it would have influ-
          enced our session. She wrote a letter to you, explaining why
          she cannot be with us anymore.

Dear Group:
     As much as I wanted to see each of you, I could not bring myself to
face you at the meeting today. I would have cried the whole time. Yesterday, I received a letter from the college about some additional paper-
work to be taken care of. It sounded encouraging. Before I could tell
Bob about it he informed me that his company had offered him a
transfer to another city more than 500 miles away. He had known about
the possibility for some time but did not share it with me. Now the offer
is firm and it will be a promotion for him. I told him that I did not want
to leave at this time. Too late, Bob had already decided that the family
would move and made the commitment to the company. His conviction
about the correctness of his decision was so strong that he did not even
consider the possibility of discussing it with me before accepting the
transfer. In fact, he has already made plans for us to spend a week in the
new town to look for housing. His company is paying for our trip out
there and our stay in a hotel. Bob thought this could be like a vacation
for us. We would leave the children with my parents for that week.
     It does not feel like a vacation to me, more like a funeral—the funer-
al of my plans and dreams about going to college. The move will strip
me of my support system. No longer can I depend on my parents or my
sister to occasionally supervise my children when I need time for myself.
Also, the emotional support I have received from you, from my friends,
and from my colleagues at work will not be available to me until I make
new friends in our new environment. I will not have the financial support from my employer for college courses as it was offered to me here.
There will not be any of our own money available for me to go to
college. Even though Bob's salary will be higher and the company will
pay for the move, living expenses in the big town we are moving to are
much higher than here.
     I am so upset I don't know where to turn. As usual, my parents are on
Bob's side, exclaiming how great his future is going to be. Although

they will miss seeing their grandchildren, they think the move presents excellent opportunities for us. As you can imagine, I am furious that Bob did not think it necessary to discuss this 'great opportunity' with me, not even when I told him about my college plans. My opinion does not matter. Of course, I could refuse to move and stay here with the children, but I am wondering if Bob would sue for divorce and—worst of all—for custody of the children. My thinking may sound paranoid, but with my parents being on his side, I don't know what a judge would say. The children are not even in school yet, so a move would not seem as traumatic as if they had to change schools. Since the news of the move I have been thinking of Anita and her pain over the loss of her children. I can't let that happen to me.

Please keep me in your thoughts. I'll miss being with you. My journey with The Group has been cut short; I hope you can continue yours.

Thinking of you
Julia.

Jody: That is awful. Just as she was beginning to map out her future and making plans to do something for herself. It was all for nothing. I wished we could help her.

Ther.:   It is very sad; we will miss her. You are correct, Jody, she was just starting out on her journey. Perhaps she will write to us and we can encourage her to look for options in her new environment. At our next meeting we will go over your stories. All of you have given me permission to disclose them. I thought you might read one another's stories. You can just draw numbers—unless you prefer to read your own story to the group. Julia's letter in connection with what you related earlier about your own considerations gives us food for thought. Among the options we have we can follow in our mothers' footsteps or we can make ourselves important enough to determine our own goals.

GROUP PROCESS: OPTIONS AND GOALS

The above session covered a wide range of attitudes, emotions, and behaviors. The changes in Betty's and Helen's outward appearances triggered a novel behavior in Anita that, in turn, led to a disclosure about her own painful past. Briefly, the concern of women's competition with other women was raised but did not receive in-depth attention at this time.

The notion of challenge was widened to include members' choices and goals as well as situations that members were faced with for resolution. The question about how women gain a sense of personal significance, which had been raised earlier, continued to be an issue in the discussion. Fears of confrontation and of abandonment were expressed. One group member reported on a coping technique she had devised for herself to help her in changing a specific behavior.

The sad news about one member's leaving was announced at the end of the session. It was the therapist's decision to prevent interference of the sad news with the work that was to be accomplished in the session.

SUMMARY

The concepts of options and goals were discussed in this chapter. For some people, choices or options symbolize a state of freedom, whereas to others they are stress producing because of the demands placed on the outcomes of pursuing one option above others. The reality of myths concerning the pressure to choose between two options was investigated. What appear to be mutually exclusive choices are not necessarily oppositional.

Time and efforts spent in the process of selecting the most favorable option can prove to be an intelligent investment in the outcome. Considering options without goals may be thought of as intriguing mental exercises, but in the overall scheme it is meaningless. Goals are the milestones that provide direction to the option-selection process and determine the probability of success.

The focus of the second half of the chapter was on how today's young girls may differ from their mothers and grandmothers in executing their options and establishing their goals for the future. Do they allow for changing directions, or are they certain about their goals from the outset? As in previous chapters, interactions in the group process concluded the chapter.

QUESTIONS FOR CONSIDERATION

What are the benefits of carefully exploring available options and selecting the most favorable one among them compared with just flipping a coin? Can you think of a recent situation in which you used one or the other method? What were the results of using the particular method?

What were the goals when choosing either method in the above question?

Consider yourself to be Renée's mother. What would you have done to facilitate trust and communication with your daughter when Renée decided to drop out of college? Would you have presented her with an ultimatum that either Renée complete her college degree or you would cut your ties to her? What possible options were available to Irene that she did not use?

RECOMMENDED READING

Beattie, M. (1987). *Codependent no more.* New York: HarperCollins.
  This book is about taking care of oneself instead of trying to control others and their problems. The author uses real-life examples, personal reflections, and exercises to illustrate her points.
Levine-Shneidman, C., & Levine, K. (1985). *Too smart for her own good?* New York: Doubleday.
  The authors explore the question of whether women have to choose between career and family. They illustrate their points with the use of case histories and interviews.
Lipson, A., & Perkins, D. N. (1990). *Block: Getting out of your own way.* New York: Lyle Stuart.
  The authors help readers to create a structure for thinking about changing undesirable behaviors by pointing out how the human mind works.

CHAPTER EIGHT

Recovering the Forgotten Self

I n the preface to her book *Reviving Ophelia,* Mary Pipher (1994) considered the current cultural environment to be a "girl-poisoning" culture (p. 12). In Pipher's opinion, today's movies, music, television, and advertising function to limit girls' development rather than to expand it. In the 1960s, Betty Friedan pointed out that many women were miserable but could not determine the source of their misery. In the 1940s and 1950s, television programs such as the *Donna Reed Show* and *Father Knows Best* prescribed a lifestyle to young women that—beyond wearing the feminine apron—was, even though or perhaps because of being restraining, next to impossible to replicate in real life. By prescribing behavioral goals for women that cannot be achieved, women will never measure up to the ideals set by culture, society, or religion. Throughout history, clergymen expressed their conviction that for the primordial crime that brought damnation to man, women deserve punishment. After all, it was Eve's defiance that tempted Adam and caused their exit from paradise (Walker, 1983). History contains various cultural trends and institutions that have determined the lifestyles of young girls and women.

TRANSFORMATION DURING ADOLESCENCE

Adolescence has been a time of increased psychological risk for girls for over a century. At the edge of adolescence girls lose their vitality and resilience, become prone to depression, and lose their sense of themselves (Brown & Gilligan, 1992). Adolescence can be seen as a time of disconnection or even dissociation in women's lives. Women often forget or repress what they have experienced and known as girls.

166

In the process of becoming young women, girls have a propensity to dismiss their experience and to modulate the strength of their voices. With increasing emotional and cognitive sophistication, young girls who previously had been courageous and outspoken tend to become reluctant to express their thoughts and feelings and even their knowledge. Pipher (1994) described how young girls change in their characteristics around the time of puberty. Whereas before they may have been curious, adventurous, exploring, exuberant and enjoying their physical energy, a transformation occurs rendering many of them preoccupied with their looks, their weight, being moody and listless. During early adolescence girls' IQ scores drop. Their personalities change from the energetic exuberance to submissive or moody rebelliousness that is often expressed in quiet, passive ways. Their voices lose their previous confident tone and become low and hesitant. Curiosity is being displaced by concerns of conformity to the norms of feminine appeal of the day.

STRESSORS THROUGH ADOLESCENCE

Why would girls still have these personality and mood changes at a time when more women are participating in sports and working in traditionally male professions as mentioned in chapter 7? Stories in the media abound reporting on successful females charting their own course through life. Accounts of achieving women are meant to serve as encouraging models to stimulate others to become equally as accomplished. Or are the examples meant to acquiesce those that have not found their success yet and to keep them from complaining?

In reality, the celebrated examples function to increase the confusion in young girls' minds even more than before. If they don't know at the age of 13 or 15 what career dreams they want to achieve, what is wrong with them? If they haven't succeeded at a spectacular position in life, what is wrong with them? For many young girls and women comparison with *superwoman* is anything but inspiring and more often than not leads to lowered self-esteem and increased depression. Some of them struggle with and against the confusion, whereas others silently capitulate before the struggle begins. They forget what it was like to be curious or to explore.

Struggles with issues of self-concept or self-perceptions can occur at any part of life, but are most problematic during adolescence. The transition from childhood to adolescence is characterized by greater vulnerability for self-critical attributions because of the emerging social-cognitive skills. The rising awareness of the self as targets of others' thoughts and feelings may make adolescents think they are transparent to others and, in turn, induce stress and anxiety.

Data from interviews and observations involving two groups of teens were analyzed to explore risk factors associated with alcohol, tobacco, and other drug use by adolescent females (Bemker, 2000). One group was composed of residents of a treatment facility for adolescent females with a history of delinquent behavior. The second group was made up of students in an alternative, educational setting. The girls were aged 13 to 15. Discussing self-esteem issues, most of the girls stated that males were considered to be more important than females. They thought that the schools' educational programs, sporting events, and career choices were male-dominant in their approaches. Another belief expressed by the participants was that girls needed a strong significant other in their lives. The right type of boyfriend would endow them with worth and status. The majority of the girls saw themselves as helpless in dealing with problems of daily living. They feared family strife and gang activities and longed for security. For many of the adolescent females, strong positive role models were nonexistent.

Similar sentiments were expressed by teenage girls at a group meeting of the Big Sisters of Central Indiana. Some of the girls live in neighborhoods where drug selling and gang activities do occur. The girls are 12, 13, and 14 years old. Few of their mothers have finished high school. Some have achieved their GED and were able to obtain good clerical jobs. Other mothers are enrolled in or considering getting their GED. Still others don't care. Good role models are hard to come by in the neighborhood many of the girls live in, but through the Big Sisters they have the opportunity to become part of Big and Little Sister Matches. Big Sisters are female mentors who will spend quality time with their little sisters at least twice a month for a whole year or longer. In addition, their weekly group meetings are conducted by female facilitators who are also effective role models. In their Life Choices group meetings, the adolescent girls are provided with opportunities to explore careers, values, and relationships. They learn to look at options and to consider consequences of their choices as they come about at a critical point in their lives. The girls come from different backgrounds and for a time they are able to step out of their neighborhoods and share their experiences with others. Most referrals are made through school counselors, teachers, and social workers, but not all that could benefit are reached and there is a continuous need for individual mentors.

DIFFERENCES IN SELF-CONCEPT BETWEEN BOYS AND GIRLS

Studies of adolescent self-concept have shown that consistency of self-evaluation was greater for boys than for girls and increases in achievement and leadership were found in boys but not in girls as they moved through adolescence (Monge, 1973). Although children's perceptions of their own ability become more accurate and less prone to overestimation as they advance in age, the perceived competence is instrumental in the choices they make in seeking challenges. The beliefs about their abilities rather than the actual abilities determine children's behavioral choices. There is no guarantee that children with high competence will actually see themselves as having strong abilities. In a study examining cross-sectional and longitudinal samples of high-achieving students in third, fifth, and ninth grades, the students were assigned to three different groups according to their own perceptions of their abilities, inaccurately low, average, and high competence. One of the comparisons in the study focused on sex differences in illusory incompetence. In the third and fifth grades there were no significant differences between boys and girls in perceived competence. At the ninth-grade level, however, significant sex differences characterized the competence group placements. The low-perceived competence groups consisted 100% of girls, whereas the high-perceived competence group included only 40% girls (Phillips & Zimmerman, 1990).

Considering the absence of sex differences in the third- and fifth-grade levels, these findings describe a dramatic shift in the perception girls have of their own abilities as they proceed through school. While boys tend to overestimate their abilities, girls consistently underestimate the levels of their competence. The actual achievement levels, as measured by composite achievement test scores, quantitative achievement test scores, and final-year grades, showed no significant sex differences among the ninth-grade students. When comparing the children's beliefs about the expectations their parents had for them, again significant sex differences were observed. Weighed against the boys' perceptions, girls thought that their mothers—but not their fathers—expected significantly less of them and held them to less stringent achievement criteria. The ninth grade—is this the time when "Ophelia" disappears? Misperceived lack of abilities, complexity of relationships, pressures to adhere to the cultural norms of beauty and attractiveness resulting in poor self-image, anxiety, and depression force her to go underground.

Social interactions and relationships become more complicated during adolescence as peer groups increase in size and complexity.

More independence and responsibility are required to make the transition from the primarily same-sex playmates of childhood to opposite-sex interests and friendships.

SOCIOCULTURAL PRESSURES

In Western societies, girls generally feel more miserable than their male counterparts. Girls experience more anxiety and insecurity than boys, which leads to increased depression in girls. Achievement is often defined in terms of how successful girls are in attracting males. Thinness is equated with attaining perfection and promotes the idea that thinness is the answer to all of women's problems. Believing that losing weight will make the female more popular and more assertive and will result in a better job places the focus for self-improvement solely on a physical basis. If the female's body does not reflect her culture's ideal body shape, her worth as a person is low (DeLucia-Waack, 1999). Thus, self-acceptance is contingent on the approval of others. Adolescent girls' greater unhappiness, poorer self-image, and role confusion may contribute to the greater prevalence of eating disorders in females than in males (Hsu, 1989).

Observations that White female adolescents feel more anxious and insecure and have a poorer self-image than Black female adolescents have been reported (Simmons & Rosenberg, 1975). The profound impact of cultural roles on developing White adolescents results in a decline of self-esteem beginning in early adolescence (Phillips & Zimmerman, 1990). In comparison, African American girls scored higher in self-worth and in social acceptance than other ethnic groups (Erkut & Marx, 1995). African American women are not as involved in the dominant culture and are thereby in a position to assess and interpret messages from the dominant culture without internalizing them.

In a study involving five African American and five Caucasian women, ages 40 to 80 years, conducted to compare the women's identity formation through life, Petersen (2000) found that Caucasian women struggle to emerge from cultural engulfment to regain a sense of identity, whereas African American women are able to sustain their identity despite oppression. Eight of the participants were college educated and two had high school diplomas. One woman was retired but the remaining women continued to work despite—in some cases—their advanced age. All of the women were considered to be achievers. The results indicated a strong sense of continuity of identity among

African American women. In contrast, Caucasian women were twice as likely to report notions of changing identity compared with having a stable identity concept.

ADOLESCENT SEXUALITY

Adolescence is also a time of hormonal changes and developing sexuality. New physical and emotional feelings bombard the young person at a time when developmental tasks of forming value and belief systems have not been accomplished and realization of consequences and replacing myths with reality have not been completed and internalized.

In the United States, 1,040,000 adolescents under the age of 20 became pregnant in 1990. Approximately 51% (530,000) of them gave birth (Coley & Chase-Lansdale, 1998). Since then the rate of teenage births has declined but teenage birth rates in the United States still far exceed those in all other industrialized countries (Maass, 2000b). A study by the Alan Guttmacher Institute in 1994 found that 42% of teenagers have had sexual intercourse by the age of 16, and 71% by the age of 18 years. Even more alarming was the observation that frequent unprotected sexual intercourse resulted in high rates of sexually transmitted diseases (STDs). One in four teenagers had become infected with an STD by age 21, leading to two and a half million cases (Valois, Kammermann, & Drane, 1997).

Female adolescents of different racial and ethnic groups show differences in childbearing rates. In general, Whites have considerably lower rates of adolescent births than Hispanics or African Americans (Coley & Chase-Lansdale, 1998). While childbearing rates in White and African American adolescents have declined, the rates for Hispanic adolescents have risen steadily in the past 15 years. Although Latina adolescents have lower rates of early sexual experience, they are less likely to use birth control and are less likely than White or African American adolescents to abort once they are pregnant. In the Hispanic culture, sexual attitudes are interwoven with magnified traditional gender roles and the cultural concepts of *machismo,* the social structure that elevates Hispanic masculinity to a privileged position, and *La Santita,* translated as "the little saint" and referring to the martyred position of Hispanic women who aspire to perfection by submitting to the requirements of Hispanic males and serving their families untiringly, without complaint (Barkley & Salazar Mosher, 1995).

Low educational aspirations have been linked to teen pregnancies; one third of teenage mothers reportedly dropped out of school before becoming pregnant (Maynard, 1995). Female adolescents who are raised in poverty, by parents with low educational attainment or by single parents, are considered to be at risk for teenage parenthood. The frequently cited assumption that adolescent pregnancy is the result of ignorance about effective use of contraception does not tell the whole story. Adolescent childbearing among some lower socioeconomic-status African American girls between the ages of 16 to 21 years may constitute a career choice and an alternative, normative life path within African American culture (Merrick, 1995).

Some investigators, focusing on the disparity of teenage girls not wanting to become pregnant and not effectively using contraception because of a lack of knowledge about reproduction and contraception, limited access to family-planning services, and inability to foresee and be prepared for protected sexual activity, seem to find comfort in expecting that many of these factors will improve significantly with age (Coley & Chase-Lansdale, 1998). They cite the fact that age is one of the strongest predictors of birth control use. Can we afford to wait for the girls to get older when in the meantime these children are facing the struggles and hardships of early pregnancies that will impede their physical, mental, and emotional development?

Educational efforts aimed at prevention or reduction of teenage pregnancy have shown various results. For instance, "Project Reality," a prevention program in rural Ohio had more than 70% of students in grades five through eight enrolled (Wilson-Sweebe & Bond-Zielinski, 2000). Comparison of pre-and posttests claimed 7% increase over the previous school year in improved communication between teenagers and their parents. Another result was that 83% of fifth and sixth graders and 88% of seventh and eighth graders, after completion of the program, stated that they believed that unmarried teenagers should abstain from any sexual intercourse. Apparently, this constituted an increase of 30% over the previous school year. On the other hand, a report from a female worker in a youth development and prevention organization disclosed that two of the girls who had been active in their peer education and mentor program since age 14 had become pregnant at age 18, despite exposure to numerous presentations from Planned Parenthood and other organizations. All the information about prevention of pregnancy and STDs, all the involvement in producing teen materials and making presentations to other teens had not been successful in. preventing their own out-of-wedlock pregnancy (Pearson, 2000).

ABANDONING THE SELF

Abandoning the self in adolescence through adopting conformity, withdrawal, and resultant depression or anger is a way of responding to cultural pressures practiced by some girls. From childhood on girls are taught the importance of looks. In fairy tales, the girl who gets to marry the prince is always beautiful. She has a sweet disposition, a pleasing smile, and tiny feet—so the prince can find her after she disappears around midnight. Miss America contestants may have different personalities and different talents that they present to the audience, but one characteristic they do not have—lack of beauty. No matter how great a contestant's talent is, without beauty there will be no crown on her head.

"I had naively confused recognition of my youth and beauty with recognition of *me*. . . . Like Sleeping Beauty, I had fallen into a trance around the age of fifteen from which I was just beginning to wake. It was becoming painfully clear that I had spent my life perfecting the game of pleasing and attracting others (particularly men) and relying on my youth and looks to do this much more than I had realized or cared to admit" (Melamed, 1983, p. 12).

During adolescence, a time when young people are expected to focus on their future amidst the struggle of transition from childhood, girls are particularly vulnerable when they abandon their selves to the worries about fitting in with the demands for female attractiveness. As a consequence of the misplaced focus, little energy and time remain to concern themselves with thoughts about a career that will provide them with mental and financial self-sufficiency. Many young women still come to the threshold of college without a well-defined goal, and once there they experience another opportunity for abandoning themselves.

Some women conform outwardly but hold on to their "real selves" on the inside. Others lose or forget about their inner selves and repress their voices. The wedding day, often thought to be the happiest day in a girl's life, is a day of resignation for some. Two of the women in Petersen's (2000) study mentioned above reported having exchanged their own identity for that of their husbands. Motherhood is another chance for a young woman to misplace her identity, as expressed by some of the study's participants.

REGAINING LOST VOICES

There are also those who are able to regain their forgotten sense of self. The lost voices can return to a woman as early as in her 20s or as late as in her 40s or 50s. After 20 years in a traditional marriage, one of the participants in the above study emerged from graduate school, remembering her parents' stories about her childhood wishes of wanting to be a garbage man and a president. The paths to discovering themselves and recovering the lost sense of self included different milestones for the women. There were divorces, moves, returns to school, and embarking upon professions—all trials in the search to regain the forgotten self.

DIFFERENT DREAMS FOR MALES AND FEMALES

Youth, a time when almost anything seems possible and dreams are limitless, can be so different for males and females. The young man curiously and excitedly may set foot on his path to destiny. For the young woman, however, who finds her prescribed destiny of marriage and motherhood not to her liking or insufficient for her own interests, youth is a time of struggle and uncertainty rather than a time of hope. Not succeeding in living the conventional life, individuals may search for an as yet unrecognized talent. When the idea of a vocation is still nebulous in the person's mind, a sense of inadequacy and deprivation is often experienced. Unlike men, who early in life enter a predictable path to achievement, women, after encountering detours and transforming themselves, may awaken later from a dormant period. There are examples of many female writers who were well into their 30s at the time of their first published work (Heilbrun, 1988).

Lisa: Return to the Forgotten Explorer

Lisa grew up in a small Southern town. Her father held a promising position at a local bank and her mother worked part-time as a high school art teacher. She was an only child until the age of 7 years when her brother was born. As a young child, Lisa liked to collect rocks and minerals. She was fascinated by the different colors and inclusions she saw in her treasures. Her father encouraged Lisa's treasure hunts and bought her a microscope so that she could enjoy details that were not discernible with the naked eye. Lisa's mother did not share her daughter's enthusiasm for rocks. When Lisa was 10 years old her father died suddenly. The family moved to a smaller house and Lisa's rock collection disappeared in the move.

While Lisa's mother extended her teaching to a full-time position, Lisa had to help with household chores and look after her younger brother. Her school years were unremarkable. She was pretty and pleasant, had a group of friends, and managed to maintain a "B" average in her grades. She showed some talent in drawing, and a college education with a major in fine arts seemed the appropriate direction to pursue. While in college she met a young man who appeared to possess the attributes of an ideal husband. Soon after graduation Lisa and Mark got married. Lisa settled down to housekeeping tasks and used her art education to tastefully furnish and decorate their apartment. After about a year of housekeeping and an increase in her waist size, she decided that she was bored with staying home all day. She remembered her education and found a job that was remotely related to her training and her degree.

Lisa was excited about her job and put a lot of energy into it. She advanced to a managerial position. Mark was not as happy as Lisa about her work because she expected him to help around the house. Mark suggested that now would be a good time to start a family. Lisa was not ready to trade her achievement in for a baby. She said she needed about a year to prove herself to the company. After that they could plan on having a child. Mark did not agree to the delay and gave her an ultimatum. Lisa accused Mark of denying her the satisfaction of a career. Their arguments escalated and in less than a year they were divorced.

Soon after the divorce became final, Lisa lost her job without much prior warning. Now she was on her own with no job. She contacted Mark to see if they could reconcile their differences. It was too late; Mark had already made a new commitment. His girlfriend was pregnant and he was finally going to have a family. Lisa embarked upon a frantic job search and found another job, however with less responsibility and less money than her previous position had given her. She dated various young men, but none of these relationships resulted in marriage. Her new job lasted only 6 months. The business she worked for was taken over by a larger company who placed one of their own employees in Lisa's position.

The next job offered her even less money than the previous one. Lisa could not afford to be choosy because she faced a stack of bills that had accumulated since her divorce. It did not help that she occasionally ran into Mark and his new family. Those encounters emphasized Lisa's loneliness. Although she could ill afford it, she did everything to portray the successful young career woman, rationalizing that this was the only way to attract a young man who would ensure her future. Lisa used her meager financial resources to purchase smart-looking clothes, and she developed skills in occasionally leaving the store with merchandise bypassing the cash register. Although she did not get caught, she was scared enough to quit this practice.

Lisa sought the advice of an employment counselor and was told that her degree was not useful on the job market unless she found a teaching position. The suggestion that she invest in additional training for a teaching job was not to Lisa's liking. She stated that she had already obtained one college degree. Lisa's plans for the future had focused on being married. Her education was meant to be an asset to her husband's position rather than a means for her own financial independence. She regretfully remembered that in the past putting importance on a career had led to the disintegration of her marriage. Now she felt cheated out of her goals again.

By the time Lisa volunteered to relate her story, she was working as a sales associate in the women's clothing department of an upscale department store. The fluctuations in her attitude regarding professional women seemed significant. In her first job, she had briefly experienced pride and excitement when she had been promoted to manager—even to the point of postponing motherhood and risking her marriage. Yet in her interaction with the employment counselor, Lisa seemed to have reverted back to the traditional ideas of women's work supplementing the husband's income. What had prompted the shift in attitude? Lisa answered that in her opinion, her short-lived attitude of independence had caused all her current trouble. Without her insistence on pursuing a career she would still be married to Mark and would not have to worry about her financial future or about finding a suitable husband. When asked if she ever wondered how soon after their breakup her ex-husband had made a commitment to another woman, Lisa replied with "Men don't have to wait around, they have their pick of women."

There was one more question to ask: "Had she ever remembered her childhood interest in rocks and minerals? She thought for a moment, with tears in her eyes, sadly shaking her head before responding, "That was in another life. I wished my dad was still alive."

About 6 months after the last interview, Lisa wrote a letter: "I just wanted to give you closure on this part of my life. After you asked me the question about my rock collection, I kept thinking back of the time I was so engrossed in it. There was a faint recollection of how it had felt to be both curious and at peace at the same time. I allowed myself an hour of exploring the emotions of the moment. It was a mixture of sadness that comes from having lost something and a longing for its return. I went to the library and got some books on minerals and semiprecious stones. One of the books included a section on gemstones. To make a long story short—I decided to obtain training in gemology. I want to learn more about the mystery behind the gems' beauty. Perhaps I can combine my fascination with 'rocks' with my skills in drawing to work in designing jewelry. It all feels a bit overwhelming but I have taken a few small steps, such as signing up for the training and requesting a transfer to the jewelry department of our store. Financially, I can't afford to give up my job, but I thought I would be able to learn something in the jewelry department that would be of help in the future. I just received word that tomorrow will be my first day among the gemstones. By the way, it is remarkable how fast Mark got into another serious relationship. Thank you for asking those questions."

Lisa's childhood recollection can be understood within the psychology of life stories (McAdams, 2001). Self-defining memories or personal event memories (Pillemer, 1998) are episodes remembered from the past that present specific events, occurring at a particular time and place. These memories evoke sensory images contributing to the feeling of "reliving" the event and linking its details to particular moments of phenomenal experience. Among the many varieties of personal event memories, those that are influential in self-definition contain symbolic messages that are interpreted by the "rememberer" as generating or affirming an interest or vocation. When the event occurred, at the time of encoding, goals determined the memory selection. The originating events can remain dormant for a period of time until a turning point episode suddenly arouses the self-defining memory and redirects a life plan (Pillemer, 2001). In Lisa's case, collecting rocks can be seen as the originating event that gave rise to the personal event or self-defining memory. The questions asked in the interview with Lisa provided the turning points that directed her back to the all-consuming interest of her childhood.

THE GROUP: WISHES AND DREAMS

The mood among the group members was subdued, perhaps due to the loss of one of their members. Nobody had heard from Julia. Liz looked around and announced that there was one chair less in the room, which made it appear as if Julia had never been with them. As the therapist entered there was still another empty chair. Members looked around with a questioning expression on their faces.

Ther.:   (With a somber facial expression): I have sad news again. Anita called to say that she had to go away for a while. It had to do with her children. She did not know when she would return. Losing two members almost at once is distressing.

Betty: Do you think Anita's gifts to Helen and me were her way of saying "goodbye"? Did she know it was going to be her last visit with us?

Ther.:   That's difficult to say, Betty. If it was meant as a farewell, she could not have done it in a nicer way. Let's remember her in her generous action. (After a brief pause): This is a good time to find out more about each of you. I have removed Julia's and Anita's notes. Each note has a number instead of a name. If you draw your own note, you can decide to read it or to put it back into the bag and take another one. Let's start with you, Cindy. Please take one of the notes and pass the rest on to Ann next to you and so on. Let's listen to each note in turn without discussions after the individual readings.

Note 1:   (Liz) When I was 4 or 5 years old, I could not dress myself yet, but I had a pretty apron that was part of a dirndl dress. I wrapped it around me and tried to dance and curtsy. My mother told me to stop and be quiet. It wasn't that I wanted to be a ballerina or anything like that. I just wanted some attention. Our home was always sad and quiet. My older sister was sick. She had a genetically determined illness. I learned that I had a brother who died of the same illness before I was born. My mother was busy taking care of my sister, not much time or attention was left for me. I clowned around, trying to cheer them—and probably myself—up. My mother did not approve. I liked going to school. It was less sad than at home. I tried to make friends, but the friendships did not last long, because I could not invite any of the other kids to my home. I liked art classes the best when I found out I could draw better than any of my classmates. The teacher thought that I had talent and asked me how my parents liked my drawings. I did not show my drawings at home, thinking my mother would not approve. All of a sudden I received a lot of attention. My sister had just died, and secretly I was almost glad that she was dead. My parents took me to the hospital even though I was not sick. They had me tested to find out if I had the same illness. They were happy when they found out that I was healthy. At what seemed to be about a year later, my mother gave birth to a baby boy. Much, much later I thought that my parents attended to me and had me tested because they wanted to replace the son they had lost or the daughter that had died. The attention was not really meant for me.

Note 2: (Inge) My dream was to become an actress. I wanted to be somebody else than myself. My mother was against it. She always told me to be modest, not to draw attention to myself—when attention was all I wanted! The few times that I was allowed to go to the movies with the neighborhood children I was just fascinated. I remember on the way home we tried to imitate some of the actors and actresses in the scenes that we had seen. But I was not allowed to go as often as the other children. My mother punished me without mercy for any act of disobedience, as she perceived it. It got worse with the birth of my younger sister; I got punished for two. Whenever my sister cried, my mother scolded or beat me because, as she said, I must have done something to upset my sister who was just a sweet little baby. My mother was not happy in her marriage and repeatedly told us that she sacrificed herself for us. There was no way I could ever become an actress. I was expected to go to work as soon as possible. I could not even run away from home, because in Europe the police have ways to find you. That's why I married so young. My mother was against it, but my father signed the papers for me to get married before my 18th birthday. My mother did everything she could to keep the rivalry between my sister and me alive; we did not speak for 20 years. We communicate now but we are not close, too much has happened. My husband and I came to America and I had opportunities for professional training. I am the best mother to my four children that I know how to be. My mother condemns me because I left my husband and deprived my children of having a full-time father.

Note 3: (Betty) My family life did not invite big dreams. We lived in the country on a small farm. Everybody had chores to do and there was not much time for dreaming. When I was in grade school, one or another of the girls would get mad at me and I would be afraid to go to school to face them. I don't know why they were mad at me or why I was so afraid. They weren't likely to beat me up. In high school, my discomfort continued. I remember there was one girl who was so angry with me that she did not talk to me for a whole year. I never found out what made her angry with me. In school I was sitting in the back, trying not to be noticed. It seemed safer that way. Regarding my future, I hoped that a nice man would find me, marry me, and have a family with me.

Note 4: (Jody) I saw myself as a mother with lovely, happy children. I would tell them stories. We would play together, run through the fields, walk through the woods, looking at flowers and trees, dancing in the meadow—just being happy. It was what I did not have in my own childhood. Looking back, it seems more that I was acting like an older sister rather than a mother. I could never imagine myself being alone. I have an uncanny ability to be what people expect me to be. It's like I exist only in the reflections of others. Last year I took a writing class. We had an assignment to write about ourselves, to describe what is our essence, as we see it. The instructor wrote on my paper that she could not find me. What I had written made her think she would have to ask others—those that I mentioned in my paper—about the real me. I was devastated when I read her response, but she was right. Will I ever find out about me?

Note 5: (Ann) Being the middle child in a family of five siblings, with parents who believe in treating all the children in the same way, may sound great but does not encourage thoughts of individual greatness. There was nothing I excelled in over my siblings—we were all in the same class, intellectually. I had to hide my burning desire to be special because my parents would not have approved of that. They often told us how lucky we were because there was no room for sibling rivalry among us. Our parents' love was identical for each of us. Because I was afraid to hurt my parents' feelings, I never talked to any of my siblings about how they felt.

Note 6: (Helen) I don't remember ever having any aspirations for the future. My life was hard work as far back as I can remember. There was no time to read books or play. There was a time that I wished I could fly, like a bird. A little gray bird would be enough to carry me away. I had no destination nor did I think about exploring anything—just to get away from the pain and ugliness of being sexually abused by my father. Now I know that it is common for victims of sexual abuse to think of themselves as floating or flying, trying to get out of their bodies, so they can pretend that what is going on is not really happening to them. I remember one day sitting outside and watching a beautiful butterfly. How pretty it looked and how gracefully it moved its wings. I wondered then why I did not wish to be a butterfly instead of the little bird. My answer to myself was: "I am ugly and dirty, I can't be a butterfly." I cried and cried. I didn't seem able to stop crying until my mother came out of the house, scolding me. I did not think of the butterfly anymore.

Years later I learned sign language in volunteer work with the deaf. One day I used my skills in church to interpret the sermon to a deaf couple in the congregation. Their daughter who was able to hear and speak normally had gone away to college. In her gratitude the woman signed back to me: "Your hands speak like a butterfly."

After my mother cut me out of the family because I had mentioned the incest, I moved away. Everybody in the family denied that it ever happened. That made it impossible for me to live in the same community. I am over the sexual abuse through the work in a victim's group. It was helpful to a point. The other group members could identify with me in detesting my father but they could not understand that I hate my mother. To me, what my mother did was just as bad—if not worse—than what my father did to us.

Note 7:   (Cindy) Growing up in the shadow of two beautiful older sisters did not encourage me to entertain extravagant dreams about myself. My mother's attempts to comfort me by saying "plain girls make better wives" did not help. I know she meant well, but it only reinforced the idea that there was nothing special about me. The only memory that could be remotely relevant to this assignment is of my sisters taking me window-shopping with them when my mother was busy. Naturally, they were always interested in pretty clothes. To pass the time, I imagined myself owning the store and decorating the store windows differently, making colorful signs to attract the people's attention. Once I made some bright posters and put them up in my room, and I rearranged the furniture to make it look like a store window. I put a chair facing the door, just off-center, and "borrowed" a very colorful dress from one of my sisters, draping it over the chair. I found some shoes and gloves to match the dress and complete the picture. For the background, I arranged a light blue bedsheet with some cotton clouds. My sister missed her dress and my mother looked for it and, of course, found it in my room. She removed the dress, gloves, shoes, and sheet and told me that the posters

were much too bright for a girl's bedroom. I never did anything like that again and did not even think about it. It did
not seem important.

Ther.:   These are emotionally charged writings. Each of you put your
feelings into what you wrote. When I first read the notes they
struck me like raw elements at the core of your very being. It
has been covered up in you for years like it was not even
relevant to your life, but it is still there and you can feel it.
These notes seem to speak louder than many other of your
verbalizations.

Jody: I felt like crying when I read the story I drew, and I felt even
more like crying when I listened to my own story. There
seems to be so much sadness in our lives.

Cindy: Listening to the stories, I found myself thinking I can't believe the pain you are feeling. My situation seems almost
trivial by comparison.

Ther.:   Yes, there is a lot of pain, Cindy, and your pain is just as real
as anyone else's.

Ann: That's right, Cindy. The need to be acknowledged as an individual or as special is just as painful when unfulfilled as other
hurts.

Ther.:   It is remarkable that most of you did not describe yourselves
in terms of a distinct individual with goals and directions.
That reminds me of what we talked about before, how important it is to know ourselves before we enter into a romantic
relationship.

Inge: But it's so difficult to focus on yourself when you have been
told over and over again to be modest, not to think about
yourself first.

Liz: I agree with you, Inge. We were not allowed to want things
for ourselves. And the very fact that we were not given special
attention made us think we don't deserve it and it's bad to
want attention, and yet we crave it! You wanted to be an
actress. It was easy to figure out your story because you mentioned growing up in Europe. An actress gets attention being
up there on the stage for everyone to see and admire.

Ther.:   I guess by now most of you have recognized one another's
stories—is it all right to talk openly about your notes? (Group
members nodding their heads in agreement): Let's look at it
logically. We know that many of us want to be special and
would like to receive attention and encouragement from

others. But there are those of you who feel guilty about this desire and try to hide it as if it were bad.

Ann: It's considered to be bad.

Ther.: By whom? Where did you learn that?

Ann: My parents, of course.

Liz: Mostly from my mother, my dad never said much about it either way.

Cindy: My mother never actually told me not to want attention, but by saying "plain girls make better wives," she confirmed that I was plain and that I should accept it. She may have been sad that I felt bad being "invisible" but she did not help me become more visible.

Inge: That reminds me of a question I had when I heard your story, Cindy. I was surprised about the way you described using colorful items when you tried to make your bedroom look like a store window. I hope you won't be offended by this: Since we have known you, you mostly dress in beige and brown colors—very subdued colors for someone who wants to be visible.

Cindy: I have dressed like this for years. Why? I don't know. I just seem to gravitate toward those colors. Perhaps my mother's comments are working on my subconscious.

Jody: Why do you think parents don't encourage us do think of ourselves as being special?

Betty: Parents think we would cause more trouble if we thought of ourselves as special. If we are not special, we don't expect special treatment and we do what we are being told to do without complaining. At least, that's how I was raised.

Helen: And if you don't expect anything great, you won't be disappointed.

Jody: So the best we can say about our parents is that they raised us not to be disappointed?

Ther.: You tracked down where the notion that wanting attention is bad came from. Now you can continue to believe that it is bad because your parents told you so or you can decide for yourself whether or not it is bad. However, as long as you do not doubt the correctness of that belief, you will not change your actions and feelings.

Ann: So what do we do about it? We can't go around telling everybody that we are special.

Ther.: It wouldn't work well if we insisted that we are the only special person in the world. But you already know that there is more than one unique person right here. While we accept each other's uniqueness, we develop and nurture our own. We talked about meaning, identity, and personal significance before—all this is related to what we are working on now. You have an opportunity to redesign yourselves. (After a brief pause turning to Betty): Betty, in your note you made quite an important connection about your discomfort with confrontations. It is a significant concern for several of you, and we want to continue to work on this issue.

Betty: Actually, writing down those thoughts helped me to realize how much of my life has been wrapped up in being afraid of and trying to avoid confrontations. If I change now, I wonder if I can make up for lost times.

Ther.:   It's worth trying. (Turning to Helen): Helen, your story about watching the butterfly was so moving. I wonder if your fear of crying may stem from that incident—when your mother scolded you for crying?

Helen: It's true, I haven't cried much since then. I didn't cry in the other group when they told me it was wrong to hate my mother.

Ther.:   Helen, your feelings are understandable in view of what happened to you. As we just discussed, parents do not always do what we think would be best for us. They don't always protect us when we need it, and some of them place their own needs before the needs of the children they brought into this world. For some of us, the storybook-mother does not exist. All the more reason that we treat ourselves well. We can all be the kind of mother to ourselves that we wished we had when we were growing up.

Helen: You mean, mothering ourselves?

Ther.:   Yes, in a way we can do that quite well because we know what we were missing. I think we can learn a lot from your notes. Most of you sounded sad when looking back into your past, sad as if you had lost something precious. You may have lost or forgotten your dreams or the opportunity to dream—both precious commodities. Liz, you mentioned drawing when you were a child, Inge wanted to be an actress, Jody thought about writing or telling stories, and Cindy liked to decorate with bright colors. You don't seem to be engaging in these activities now. Your notes have raised those memories; perhaps you would like to think more about them and how they might fit into your lives at this point.

GROUP PROCESS: WISHES AND DREAMS

The session began with the therapist's announcing that another member had dropped out. Reading the group members' notes evoked emotional reactions within the group. The discussion that followed centered around parents' teachings and hurdles to focusing exploration on self. The therapist gently responded to selected items contained in the members' notes. With the sadness over past experiences, some hope for the ability to change arose.

STIMULATING THE SEARCH FOR THE FORGOTTEN SELF

As seen earlier in the case of the volunteer Lisa, her early childhood memories did not come to the surface automatically but were prompted by the interviewer's questions. The struggles of adolescence often function to displace earlier memories into hard-to-get-to compartments of the brain. For young girls, the self-doubts and faulty perceptions of lack of competence, the concerns about socially prescribed appearance and behaviors—function to push other issues into the background. As the self becomes abandoned so do the memories. The individual most often does not know what would trigger the reappearance of displaced or forgotten materials. Sometimes hypnosis is of help. However, if one is not aware of having lost or misplaced something, one is not going to search for it—with or without hypnosis. For the group, the assignment to write down their thoughts served as catalyst for the emergence of the group members' forgotten moments. Because two sessions dealt with the assignment and the individuals' responses to it, both group sessions are appropriately placed in this chapter.

THE GROUP: FORGOTTEN MOMENTS

Group members seemed to gravitate more closely to one another as they entered the room. There was an atmosphere of acceptance, openness, and even excitement as the women greeted one another with warm smiles. Inge eagerly removed her handbag from a chair to make room for Ann to sit down next to her. Cindy walked in wearing a pink sweater with her beige skirt. Pointing to her sweater, she was trying to attract Inge's attention. Inge gave her a big smile of approval and motioned her to sit down next to her. It was interesting to observe that Inge, who was generally polite but had never overtly invited any of the women to sit next to her, now actively encouraged two of them to be close to her. Jody, Liz, and Betty were sitting together and made room for Helen, who was the last one to arrive.

Ther.: I am sure the previous session stirred up a lot of emotions in you. I wonder if anyone wants to talk about reactions you may have had.

Jody: I had been working on my closet. Most of the stuff that was in there I was able to remove. I painted the walls because they looked kind of stale. There is room for a tiny desk at one end and a couple of bookshelves on the wall above it. That's along the narrow side of the closet. On the other end, under the narrow window, there is enough space for a comfortable chair and a little table to hold a book or writing pad. With a couple of small lamps, the place looks rather cozy.

Ther.: Congratulations, Jody. You worked hard to provide a space for yourself. I hope it will accommodate your search for what you want to find out about you.

Liz: How did your husband respond to your new space?

Jody: He does not know it yet. I keep the door locked when I am not alone in the house, and I painted the walls when he was out of town so that the smell of paint would not give me away. You probably think I am a coward—and you are correct. I am not strong enough to confront him.

Ther.: How will you be stronger in the future? Are you allowing yourself time to find out what it is you want to try for yourself?

Jody: Yes, I want to concentrate on myself with as little interference as possible. Then when I know what I want to do, I hope I will be better able to assert myself, and I will also work more intensely on my feelings for him. First I need to know myself better.

Ther.: You have learned to define your initial steps and the pace with which to continue along the path. When you feel ready to discuss your plans, you can decide how to approach the communication.

Jody: I feel I am heading that way. Several weeks ago when I was writing my story for the group, I remembered a photograph of myself as a child of about 12 or 13. It was just a fleeting thought then. But when I heard my story read out loud in our group session it hit me. I had to find the picture. This is the only picture that I have ever seen of myself where I don't smile. In all other pictures I am smiling because I knew I was being observed. I needed to look happy so nobody would accuse me of being mean to the baby-sitter. In fact, the picture must have been taken by one of the many baby-sitters we had. The picture shows me sitting, writing—probably a letter to a friend. I am not sad looking, just not smiling. It seems I was really engrossed in writing and did not put on my usual performance because I felt safe and unobserved.

Ther.: It was a significant moment for you to remember the picture. It may provide the turning point for redirecting a part of your life plan.

Jody: That's just it! When I wrote the story I remembered the picture but it did not make the big impact that it made when I heard someone else read the story. That's when it hit me. Is that why you had us read one another's stories—so we would experience it differently?

Ther.: You made a good observation, Jody. We often respond differently when someone else talks about our experiences, even if it is in our own words.

Jody: I wonder if the picture shows the real me, the "forgotten" Jody? I put it on a shelf above my tiny desk to remind me that I don't always have to smile, that I don't have to be what others expect me to be.

Ther.: Perhaps the picture will guide you in your search. You have developed two devices that can assist you on the path toward your goal. In addition to the imaginary zipper on your mouth, you have the picture of the forgotten Jody. That is great work. (Turning to Helen): Helen, you look as if you want to tell us something.

Helen: What you said earlier about staying a victim made me think. Anita's kindness had a great impact on me, too. Here she had her own problems, losing her children, yet she had it in her to look at Betty and me. After listening to my story, it occurred to me that the best way to end my victim stance is to do something for others. I am not trying to become a saint or martyr. It's just to focus away from my own misery. After our last meeting I had an idea.

Ther.: Helen, that is great! Please tell us about your idea.

Helen: I contacted the school for the deaf and made an appointment to meet with the administrator. He did not have a job for me and that is not what I went there for. He said they would be happy to have me help on a volunteer basis and that my ability to communicate in sign language would be an asset. He suggested I attend the church service on Sunday morning to get an idea about the children and their parents. This is not a residential facility, but many of the children and their parents attend church on the school grounds.

Cindy: Did you go?

Helen: Yes, I did. I was a bit anxious, but this was my chance to start something different. Before the service, the administrator took me aside and told me he had talked to the minister about me. They both thought it would be a good idea if I could briefly introduce myself to the congregation, using sign language along with my words.

Cindy: How did it go? Did you like it?

Helen: I was nervous at first being in front of all these people I didn't know. But they seemed friendly and I began to relax. After the service a young boy—about 8 or 9 years old—came up to me with his father trailing behind him. The boy looked sad. He wanted to know if I could hear. I was surprised that he asked me verbally, although it sounded a bit different from the way people normally pronounce words. When I told him yes I could hear he wanted to know why I had learned sign language. I said I learned it to be able to listen to what children like he wanted to tell me. He slowly stretched out his hand and thanked me. His face briefly reflected the shadow of a smile. There was a heartbreaking quality about this boy. I kept thinking about him for the rest of the day, wondering what had happened to him.

Betty: Are you going to see him again when you do your volunteer work there?

Helen: I hope so. I feel I can give him something—warmth, care, attention . . . I don't quite know.

Ther.:   How do you feel right now? You have this soft smile on your face, it's like a glow.

Helen: I feel soft on the inside—as if there is a small crack in my wall and some warm air is coming through it. But it's also exciting. I don't know if that is the right word. I have done something to get away from my misery.

Ther.:   Helen, you have actively stepped away from the victim. You have made a door in your wall and you have opened it to take a step outside and to invite something new to come into your life.

Betty: Helen, I am so impressed with what you did. When we both got our new hairstyles that was an outward sign of our wish to change and you have taken a big internal step. I hope I can do the traveling with Nancy. That will be my start. Then next year I am going to take computer and accounting classes to improve my job skills.

Helen: That sounds interesting, Betty. I sure could use more training, too. Maybe we can find some classes for both of us.

Ther.: Additional training may be options you can create for yourselves. The same applies to past interests that some of you had mentioned in your notes. Inge, did you ever consider joining a local acting group?

Inge: Funny you should say that. A colleague of mine is a member of a lay theater group. He had a few roles in local productions and has invited me to come along to one of their meetings. I am very nervous, though, because I have never really played a role.

Cindy: You could learn. With your looks, they would probably be glad to have you. You would look great on the stage.

Inge: Thank you, Cindy. I sure appreciate your encouragement. Why don't you come along?

Cindy: I might just do that. After our talk about observing how other people get to be noticed, I have studied a few people and the behaviors that I thought attracted others. It was really interesting to watch and analyze what makes people noticeable. It reminded me of an exercise in school. The teacher told us to write a few sentences about each of the other students. I think she had in mind that we would all say complimentary things about the others. There were several of us—I was among them—the other kids did not know what to say about. Most of them said about me that I was quiet or agreeable. One kid worked hard and came up with "she has a nice smile". In my observations about people who draw attention, I also found a few who seemed to be as invisible as I. I studied them, too.

Liz: What a fascinating observation! Did you find similarities to yourself in their behaviors?

Cindy: Yes, I did find similarities. I also noticed people getting attention for different reasons. There are the beautiful ones who obviously attract attention. Then there are the good listeners, the ones that make others feel comfortable, and finally the ones that have something interesting to say. They have an all-consuming passion, something extremely meaningful to them that they are deeply involved in. Their excitement about it is almost contagious. It made me envious to see their passion. I learned a lot by observing.

Betty: I am glad you explained that, Cindy. Earlier when we dis-
          cussed observing others to adopt some of their behaviors, I
          was wondering how outside behaviors would connect to the
          feelings of being special that come from within. (Turning to
          the therapist): So in your suggestion there was more to it
          than just looking at the outside behaviors. You thought a
          good observer could make inferences about a person's men-
          tal involvement on a deeper level, is that correct?

Ther.:   You explained that very well, Betty. Thank you for your astute
          observation. Yes, there is more than imitation of superficial
          behaviors. (Turning to Cindy): Cindy, you accomplished a
          valuable task with your observations. What are your plans
          from here?

Cindy: I took notes about the different groups, the ones that drew
          attention and how they did it, and the ones who did not get
          noticed. Realizing that I am not the only one who fades into
          the background, I had an inspiration. What if I seriously study
          these different behaviors and try them out on myself? Respons-
          es from the people around me would provide feedback and I
          could develop it for a workshop to help people like me.

Liz: That is a fantastic idea! Cindy, you could write a book about
          it and sell it at the workshops.

Ther.:   You are making exciting plans. (Turning to Ann): Ann, you
          haven't said anything today. How did your date go?

Ann: I don't think I got off to a good start with that.

Ther.:   Would you rather wait for another time to tell us about it?

Ann: I might as well get it over with. I did a stupid thing. Ron is so
          sophisticated and I wanted to impress him. So I bought a
          beautiful outfit that is much too expensive for my budget. I
          charged it on my credit card, and my plans were to return it
          to the store after the date, saying it did not fit. Friends of
          mine have done that and had no trouble. You just have to be
          careful not to get any spots on the garment.

Betty: You mean you wore the outfit knowing you could not afford
          it—weren't you nervous?

Ann: Of course I was nervous. Ron took me to an elegant restau-
          rant and we had a fabulous meal. He complimented me on
          my outfit and said what attracted him to me were my intelli-
          gence and my excellent taste. He thought that was a rare
          combination in a woman. It made me feel special. The rest of
          the evening I did not say much because I was so worried
          about the dress and—of course—I spilled some gravy on it. I

went to the ladies' room to see if I could get it out, but it left a stain.

Jody: (Breaking in): How awful, what are you going to do?

Ann: I have to keep the outfit and pay for it. I hope the stain will come out in the dry cleaning so that at least I will have the use of the dress. But it will set me back financially. You don't know how often I heard your voices in my head, saying that being special comes from within. Ron did not seem to notice my quietness. He talked about himself and his work. He has written several articles and is working on another book about his newest discoveries. My being in the medical field was interesting to him. Perhaps I could help him with the editing of his book. I would have a better comprehension of the content than most editors. In his experience, the editors that the publishing companies assign to a writer are mostly women who have a degree in English and know where a comma should be, but that is the extent of their knowledge. Rather than concentrate on the meaning of the content, they argue over punctuation. Of course, I felt flattered that he considered me intelligent enough to edit his work.

Liz: It sounds as if he is buttering you up for some work. How did the evening end?

Ann: I think it would be interesting to read his writings, although I am not sure that I'll understand it. He asked me if I wanted to go to a bar for a drink, but by that time I was too nervous about the dress. I just wanted to go home. We did make a date for the next weekend. I wouldn't be surprised if he called it off, I wasn't very entertaining.

Ther.: It sounds as if your worry about the dress did not let you enjoy the evening. What a stressful situation you put yourself into. Do you remember while you were in the store what thoughts prompted you to take that outfit with you?

Ann: I thought, this is my chance to go out with a real accomplished man. I have to impress him at the first opportunity because I may not get another chance. He can have his pick; I have to be really special. I also thought that my intentions to wear the garment and return it as if it were still new were not quite honest. But my friends got away with it.

Ther.: You believed the dress would make all the difference even though you had already attracted his attention in your regular clothes?

Ann: I just wanted to make sure to put my best foot forward.

Ther.: That sounds logical on the surface. What if we look at the
        cost of your "best foot"? You did something you did not really
        approve of. Something that is not congruent with your val-
        ues. You risked embarrassment if the store would face you
        with the fact that you had worn the garment or you risked a
        financial setback if the dress got a spot on it.

Ann: Which it did. Now I have to pay for it.

Ther.: Yes, you will pay for it but it can be a learning experience.
        Those consequences that I mentioned may follow if you act
        on the belief—which you did—that the dress would make the
        difference between impressing or not impressing this young
        man. But where is the evidence that it would work? As a
        matter of fact, you already doubt that he will keep the next
        date because you were not entertaining while you worried
        about the dress. Another belief that rests on shaky ground is
        that because your friends got away with it, so would you.
        Acting on these two beliefs put you in a difficult position. You
        mentioned that while you were aware of the spot on the dress
        you heard the group members' voices, reminding you that
        uniqueness comes from within. That was a reminder of reality.
        Reminders of reality are important signals.

Ann: If I had had those reminders in the store, if I had thought of the
        possible consequences as you described them, I would not have
        taken the outfit. That is what you are trying to teach us, right?

Ther.: Right. Checking out beliefs before acting on them. As we dis-
        cussed before, usually we don't question our beliefs, but just
        because we hold certain beliefs does not mean they are based in
        reality or—even more important—that acting on them would
        be in our best interest. While we are talking about challenging
        our beliefs and considering consequences of our behaviors be-
        fore we act on those beliefs, we can also consider alternatives. In
        addition, let's also think of the forgotten moments mentioned
        earlier and hold on to the promises of the forgotten moments.

GROUP PROCESS: FORGOTTEN MOMENTS

This session was a lively continuation of the previous meeting. The
material disclosed in the earlier meeting functioned as a catalyst for
further discoveries. The therapist encouraged members to continue
with their explorations. The session ended with a demonstration about
how acting as if our beliefs are true can lead to self-defeating behaviors and a reminder about the forgotten moments.

SUMMARY

This chapter discussed the transformation that young girls experience during adolescence. The child they leave behind to become the young girl who needs to find a place in the world undergoes many changes, some of them poorly understood. Values and beliefs are being tested, confirmed, or rejected. There is an expansion in complexity of relationships from the protective family circle to increased peer involvement where different rules of conduct and interaction are operating. In this turbulent period of transition valuable parts of the girls' identity may get misplaced or forgotten. But the memory of treasured moments can be recaptured for some, opening the door to rediscoveries and reinterpretation in the current light. Recoveries occur at different times, often taking decades until an identity is reestablished.

The interaction in the therapy group was used for illustration of how powerful the forgotten moments from a previous period in a person's life can be. Whether conscious or unconscious, those moments still impact the individual's existence in various ways.

QUESTIONS FOR CONSIDERATION

In the case of Lisa, should she have given up her job and start a family, as her husband requested, instead of letting the marriage deteriorate to the point of divorce?

Using your own experiences, would you agree with the findings of the Erkut & Marx study that African American women are better able than Caucasian women to avoid internalizing negative stereotypes?

Imagine you are a member of "The Group." What are the memories or dreams you would write down for the assignment?

RECOMMENDED READING

Heilbrun, C. G. (1988). *Writing a woman's life.* New York: Ballantine Books.
  The author writes about women who do not make a man the center of their lives, but are adventurous, pioneering women in search of their fulfillment.
Petersen, S. (2000). Multicultural perspective on middle-class women's identity development. *Journal of Counseling & Development, 78,* 63–71.
  The article is a comparison about African American women and Caucasian women in their different ways of experiencing their identity development.
Pipher, M. (1994). *Reviving Ophelia.* New York: Ballantine Books.
  The author describes females' struggles from preadolescence to adulthood amidst sociocultural pressures.

CHAPTER NINE

Understanding the Structure of Gender

From birth, the child's movements and sounds are interpreted through the power of gender-role expectations. Different colors and different toys are reserved for boys and girls. Little girls wear pink, play with dolls, and push doll carriages. Little boys are usually dressed in blue and other nonpink colors; they play with balls, building blocks, toy soldiers, and guns. By the time they are asked what they want to be when they grow up, most boys and girls are already aware of the necessity to give gender-appropriate answers (Burke, 1996). By the time they can supply these answers, everything about them has been subjected to rigorous and constant gender training, emphasizing differences rather than similarities between boys and girls.

GENDER GAP

The term "gender gap" is applied to differences in conceptualization and differences in achievements between males and females. What are the reasons for the pervasiveness of the gender gap in our society? Researchers in sociology, psychology, and education are involved in studies identifying and examining the underlying causes (Hanmer, 1996). In the preface to his book *The Gendered Society,* Michael Kimmel (2000) stated that he wanted to correct myths, half-truths, and misinterpretations of collected evidence by saying that women and men are more alike than different. Observed differences between men and women are not biologically determined or due to some universal psychological developmental processes. In fact, Kimmel argued that gender differences are produced by the practice and maintenance of gender inequality. The above statements comprise the reason for providing a discussion on gender structure before focusing on the tasks of designing and constructing a life. The intent is not to cast blame on anyone or any institution but to repeatedly remind women that the gap is an arbitrary one that is there for the individual woman to challenge rather than to adhere to.

CREATION OF THE GENDER CONCEPT

The concept of gender is created, defined, and maintained through social influence and social interaction (Geis, 1993). Usually as overt demonstration, it is thought of in terms of behaviors, such as masculine or feminine behavior patterns. In addition to the overt behavioral elements, cognitive factors, such as beliefs, attitudes, values, and expectations, play important parts in the development and maintenance of gender-related notions, leading to gender stereotypes. As much as behavioral elements of observed individuals are congruent with the cognitive elements of the observer, gender stereotypes become reinforced in the mind of the observer. The observer's behavioral responses to the observed person will most likely be congruent with the perception and beliefs—or cognitive elements—of the observer. Behaviors of the observed that are incongruent with the beliefs and attitudes of the observer are likely to be overlooked or explained away to avoid a state of cognitive dissonance in the observer. Beliefs and attitudes related to any stereotype condition are difficult to extinguish.

GENDER AND THOUGHT PATTERNS

Social science in the 1940s embraced a system of inventories developed by Lewis Terman and Catherine Cox Miles to assess behaviors, attitudes, and traits that would place individuals along a continuum from masculinity to femininity, providing the individual with a gender identity. Responses to the inventory that were considered to be masculine in nature were scored with a "+," and responses that were thought to be feminine received scores of "–" (Kimmel, 2000). Some time during childhood, the individual arrives at a switching or decision point in which the world is seen in terms of gender. Although this occurs well within the first decade of a child's life, it does not end with adolescence or early adulthood. Instead, the labeling process "I am female" or "I am male" continues and is reinforced throughout most of the individual's life.

If overt behaviors are gender typed, thinking and cognitive functions are also often classified as following distinctive gender patterns. As gender is part of the individual's self-concept in terms of a group identity, it could be conceived of as impacting the individual's way of thinking (Cross & Markus, 1993). Gender schema research has focused on how individuals incorporate gender-related characteristics into their self-concepts. Characteristics of the feminine gender schema include understanding, caring, nurturance, and sensitivity to others' needs. These attributes focus on another person for the experience and expression of these characteristics. On the other hand, masculine gender schemas are thought to include independence, assertiveness, and competitiveness as factors. Those characteristics set the self apart from others. Different sets of characteristics would influence different patterns of cognitive activities. Persons with feminine self-schemas are thought to focus on information about others and about the self in relation to others more than would persons with masculine self-schemas (Markus & Oyserman, 1989).

In a similar vein, Carol Gilligan (1982), arguing with Kohlberg's ideas about the stages of cognitive and moral development, stressed the point that women and men use different criteria when making moral decisions. In addition to the "ethic of justice", the paradigm Kohlberg proposed as the final stage of moral development, there is the "ethic of care"—concerned with intimacy and connectedness—that women prescribe to. The gender-related thought patterns are believed to enable men to have better memory function for information related to the self and women to have better memory function for information of self as related to others.

Although evidence confirming these hypotheses is scarce, the feminine thought patterns or gender self-schemas may be what is operating in *women's intuition,* as we have seen in chapter 3 in Jody's case, concentrating thought on self in relation to the significant other, to the point where consideration of the other becomes the overriding target and the self serves mainly the target person.

As has been stated, gender is a socially constructed concept that is reinforced by cultural forces and human cognitive mechanisms. The socially constructed gender categories influence individuals and their perception of the world (Beall, 1993). In contrast to biologically constructed categories, gender concepts can conceivably be altered or modified through cognitive mechanisms. Individuals with feminine thought patterns could benefit from learning to shift their cognitive style to one that includes awareness of their own wishes, needs, and goals and their options for the attainment of their goals.

PARENTAL INFLUENCES ON GENDER-ROLE FORMATION

Birth marks the beginning of gender socialization. The birth announcements for a new child usually start with telling the world the sex of the baby before any other characteristics. Parents have strong gender-specific ideas of what their children need. There are marked differences in the way parents treat boys and girls. Mothers encourage independence in boys earlier than they do with girls (Kimmel, 2000). Girls are encouraged to express emotions but "big boys don't cry." The benefits of physical attractiveness are stressed for girls, whereas for boys performance and athletic ability are important attributes. The list of gender-specific characteristics is long and well-known.

How strong and how durable are parental influences on young persons' attitudes toward gendered family roles and what is the mechanism that keeps them alive? Rituals—through their repeated applications—constitute the mechanism that strengthen and maintain gender-related attitudes. Chapter 1 included a general discussion of the establishment of gender roles and the power of gender as it relates to the division of household labor. Social and cultural institutions may prescribe general rules for gender-appropriate behaviors, but the most influential agents of gender socialization are usually parents because they reinforce gender-related learning on a daily basis.

In a recent study exploring parental influences on attitudes toward household labor and gender-differentiated family roles, the investigator attempted to demonstrate the process that mediates the symbolic significance of gendered behaviors to individuals (Cunningham, 2001). The hypotheses under examination included the following: Parental behavioral models observed by children early in life predict the children's attitudes toward household labor during their young adulthood. Parents' increased participation in religion leads to less egalitarian attitudes about gender specialization in the family. Higher levels of parental education and higher income tend to expose families to egalitarian ideals as well as to a greater number of women engaged in nondomestic activities. Young adults' attitudes toward gender roles and housework will be influenced by parental attitudes and behaviors during adolescence in addition to the effects from observation in early childhood.

A cohort of mothers was selected from a probability sample of the July 1961 birth records of first-, second-, and fourth-born White children in the Detroit area. These mothers were interviewed in 1962. A second-generation sample was made up of the children of 935 of the mothers first interviewed in 1962, representing 85% of the originally interviewed families. The parental information was assessed when the children were 1 and 15 years old. All mothers interviewed in 1962 and in 1977 with an 18-year-old child who had been interviewed in 1980 constituted the sample to be analyzed.

The results indicated that mothers' early gender-role attitudes exerted a steady influence on the attitudes of their adolescent children, especially regarding the children's ideal division of tasks. Modeling interactions in the family context function to define and identify gender-relevant behaviors. The findings demonstrated that parental division of labor during the children's midadolescence significantly impacted the children's interpretation of how stereotypically female household tasks should be divided between men and women. For intergenerational similarity in attitudes, parental behavioral influences later in the child's life were more important than modeled behavior observed early. Fathers' participation in housework during the years when the children are likely to be assigned greater proportions of the domestic labor is important. The variable "parents' educational level" was positively correlated with the children's gender role attitudes and their ideal task division, but parents' religious involvement did not show significant correlation with the children's attitudes.

GENDER EXPERIENCES IN SCHOOL

Gender socialization continues beyond the family circle. By the time children start school, they learn—in addition to reading, writing, and math—what it means to be male and female. "Schools are like old-fashioned factories, and what they produce is gendered individuals. . . . the message students get . . . from both the content and the form of education, is that women and men are different and unequal, and that the inequality comes from those differences, and that, therefore, such inequality is justified" (Kimmel, 2000, p. 151). That teachers call on boys more often than on girls for answers to questions and that they spend more time with boys has been stated repeatedly. Boys not only demand more attention, they get it too. In textbooks, males are more visible than females and their portrayals still reflect gender biases.

In elementary school, girls demonstrate higher self-esteem and higher achievement levels than boys. But by the time they reach junior high school, girls lose their self-esteem and their IQ scores go down by about 13 points, compared with boys whose IQ scores drop about 3 points (Kimmel, 2000). Brown and Gilligan (1992) in their work with girls found that younger girls were confident, outspoken, likely to take risks and to express a wide range of feelings. As the girls moved into adolescence, they became less sure of themselves and their opinions and their self-esteem was connected to the degree of popularity they experienced. The Commonwealth Fund survey of 3,586 girls and 3,162 boys found that by the time they reached high school, only 39% of girls appeared highly self-confident. Younger girls seemed to possess higher self-esteem than their older counterparts. In contrast, more than half the boys in high school were very self-confident, with older boys being more highly self-confident than younger boys. Thus, whereas boys seem to gain self-confidence with increasing age, girls lose it.

For girls, the transition from childhood to teenage marks the beginning of dealing with the forces of adult femininity. The rules of popularity and becoming attractive to prospective boyfriends facilitate girls' subordination on the basis of gender (Thorne, 1993). The rituals and rules of heterosexual romance often undermine real friendship among females. Efforts to keep a boyfriend may result in the girl's lowering of her ambitions. Thus, the culture of heterosexual romance serves to perpetuate male privilege. Girls learn that a higher value is placed on their appearance than on their talents.

GENDER CHARACTERISTICS REFLECTED IN THE MEDIA

Television functions as another agent of gender socialization. Cartoons and shows that are generally considered acceptable for children emphasize gender-role stereotyping. Characters and themes portray gender-differentiated situations, with females pursuing more goals related to altruism, home, and family, whereas male characters go after professions, such as attorneys, physicians, or scientists and self-indulgently chase achievements and wealth. Children's television is supported by commercials targeted to children, such as toys, candies, and cereals (Lindsey, 1990). Commercials on children's programs usually show children playing happily with gender-specific toys. Toy manufacturers produce and sell gender-linked toys. Little girls are supposed to want the dolls, little boys are expected to request the trucks or building blocks, and the parents buy them or they are made to feel guilty by advertisers and children alike.

Once grown up, the gender stereotyping in the media continues to influence people. Advertisements portray women mostly purchasing cosmetics, food, household items, and child-related goods. With the exception of one short-lived TV commercial for an automobile, cars are apparently bought by men. Women are placed in or around the cars as adornments. In general, young girls do not find encouragement for independence or autonomy in advertisements.

GENDER INEQUALITY MAINTAINED BY HOSTILE AND BENEVOLENT SEXISM

Recent explorations have focused on the role played by benevolent sexism in deepening gender inequality (Glick & Fiske, 2001). Benevolent sexism is viewed as a subjectively favorable form of chivalrous ideology that expresses affection and protection to women who embrace conventional female roles. In comparison, hostile sexism is considered to be an adversarial view of gender relations in which women are perceived to be seeking to control men through sexuality or feminist ideology. In benevolent sexism, women may be described as adorable pure creatures that need to be protected and whose love is necessary to complete a man's happiness. Some women may even agree with men in interpreting this "protection" as cherishing rather than limiting.

Benevolent sexism—although just as constraining to women as hostile sexism—serves to pacify women's resistance to societal gender inequality because of its disarming expression. By characterizing women in a favorable light and promising advantages to those who are able to align themselves with a high-status male protector, benevolent sexism reduces women's resistance to patriarchy. Women who depend on men for their well-being are less likely to challenge men's power or to pursue their own independence. In general, women who acknowledge and reinforce traditional gender relations serve men as wives, mothers, and romantic objects. In return, they become recipients of benevolent sexism behaviors and attitudes. In contrast, women who are regarded as challenging or stealing men's power become targets of hostile sexism. While polarizing women's images into distinct female subtypes, benevolent and hostile sexism incorporate reward and punishment systems and may function in complementary ways to maintain gender inequality. Polarization by splitting women into two subtypes also effectively leads to isolation among females, rendering them weaker than they could be united.

Glick and Fiske (2001) considered benevolent sexism to be "a particularly insidious form of prejudice for two reasons: (a) it does not seem like a prejudice to male perpetrators (because it is not experienced as an antipathy), and (b) women may find its sweet allure difficult to resist. Benevolent sexism, after all, has its rewards; chivalrous men are willing to sacrifice their own well-being to provide for and to protect women" (pp. 114–115). Benevolent sexism—being a gentler form of prejudice—"is pernicious in that it is more likely to be accepted by women, as well as men . . ." (p. 117).

An example of benevolent sexism is described by Tanya, the volunteer encountered earlier (chapter 4). Tanya reported in her interview that Ralph, her husband, had complimented her on her intelligence which was "remarkable for a woman" and on her efficient handling of shopping and household tasks. Of course, the running of the household was really Ralph's accomplishment because he had successfully trained Tanya by citing his beloved deceased aunt as a role model for Tanya to emulate. The aunt was far superior to his mother in qualifications for the ideal woman. Tanya was eager to become a worthy successor to her husband's aunt. For a while she believed the training was all for her own good. Her husband's ingenious manipulation and Tanya's willingness to conform to the described ideal ensured him of a life relatively free from household chores even though both of them were employed full time.

THE GROUP: GENDER EQUALITY?

The group members were sitting closer together than in previous meetings. They had pulled their chairs closer around the table and leaned toward one another during their conversations. Ann entered the room together with the therapist.

Ther.: (Turning toward Ann): Ann, you looked rushed when you came in today. Is our meeting time making it too tight for you?

Ann: (Blushing): No, I don't have difficulties with our schedule. I was late on purpose—I might as well admit it. I wanted to avoid questions about the stained dress. I feel quite embarrassed about it.

Liz: I think I know how you feel, Ann. When you told us about the dress I thought you were talking about me. Just like some of your friends, I charged clothes on my credit card that I knew I could not afford. And just like you, I wanted to impress some men I dated. A few times I returned the clothes to the stores after I had worn them. Like your friends, I got away with it. But the stress became too much for me to handle.

Ann: You did the same thing? Thank you for telling me. You are
          such a nice person!
Liz: (Grinning): Yeah, real nice. And you know, none of the men
          I tried to impress with my 'borrowed' clothes worked out for
          a relationship. One of them even made me pay the bill for
          the evening. It was our second date and he had compliment-
          ed me both times on my beautiful outfits. Strangely enough
          when it came to pay for our dinner and wine he discovered
          that he had left his wallet at home. He apologized profusely
          and asked me if I could charge it on my credit card. He
          would reimburse me as soon as I got my bill.
Cindy: I hope he paid you back.
Liz: No, I never saw him again. He stood me up on our next date.
          When I received the statement from the credit card I tried to
          call him but never reached him, and he did not return my
          messages that I left on his answering machine. I had no evi-
          dence that he owed me the money, so I was stuck. I quit my
          habit of borrowing clothes after that.
Ther.:   That was an expensive lesson for you, Liz. I am glad you told
          us about it, we can all learn from it. Pretending that we are
          wealthier or more successful than we really are can be pricey.
          It can cost a portion of our freedom. As Ann and Liz indicat-
          ed, when you wear something that does not belong to you,
          you have to be very careful not to spoil it. You are not free to
          behave as you normally would and your level of tension and
          stress rises. The other issue is why are we willing to engage in
          behaviors that are harmful to us just to impress a man we
          don't even know yet? On our own, without borrowed attire,
          are we not good enough to deserve his attention?
Ann: That is a heavy question! I guess, my behavior would answer
          it with "No".
Cindy: Ann, did you have another date with Ron? You thought he
          might cancel.
Ann: Yes, we met Friday evening. He told me about his interesting
          projects. He really is intelligent and he seemed pleased that
          he could talk to me about his work. He said he had not met
          many women who comprehended his ideas and were such
          good listeners. After dinner he asked me if I would agree to
          stop by at his place. He wanted to give me the draft of two of
          his book chapters to read. He assured me that he valued my
          opinion. As it was quite late he suggested that I take the
          chapters home with me and perhaps read them over the

weekend. He had to go out of town but would be back on Sunday evening. If I had comments or questions, I could leave messages on his answering machine and he would call me back on Sunday after his return.

Inge: That sounds exciting. Did you read the chapters? Can you really understand his ideas?

Ann: I think I understand his ideas, but it is confusing. There were two or three places where I thought it did not make sense. So I left messages on his answering machine, referring to the pages and paragraphs I had questions about. I also read what I thought would be corrections in over the phone. I was very careful not to hurt his feelings and I wanted him to be proud of me that I was able to comprehend the development of his ideas.

Jody: So, what happened?

Ann: Nothing much happened. Ron called me back on Monday. He sounded a bit irritated but explained that he had returned later than expected. About the corrections, he said he had already changed them in his copy of the draft. Apparently, he had forgotten to make the changes in the copy he gave me. He added that he also wanted me to be sure to correct any incorrect grammar and punctuation that he might have overlooked, so that the 'punctuation editors' would not overreact again.

Jody: Ann, do you think Ron belittles the editors to make you feel good?

Ann: What do you mean?

Jody: Well, I remember Liz saying the other day that Ron was buttering you up. If Liz is correct, perhaps he wants you to feel good enough to continue proofreading his stuff.

Betty: I think Jody has a point. The young man did not even sound all that grateful for the work Ann already did for him. In fact, it sounded like he wanted her to focus on the grammar and punctuation more than on the content of what he is writing.

Ther.: Those are all valid observations. However, we don't have any evidence about the young man's intentions. Ann may learn more as she gets to know him better.

Ann: I am afraid it's true. How could I be so blind! It reminds me of something I read a long time ago, in a book about women's masochism. By telling me that I am more intelligent, a better listener, and have better taste than other women, Ron made me feel special. Someone as brilliant as Ron praising

me and choosing me to proofread his book made me think
I was better than other women. I swallowed it all.

Ther.:   I think I know what book you are talking about (Caplan,
1985). I remember the part you are referring to. By selecting
a particular woman, the man whom she admires makes her
feel special and better than other women. With this maneu-
ver she becomes set up against other women and isolated
from them. Then he uses the woman's loyalty to his own
advantage. At the time, I thought the author made a very
strong point. We talked before about women being isolated
from other women in connection with Anita. Perhaps you
remember it. It is something we should be aware of because
it can be essentially harmful. Can we afford to be isolated
from each other?

Jody: That's why a group like this is so helpful. We learn from one
another's experiences. I read in the paper the other day how
women in the past realized that they needed each other. Young
women now still face the challenge of establishing a balance
between their personal and their career lives, but they have
more of a tendency to go it alone. In the paper they quoted
the first female federal chief judge in the state of Indiana
who said how grateful she was to other women for supporting her (Jesse, 2001).

Ther.:   You made an excellent point, Jody. If you still have the article, it would be nice if you would share it with us.

Inge: I still think we are too harsh on Ron. What if he really appre-
ciates Ann's help but does not know how to express it correctly. She should give him a chance. Perhaps if—because of
Ann's help—his relationship with the editors improves, he
will love Ann for it and will be grateful to have her. What
does it matter what she is helping him with? If he is such a
brilliant person, he deserves more patience and good will.

Betty: Doesn't that sound like because he is so brilliant he should
be treated differently? I thought we are all here to learn how
to treat ourselves as important persons. Inge, aren't you turning back to the double standard that some of us are trying to
get away from?

Inge: Call it double standard if you want, but I would give a lot if
I could be with David. I have lost two men and it is very hard
to struggle by myself to raise my four children.

Cindy: What happened between you and David? You never talked
much about it to us.

Inge: I talked about that in my individual therapy. David seemed like such a wonderful man and he promised to help me and be there for me. I believed him but when I needed help with the household chores and my children's homework, he was busy with other things or just left the house. Eventually it all became too much for me to handle. I had some very nasty angry outbursts that I am not proud of. When we made up after the fights we were very passionate, probably because the danger of a breakup was gone.

Ther.:   Inge, that sounds very similar to the worry-relief cycle we were discussing earlier. During your arguments you were worried about losing each other, but when you made up the relief was so passionate that it overshadowed the argument—except that it may have reinforced the likelihood of new arguments—just because it felt so good afterward.

Inge: Perhaps that was the case. We had one argument too many after which I told him to leave and he did. He never understood how frustrated I was by his withdrawal from responsibility.

Cindy: Is there any chance for reconciliation?

Inge: No, it's too late. David is a brilliant research scientist in the field of electronics and computers. When we were married he was offered a promising position with a company in another state. My first husband threatened me that he would sue for sole custody of our children. I was afraid I would lose them and I refused to move out of state. David rejected the offer but it was a sacrifice to him. He really wanted to go. Then when our marriage did not last he was even more disappointed and resentful. He is not responding to my calls or letters. But my first husband has asked me to marry him again.

Jody: But you don't love him! You are not considering going back with him, are you?

Inge: Love hasn't worked for me. Perhaps I am better off with someone I don't love. At least my feelings will not get hurt so much. If I didn't care much, I wouldn't get so angry.

Jody: You could work on resolving your anger and expressing it differently. It does not seem a good reason to marry someone you don't love just so you won't be angry. There has to be more to life than not being angry; there has to be some happiness.

Betty: If your first husband treats you right and he is the father of your children, perhaps you can learn to love him by applying

Ther.:   some of the loving behavior you experienced with your second husband to the relationship with your first husband.

Ther.:   Jody and Betty, you have raised important issues for Inge to consider. Betty, your point is interesting. You are saying that Inge could transfer some of the behaviors that she engaged in while she was happy with David to her relationship with her first husband to make it a different relationship—is that what you mean?

Betty: Yes, that is exactly what I mean. I have been listening and learning a lot lately. I try to learn from what others bring up by applying it to myself. In previous sessions, I mentioned how angry I was about my husband's behavior and the different treatment he gives to his second wife. I remember how Cindy said that she wants to be 'visible' and Ann and Liz—I guess, all of us—wanting to be special. If I had made myself special, perhaps I would have been more fun to be with. If I had been happy instead of being—say, content, for lack of a better word—maybe my husband would have enjoyed my presence more and I could have enjoyed more activities with him. There has to be a reason why his second wife was so enticing to him.

Ther.:   Betty, I am so glad you spoke to us like you just did. At times I was wondering if the group was really beneficial to you, because you seemed to participate more sparingly than others. However, your responses always indicated that you thought seriously about what was said and tried to apply it to yourself. Your comments imply a growing awareness in you. You are looking at yourself and what you might have done differently instead of focusing on what others did to hurt you. Like Helen, you have truly stepped out of the victim role.

Betty: You are correct; I don't look at myself as a victim anymore. But it goes even farther than that. When I got married I accepted my husband's behavior as the lead for how we ought to live. It never occurred to me that I could be equally entitled to have wishes. I did not know about gender equality; nobody talked about it then. Our responsibility as women was to keep peace and harmony in the family—often at the cost of our own wishes. If I had known then what I am learning now, I would have tried to insist on making it a happier life.

Ther.:   Yes, we can and should take at least part of the lead and responsibility for a happy atmosphere in our lives. Gender equality includes that responsibility. (Turning to Inge): Inge, do you think that some of Betty's considerations could be of help in the decisions that you face?

Inge: I know Betty means well and I thank her for that. I don't see how I can create a happy atmosphere when I know that my first husband is considering suing for full custody of my children so that he can take them to Europe with him and let his parents take care of them. That's the easiest for him and he would not have to pay child support; instead I would be the one who pays.

Ann: The judge would not just hand over the children to their father, especially if it includes a move to another country. Your first husband would have to prove that you are not a competent parent.

Inge: He may have some grounds for that. He is citing my brief volatile second marriage as indicating my emotional instability and that I had thought about moving with David. What is worse, he thinks I made a suicide attempt. I did not really try to kill myself. I was so tired of not being able to sleep and stop my ruminating thoughts, so I took more of my anxiety pills than the doctor prescribed. I had a brief hospital stay and the documentation mentions possible overdose. My doctor was quite upset about it and immediately referred me to therapy. According to my husband, being in therapy is another indication of emotional instability. His life, on the other hand, looks quite stable on the surface.

Ann: That sounds like your ex-husband is trying to blackmail you. Have you consulted a lawyer about your situation?

Inge: Yes, I have when David and I originally thought about moving to another state. The attorney thought that there would be a good chance of losing custody to my ex-husband. I consulted the same attorney again when my ex-husband mentioned the move to Europe. He thought that my husband would have a tough time suing for custody and then taking the children out of the country. However, the fact that he would still be an employee of an American company would have some influence and if he could make a valid case for my unfitness as a parent due to emotional instability, his chances of obtaining full custody were at least 50-50.

Ther.: Inge, you have an excellent work record; that would be a reflection of your competence. You have many responsibilities and decision-making duties, which you are handling very well. Perhaps another attorney could be of help. Also, at the point of divorce we learn a lot about the person we were married to and how good or bad the marriage really was. You have more information about your ex-husband now than when you first married him. Please consider all your options before making a decision, and don't hesitate to discuss the situation further with the group.

Cindy: I have been thinking about what Betty said earlier today. It is very difficult to get away from the double standard—even here with us. Ann and Liz have told us what extremes they went to in order to impress some men. Jody was looking at intelligence in men, even though she has plenty of it herself. Ann was intimidated by Ron's mental brilliance, and Inge agreed that a man's intelligence justifies different treatment but Inge is probably just as intelligent as the two men in her life. Why is a man's intelligence more important than a woman's? I remember my two beautiful sisters whom I envied all my life. They always tried to hide their brains under the newest hairstyle of the time.

Ann: Cindy is correct. We are still in awe of men's intelligence but shortchange our own. As in my case, when a brilliant man pays attention to me, my self-esteem grows, even though it does not make me any smarter—actually, just the opposite— because with my admiration of his brilliance, I may invite him to take advantage of me. That is a hard lesson to learn; it seems so ingrained in us.

Cindy: We are all too ready to agree with society around us in endowing men with special powers. We are perpetuating the gender gap to our own detriment. When you come right down to it, it seems ridiculous. Our level of self-esteem becomes a function of the power we give to men to judge us.

Ther.:   Cindy, you described the situation very well; that shows excellent thinking on your part. You are not hiding your brain under your hairstyle as your sisters did. It would be a worthwhile exercise for all of us to determine what criteria we base our self-esteem on.

Cindy: Actually, I have been learning a lot lately, just by observing people—as you had suggested. At work we have monthly meetings to give interim reports about the status of the accounts we handle. It frequently happens that a woman who is the only female in her department does not have a typed report when she comes to the meeting. The regional manager commented on that and she defended herself by stating that the clerical person in her department did not get it typed in time. Last week after the meeting, she asked me how I get my reports done in time, even though I was one of the newer employees in my department. I told her that I do them myself on the computer because I type faster than I write by hand. She complained that she gave her reports to the female clerk as early as her male colleagues did, but the clerk automatically processed the men's reports before even looking at hers. Just as I was about to feel sorry for her, she asked me if I would mind typing her reports if she could not get the clerk to do them on time.

Liz: Wow! First she accepts the differential treatment from the female clerk and then she turns around and tries to do it to you. How did you respond?

Cindy: I admit I was stunned. After a moment I suggested that she might discuss it with the colleagues in her department. I agree with you Liz, I thought she was trying to use me because I am another female and having less seniority than she has places me lower on the totem pole. Actually, before she came up with her request I was ready to support her in whatever way I could, perhaps by being a witness to when she turned in her report to the clerk. I have received similar treatment in the past by being given assignments that were not congruent with my training, and by typing my own reports I steer clear of the gender issue in this instance. But I have changed my behavior slowly by increasing the level of firmness and reducing the number of questions in my communications. I am learning from Jody's example of imagining a zipper on my mouth before I speak, especially regarding questions. In my mind I ask myself whether this needs to be in question form or whether a statement form would be appropriate to express my thought.

Ther.: That is a great method, Cindy. You are learning so much through your observations. Your example is well chosen; in the workplace we still have a long way to go toward gender equality. It is sad that women are not always cooperative with one another.

Cindy: I know I am monopolizing this session, but I am excited about my observations and want to see what the group members think of them. First of all, I appreciated Inge's remark some time back about my dressing in drab colors. That remark—combined with the suggestion of observing people—has opened a whole new world for me. It does not only apply to my way of dressing or finding out what makes an interesting listener or speaker. It goes beyond that and actually fits in with what we are discussing right now—gender gap or gender equality.

Ther.: You do sound excited, Cindy. What other things have you discovered?

Cindy: (Turning to the therapist): As I was describing some of the dynamics in my work situation, your comment about having to go a long way toward gender equality in the workplace put some of my observations into perspective. Anyway, here are my thoughts: Many women at the middle-management level and beyond appear to wear a uniform, just like the men do. But unlike the men's uniforms, the women's clothing with short narrow skirts seems inappropriate for the movements in the workplace as they often reveal more of the women's legs than is conducive to keeping a neutral work atmosphere.

Inge: I don't see why women should not dress the way they want to, as long as they wear street clothes. The men shouldn't look at the women's legs in the office. They should concentrate on their work.

Cindy: That's just it! The men are responsible for their own behaviors. But the men at the top who decide about advancement may use this factor as justification when they unfairly advance men over women. They may even be concerned about the development of sexual harassment issues if male employees make remarks about female employees' appearances.

Ther.: Cindy, when you said that clothes worn by men and women appear to be uniforms in their styles, are you alluding to the functional aspects of these uniforms?

Cindy: Yes, that is my point. Traditionally, women have been and still are perceived as physically weak or helpless. Often, with their clothes, women emphasize this helplessness. With narrow skirts it is difficult to bend down. Other items that handicap women are the large colorful shawls or scarves they often wear to perk up their suits. Rarely do these scarves stay in place when the women move. Probably the worst examples of women's helplessness are high-heeled shoes. Men's shoes are made to stride in when walking and to maintain balance when standing. The opposite is true for high-heeled shoes. Watching a man and a woman in high heels walk side by side, most women look ridiculous with their tiny steps trying to keep up with the man's walk. Why do women wear those shoes at work?

Inge: Well, high heels make the legs look longer and by increasing the arch of the foot, the whole foot looks smaller and prettier.

Betty: Isn't that similar to what they did in China when they bound the girls' feet so they would not grow to their full size?

Ther.: That's an excellent comparison, Betty. The Chinese girls and women were not able to walk very far after they had successfully undergone that procedure.

Inge: A polite man will slow down in his walk to accommodate the woman.

Cindy: Yes, the man can do that; but in business, he may not want to be that polite and if he does, it may be in a patronizing manner. My issue is not that women should not wear what they want, but at work, where we want to be equal to men, we often choose our wardrobe to emphasize the difference in gender in a way that is not beneficial to our goals. We want to appear as competent and efficient as men but we may handicap ourselves with our clothing.

Ther.: Cindy, you are becoming quite an expert on human behaviors with your observations. We want to be aware of how gender structure affects our lives as it may influence our thoughts, attitudes, and beliefs and we also want to be aware of how we may contribute to keeping the gender gap alive.

GROUP PROCESS: GENDER EQUALITY?

In this meeting, members seemed to feel an emotional closeness, which intensified when one member revealed past situations of self-defeating behaviors similar to the ones reported by another group member at the previous session. The issue of women's isolation from other women was raised once more. It can occur in many settings, and the therapist emphasized again the disadvantage it holds for the individual woman and for women in general. Issues of gender inequality and women's own role in maintaining the inequality provided the content for discussion during the second half of the session.

SUMMARY

Aspects of gender concepts were explored in this chapter. Factors that contribute to the development and maintenance of gender-role formation and its resultant functional features were outlined with the help of examples from female volunteers. Explorations about the structure of gender and gender-related concepts at this point in the book provide a structural foundation for understanding a concept that so profoundly influences the lives of women. The emphasis of these explorations is on the awareness of the gender gap existence in the public opinion. This awareness serves a preparatory function to the task of designing and constructing a life, the topic of the following chapter.

QUESTIONS FOR CONSIDERATION

Characteristics of the feminine gender schema include understanding, caring, nurturance, and sensitivity to others' needs. These characteristics are important traits in the nursing profession, which is predominantly female. Does the increase in male nursing professionals indicate a change in the overall gender schema?

Are gender-linked toys initially requested by the children or provided by the parents in response to media influences? What is your opinion or experience?

RECOMMENDED READING

Beall, A. E., & Sternberg, R. J. (Eds.). (1993). *The psychology of gender.* New York: The Guilford Press.

> *The book is a collection of several contributing writers addressing various aspects of gender and the influences on human thought and behavior. The different articles explore a variety of theories.*

Kimmel, M. S. (2000). *The gendered society.* New York: Oxford University Press.

> *The author examines basic beliefs about gender, emphasizing that gender is not a quality inherent in individuals but is embedded in society's institutions, such as the family, school, and the workplace. Men and women are more alike than we have ever imagined.*

CHAPTER TEN

Designing and Constructing a Life

C hildren who early on tend to do things for themselves seem to have a capacity to enjoy themselves and their activities. They feel a sense of triumph connected with their interactions with the environment, whereas children who are the passive recipients of attention from others do not share the joy of triumph and mastering one's activities. The experience of mastery constitutes a gratifying exchange with one's environment, leading to increased motivation to interact with the environment and to optimistic expectations of future mastery. Competence develops as the child adjusts to the changing environment and achieves developmental tasks (Masten & Coatsworth, 1998). The development of competence, and with that the experience of mastery, are functions of the environment as well as of the child's inherent characteristics. To the extent that the small child is dependent upon its environment, the environment is a source of strong influences and determining factors in the process of achieving mastery.

DETERMINING FACTORS IN THE LIVES OF WOMEN: ARE THEY CHANGING?

How and by whom is a woman's life determined? By parents who foster early independence? By teachers who encourage curiosity and explorations? By society, religion, fate—or by the woman herself? In general, the answer is "all of the above." Socialization—with the influence of parents, teachers, and others—rather than biology, determines women's assessment of their own abilities. Considering themselves within their social context often obscures women's recognition of what is in their best interest. If their self-interest is in conflict with the interests of others, how are women to choose? What choices will be sanctioned by those important to them and what choices will be disparaged—if not punished? The decision whether to lead a self-determined or other-determined lifestyle is the task of the individual woman. Whether to live according to personal authority or the authority of others is to be decided by the individual woman without reliance on changes initiated by social or political movements that may not occur at the speed desired by women.

OPINIONS OF OTHERS

During the earlier years of their development, various forces were in operation to render females dependent on the opinions of others. Traditionally, women's identity has been formed through the appraisals of others, as discussed in chapter 8. Women have let themselves become vulnerable to the pressure to change according to guidelines set up by others. In addition to behavior guidelines, there are widely advertised standards of female beauty, pressuring women to attain unrealistic ideals of slimness (Hare-Mustin, 1986). Women's preoccupation with their body shape may drain their mental energy and interfere with their academic performance as indicated by a study investigating the effects of girls' self-conscious monitoring of their looks on their performance on a math test (Murray, 1998). Many of the guidelines about female attractiveness are difficult to fulfill. They represent a control mechanism that keeps women trying to come closer to the "perfect" state, without ever reaching it. Women have the option to develop their own opinions and to determine how perfect they want to be.

The options for lifestyles of female adolescents who were born during the time period of 1954 to 1960, as well as their mothers' options, were different from those of generations before. These adolescents were the first to be exposed to the new feminist movement of the late 1960s and early 1970s. They have demonstrated less interest in marriage than earlier generations (Bernard, 1975). Motherhood is no longer monopolizing their whole life.

VOLUNTARY MOTHERHOOD

Whereas in the past socialization for motherhood had been all-pervasive, now motherhood has become voluntary. In 1972, 70% of sexually active teenage girls worried about becoming pregnant, but fewer than half were inhibited by such fears. Almost a fourth of the girls had pregnancies. Twenty years later, statistics showed that among U.S. females aged 15 to 19 years old, approximately one million pregnancies occurred per year, translating to 1 of 10 teenage females becoming pregnant yearly. Of those pregnancies, 84% were unintended. In recent years, the birthrate among teenage girls dropped as did the number of teenage mothers who have more than one child, and 1999 saw the lowest birthrate in 40 years among American high school girls aged 15 to 17. But, as mentioned in chapter 8, teenage birthrates in the United States still far exceed those in all other industrialized countries (Maass, 2000b).

Bernard (1975) described a young woman's notion when entering marriage prior to 1977 as wanting to bear two or three children for her self-fulfillment with support from a husband for her lifetime in exchange for taking care of his personal needs. Now she would want one or two children for her self-fulfillment plus help in her career or job through the man's sharing the costs of motherhood. In turn, she would be willing to share the provider role for the family and also help her husband in his career. Aside from the question whether or not his predictions will be on target, it is interesting to note that the author still envisioned motherhood as the primary agent for women's self-fulfillment.

LIFE AFTER MOTHERHOOD

For many, the role of mother is still seen as the most important role in the life of the adult female (Williams, 1983), even though it will not be sufficient for most of their lives and may leave them with a sense of emptiness for the second half of their existence. The requirements in terms of time, effort, and involvement shrink continuously as the children achieve their own independence. Women who have prepared themselves for that stage in life may experience a sense of liberation rather than the depressed feelings that accompany the "empty nest" syndrome. If indeed there is a condition of emerging adulthood as proposed by Arnett (2000), it could provide a good opportunity to prepare women not only for the years of childbearing and childraising but—even more important—for the season thereafter. The years of intense motherhood could be conceived of as a time with a double-layer purpose: While raising children, to also plan and prepare for the second period of freedom many women can expect to experience.

WOMEN'S SOCIAL STATUS: TRANSFER FROM FATHER TO HUSBAND

In patriarchal societies, women's social status is considered to be inferior to that of men. Despite the growing number of women participating in the labor market, sex segregation and discrimination in placement and pay still put women in inferior positions to men. In the late 1970s, American women of working age constituted more than 50% of the labor force. This was the beginning of an era in which employed women were part of a majority—although of lower status than their male coworkers. The decade of the 1970s also marked the start of minority status for women who were devoted exclusively to domestic labor at home (Bergmann, 1986).

Women's social status and standard of living have largely been achieved through relationships with men. Fathers are the first to provide these, and husbands continue. Some developmental theories reflect this opinion when proposing that women achieve their identity through the men they marry (Erikson, 1963). A statement such as this today would likely meet with disagreement. As mentioned above, more women than ever are active participants in the labor market and are capable of providing for their own needs. Still in dual-earner families, it is most often the husband who holds the more prestigious occupation and receives the higher income. Women have been offered many jobs, but usually in categories of "women's jobs" with lower pay than that paid in jobs open to men and with inferior promotion opportunities (Bergmann, 1986). Even in dual-earner families in which the wife's salary is higher than the husbands', wives do not experience equal standing, as was seen in chapter 1.

CLASS IDENTIFICATION AMONG EMPLOYED MARRIED WOMEN

In situations in which women are housewives, they take on the social standing in the community from their husbands. But with more than half of all women participating in the labor force, many of them possess independent sources of income and status. The literature regarding class identification among employed married women includes two competing arguments with claims of empirical evidence supporting each of them (Beeghley & Cochran, 1988). The status-borrowing hypothesis proposed that employed married women consider only status characteristics of their husbands when deciding which class to identify with. But the status-sharing hypothesis suggested that employed mar-

ried women consider their own and their husbands' status characteristics in deciding on class identification.

Applying gender-role norms to the situations of employed married
women, Beeghley and Cochran (1988) proposed that employed married women who adhere to traditional gender-role norms will base
their decision about which class to identify with, only on their husbands' status factors. But employed married women who believe in
egalitarian gender-role norms will consider both their own and their
husbands' status characteristics when deciding about which class to
identify with. The authors explained that the research on class identification among employed married women had been conducted in
specific historical contexts; but it could be predicted that in the future
more and more people will accept egalitarian gender-role norms.

METAMORPHOSIS: TRANSFORMATION TO WIFE

When we consider the passive role even today's brides play at their
own weddings, Erikson's proposal still appears to have some basis in
reality. In traditional weddings, the bride is "given away" by her father—or some other significant male—to the husband. Following the
"hand over" of the bride, her former self ceases to exist, as it did with
her sisters in ancient Greece. In Athens, it was the custom to refer to
a married woman not by her name but her husband's name (Kitto,
1951). The former Nancy Brown becomes Mrs. Robert White. What
happened to Nancy? Where did she go? Is society conditioning women
to believe that by marrying they become different persons? Upon divorce, Mrs. Robert White would undergo another metamorphosis.
Leaving the divorce court, she is no longer Mrs. Robert White. This
name is reserved for another woman if Robert White marries again. As
she automatically becomes Nancy White (unless she assumes her
maiden name), she may ask, "If I am not Mrs. Robert White anymore,
who am I?" In general, women tend to identify more strongly with the
role of wife than men do with the role of husband and some of this
may be due to the name change a woman undergoes at marriage
(Neumann, 1992).

One could argue that this is just a matter of a different name and
therefore a superficial issue. But it goes deeper than that. Gradually,
Mrs. Robert White becomes a different person from Nancy Brown.
She learns that her behaviors will be regarded as a reflection on her
husband and that it is her responsibility to act in accordance with his

position in life. Even if husbands do not demand this change, women seem to assume that the conversion is expected of them.

Carolyn Heilbrun (1988) has discussed this issue in the following way: "In the last years of the twentieth century, it is unclear whether women who refer to themselves as, for example, Mrs. Thomas Smith, know what servitude they are representing in that nomenclature. The same might be said today of women who exchange their last name for their husband's. Particularly with the statistical chances of a marriage ending, it is confusing for women not to keep the same name throughout their lives. Any possible ambivalence about this matter should surely have ended by the beginning of the 1980s at the latest" (p. 85).

MARRIAGE SHOCK: WHO IS THIS WOMAN?

Dalma Heyn (1997), in her book *Marriage Shock*, writes about the transformation of women into wives. Girls and women change themselves into what they have come to believe wives should be like. In the transformation they may lose what was exciting and enjoyable to themselves and their husbands. They don't allow themselves the luxury of asking for or getting what they want. Before they can utter a word about their wishes, they have already decided that this would be "selfish" and good wives are not supposed to be selfish. What could have been a pleasant experience gets drowned in silence.

Tanya: The Loss of Self During Transformation

The volunteer Tanya, mentioned previously, could have stepped right out of Heyn's book. Tanya's mother became widowed when Tanya was a baby. Raised in the Lutheran faith, she was still a virgin in her early 20s when she met Ralph, her future husband. Tanya was attractive, bright, outgoing, hardworking, and independent in her decisions. She enjoyed ballroom dancing and had sufficient energy to keep two partners busy. She liked to travel and was not afraid of taking trips by herself as her small income would allow. Motherhood was not high on her list of goals. Although she did not rule it out completely, she did not consider it necessary for a fulfilled life.

Tanya's disclosure about her virginity evoked a surprising reaction in Raph. He seemed disappointed. As he stated, he was sexually quite experienced and thought it inconvenient to be starting with a virgin. Tanya was impressed with Ralph's intelligence—she thought he was brilliant. She looked up to him. The way he responded to her virginity made it appear as if she did not quite measure up. She was confused: Her religion taught her that being sexually untouched was a virtue but now it became a liability! After a short engagement period they got married. Tanya learned that Ralph did not like certain colors. She eliminated all garments in those colors from her wardrobe.

Ralph had definite ideas about a good wife. She had to be efficient—never went shopping without a list. Cleaning had to be done when the husband was not at home. This was difficult to accomplish because Tanya continued to work full-time and both had the same work schedule. Ralph tried to be accommodating, on some evenings he visited with friends so Tanya could clean house by herself. There were other rules that Tanya adapted to over the years. Ralph's sleep was sacred. He needed absolute quiet to restore his energies and his brainpower. Finally, the ideal wife would play the role of a different seductress every night.

Tanya was shaking her head as she told her story, "I can't believe I did all that! Our household ran very smoothly. I usually do things to the best of my ability and I sincerely tried to be the best wife I could be. Ralph's expectations did not seem exaggerated to me because I had nothing to compare them with in my past. I do remember one time that my mother-in-law made fun of me for working so hard to please Ralph. Most of the time I anticipated what he wanted before he told me. He was really impressed with my ability to read his mind—as he called it. The one task I was not able to perform was to play different roles in our sex life. Although Ralph was so experienced sexually, I never enjoyed our lovemaking. It was not interesting. I did not get aroused. Of course, I blamed myself for this failure. Today, I know better.

Tanya's final words were, "I don't want to blame Ralph for the change in me. By wanting to do the best for the marriage as wife, I did poorly for myself. My intentions were good, but I guess, my judgment was distorted. For a number of years I became a totally different person. I even looked different. Comparing photographs from that time with those from before my marriage, people would not think it was the same person—and it really wasn't."

Tanya has reclaimed herself, however, at the cost of her marriage. Just like Jody, the group member, she tried to anticipate and fulfill her husband's every wish. If she had preserved an independent attitude about herself during the marriage to a domineering husband, would the marriage have survived? Would she have been able to attain a status of equality? Would she have been able to maintain her loving feelings for Ralph? Answers to those questions are difficult to come by. It is important that Tanya gained the insight of her own involvement in the deterioration of the marriage. It was not all Ralph's fault. Her voluntary change into the perfect wife—at the very least—encouraged the continuance of Ralph's domineering behaviors. We are also reminded here again of Jody's (and Inge's) case history. Women's adoration for a man's intelligence may pave the way for—or indeed invite—the possibility of their inequality in the relationship.

Tanya was not a client involved in psychotherapy; she is one of the women who volunteered to tell their stories. Would psychotherapy have been beneficial to her in preventing the loss of her identity and subsequently the death of her feelings for her husband in the process of adaptation to the role of wife? Possibly so, but we don't know much about Ralph and his intentions beyond what Tanya has told us. Tanya, as she later realized, had chosen the option of submerging her own personality to become the "perfect wife."

RELATIONSHIP OF DIFFERENT PROFESSIONS TO THE LIKELIHOOD OF FAMILY BUILDING

Women in different occupational groups appear to have different marital and family-building experiences. There is an increasing connection between high levels of educational attainment and childlessness. Furthermore, for women, educational attainment and the likelihood of divorce are related. Women's pursuit of high educational levels and professional careers is linked to delayed and reduced involvement in marital and parental roles. In general, for women who married prior to engaging in professional training, their marriages were more likely to end in divorce (Houseknecht, Vaughan, & Macke, 1984).

Cooney and Uhlenberg (1989) compared family careers of professional women 30 to 39 years of age in law, medicine, and postsecondary teaching. The sample included 1,120 postsecondary teachers, 839 lawyers, and 486 physicians. The age range was broken down into two categories for women—age 30 to 34 and age 35 to 39. The younger group included more than twice as many lawyers as the older group and significantly more physicians, but a somewhat smaller number of teachers. In both age groups, the percentage of divorced lawyers was significantly higher than that of divorced physicians and teachers. The percentage of separated or divorced women remained stable through the entire age range and was of about the same likelihood as for women of comparable ages in the general population. Among the three professions the percentage of never-married women was similar. In all professional categories, the divorce rate was much higher among those women who married early than among the ones that delayed marriage.

When remarriage after termination of the first marriage either through divorce or death of spouse was considered, across both age groups physicians were the most likely and lawyers the least likely to remarry. The findings indicate that even though female physicians marry later, their attachment to married life is stronger than for the women in the other two professional categories.

Among the professional women who were or had been married, these women were two to three times more likely to either be childless or to have fewer children than their age peers in the general population. Within the older age group of the sample, female physicians were more likely to have children and tended to have more children than the other female professionals. Among women in the older age group, teachers were significantly more likely than women in the other two professions to remain childless.

Across the entire age range, approximately 39% of the female lawyers were married to men who had attained lower educational levels. Only 30% of the teachers and about 25% of the physicians were married to men of lower educational grades. The authors expected that the difference in educational level between female lawyers and their husbands would lead to less marital harmony and thus increased likelihood of divorce. In addition, a look at the work schedules of the professional women and their husbands revealed that both the female physicians and their husbands tended to work more hours than the couples in the other professional categories. Yet, as mentioned above, the physician couples were still more likely to have children, and more of them, than the other couples. Exploring flexibility of work schedule and possibility of part-time work as an explanation for differences in family-building patterns among the three different professional groups, the authors did not find this to be a determining factor.

When looking at the overall costs and benefits of marriage, women may consider the potential gains from a husband's income. Their own diminished earnings after marriage may be offset if their husbands' financial contributions are high. Women physicians apparently experience only small losses in their human capital investments and large net gains when they marry and have children. On the average, female physicians who adopt a family path earn higher incomes than female lawyers and teachers who forgo family roles.

Although it is not known whether the women in the sample had planned their training and family involvement to occur as it developed, the thought about higher risk of divorce when marrying prior to career preparation appears logical. Increased exposure to education and professional experiences can be expected to have an impact upon women's attitudes and values. In addition, it presents different lifestyle options. Therefore, it is logical to assume that the same young woman may find a different type of man attractive as a husband before completing professional training than after she has established herself in a profession. When designing a life, the above findings are relevant factors to consider.

TIMING AND VARIATIONS IN THE PROCESS OF CHANGING OR REINVENTING ONESELF

The decision to take the initiative to be self-determining and to make significant changes can occur at different times in a woman's life. To be independent and self-sufficient at a young age is, of course, an ideal situation but it may appear impossible for some women. Opportunities for increased meaning and independence can become apparent at almost any time. After children are grown and have left the home, many women finally have the time to focus on themselves and their interests. Changing or reinventing oneself can take many forms. Choosing models or mentors to follow in their footsteps is part of changing oneself. Making oneself over in the image of another person or ideal is an attempt at reinventing oneself. Learning new skills, trying out new behaviors, even imitating behaviors we admire in others, are elements of designing a life. For women, it is beneficial to construct as early as possible a well-rounded life with many rewarding interests and activities. In addition to the stimulating aspects of leading a well-rounded life, it facilitates the maintenance of mental and emotional independence.

Judy: A Head Start on Planning

Judy, a lovely young woman who is one of the group facilitators with Big Sisters, was excited about volunteering the experiences of her young life. Her family of origin was financially comfortable. Her father was a good provider but emotionally distant and even verbally abusive to Judy's mother and her older autistic brother. Judy saw herself simultaneously as the oldest child mentally while chronologically being the youngest. In other ways her life was that of an only child because of her brother's condition. Judy had dance lessons from age 3 and continued with it until high school. She was in stage productions and devoted about 6 hours daily to practicing dancing. In school, she was popular and engaged in many extracurricular activities.

When she was 15 years old her life changed. During her first week in high school, Judy's father left the family to live with another woman. Judy's mother—although having been trained as a teacher—had not worked outside the home and did not have many practical life experiences. Her husband had taken care of all the finances. She did not know much about handling a checking account or making mortgage payments. Judy's mother was devastated and in a state of shock. It was Judy's turn to keep the family together. Without the help of all her good friends she could not have done that. Judy, her mother, and her brother had strong bonds to one another. After her mother recovered from the shock, she returned to school to obtain a master's degree and continue her career as a high school teacher, which she enjoys to this day.

Judy's father moved to another state with his second wife. The relationship between him and his children became even more tenuous. He complained bitterly about his children being selfish, and today he does not even respond to his daughter's communication efforts. Judy is now 24 years old. She graduated from college with a degree in speech pathology and audiology. But she always had a strong interest in counseling. She was part of the student council during high school and became involved in providing for the needy. She was a candy striper in the hospital and volunteered in nursing homes. Perhaps her interest in counseling evolved because of her brother's impairment. She decided to follow her interests and to obtain graduate training in counseling and is now enrolled in the master's degree program in the school for social work.

Judy is not afraid of obstacles. After graduating with her speech pathology degree, she drove by herself from her hometown to the state's capitol to investigate the university for an appropriate program for her further studies. She applied, inquired about financial aid, enrolled in classes, and found herself an apartment, all ready to start her graduate studies that fall. Having accomplished all that, she returned home to inform her mother and her fiancé about her decisions. And while she was apartment hunting, she found one for her fiancé too who had arranged his life to fit in with hers. True to her past, she found opportunities to volunteer her time and services with the Big Sisters. She enjoyed the contact with the teenage girls and the opportunity to help them in their struggles to build a better life for themselves. Her excitement is contagious; the girls love and trust her. From the volunteer cofacilitator, she has advanced to be one of the main facilitators, conducting two groups every week.

After her father deserted the family, Judy's trust in men and marriage was badly shaken. She slowly worked through any abandonment issues that may have affected her. She had a stable longtime dating relationship in high school. She gives credit to the young man's devotion and respect toward her for the confidence she built up in herself. The relationship did not survive the changes of college and the different environments the two young people faced. Judy ended the relationship but gratefully remembers the strength she derived from it. She is engaged to be married soon to a young man who recently graduated from law school. They have dated for several years and feel secure in the fact that they have taken so much time to know each other.

When asked about the person who had the most significant impact on her life and the decisions she made, Judy names her mother. She admires her mother's strength. After the devastating blow of being deserted by her husband, Judy's mother has created a new life for herself. Judy wants to have children, but this is sometime in the future. First she wants to work on her career after graduation. She wants to continue with the work she is so interested in. She and her husband want to travel and learn about different people in different places. She is not planning to devote her whole time to her children, although she considers staying home when the children are very young. With a wistful smile she adds, "If I cannot work in a regular full-time job while my children are small, I may consider going to law school part-time. Family law would be a good and related field to my interest in counseling. Because of my father's resistance to continue with support payments for my disabled brother, my mother had to consult several attorneys. I could be of help to people with similar difficulties."

Whatever Judy's plans will be, they always seem to focus on contributing to others by helping them to find ways to become as independent, confident, and self-determined as she is. Her example is inspiring to the teenage girls she works with. The "Little Sisters" have a much needed and much appreciated role model in this young woman. Did she ever wonder how her life would have been had she continued her dancing? Judy becomes reflective, "There are moments when I wished I had continued, but when I stopped it was at a time when life was very stressful for me." Through the pain and the struggles of her parents' divorce, Judy learned to appreciate the value of a woman's independence. What are the reasons for volunteering for this book? The wish to encourage others who face similar struggles and to convince them that it is all worth the effort.

THE GROUP: DESIGNING A LIFE

Group members entered the room and looked around in surprise. The table was missing. Hesitatingly they selected chairs to sit in.

Betty: (She was the first to speak): Where is our table?

Ther.: We used it in another room and did not have time to bring it back here.

Betty: I miss the table. It makes me feel that I ought to do or learn something, take notes, write down questions or thoughts. It also makes me part of what is going on even if I have nothing at the moment to contribute. We are all so different in age and experiences, but when I sit down here at the table, I feel like I am part of a family. Can we get it back?

Ther.: Sure, if we all take a few minutes to move it, we can have it right back. I am glad you spoke out, Betty. It is important that we do whatever we can to facilitate our learning.

Cindy: (After replacing the table everybody settled down to continue with the session): I like Betty's suggestion of bringing the table back in. It helps me to focus on what I want to process. (After a brief pause): But where is Inge? She is not here yet.

Ther.: Inge called to say that she will not be with us any longer. . . .

Cindy: (Interrupting the therapist's statement): I was wondering if she was offended by my observations regarding women's clothes and shoes. Perhaps I can explain it to her in more detail so that she wouldn't take it personally.

Betty: Some of the things you mentioned applied to Inge. When she came here directly from work, she wore high heels and suits or dresses as you described them. Personally, I think you made a good point with your observations. We can all learn from them. Actually, your excitement was contagious; you are becoming quite 'visible.'

Ther.: If she was upset by those observations, that is not the reason why she dropped out from the group. Inge told me that she had decided to marry her first husband again. She had to terminate her group participation because of time pressures.

Arranging the wedding and getting herself and the children ready for the move to Europe will demand all her time now. Betty is correct, Cindy, your observations are relevant and you are visible.

Jody: I think Inge is making a mistake by giving up her career for a man she does not love.

Betty: She may be able to continue with her career working for an American company there. With her college degree, her work experience, and her bilingual abilities she would be an asset to any business.

Ther.:   Yes, I think she might be able to do that. At our last time we talked about gender-role formation and other gender-related concepts. It is important to understand the underlying structure and ideas and how they still influence the people around us. As we set out to design and build a new life, we may need to be prepared to face resistance to our objectives. Our focus is how to achieve our goals despite the resistance. Therefore, preparation and careful planning are important steps in the process.

Betty: Before we get into a new topic I would like to tell you that Nancy wants me to be her assistant on the trip with the art study group. She told them about my friendly nature and they are looking forward to having me around. A year ago nobody would have said anything about my "friendly nature." It is amazing what a change in attitude can do. The next trip will be in October, to London. The group has been there before but now they want to see the new Tate Gallery, an addition that has been designed to make room at the original Tate Gallery for the older art works.

Ann: You will be an art connoisseur and world traveler before long. Perhaps you can become our very own travel agent.

Betty: That would be great but I have a lot to learn before that. I am really excited about it. What a way to use my vacation. If I do well, Nancy might take me along on other trips with the art study group. I would like to make this a part of my life. By helping Nancy I could earn a substantial part of the travel costs. I would never have been able to afford trips abroad. The remarkable thing is that it would not have happened before. I never talked to anybody in the apartment complex. I never smiled much—as you know. Now that I am not so absorbed in my misery and anger, being in the group has made me more open, outgoing, and even adventurous.

Ther.:   We are proud of you, Betty, and expect postcards from your trips. After all, everybody here has had a part in the development of your new attitude toward life.

Helen: There is hope for me, too. I can tell you about an interesting development after my interchange with the little boy at the school for the deaf. The administrator called and asked me if I could spend a few hours on Sundays at the school for some special tutoring. The father of the little boy had approached the administrator to find out if I would be willing to tutor his son in speaking. The boy had lost his hearing through an accident, but he is able to speak. However, since he cannot hear himself speak, his pronunciation skills have deteriorated over time—as I had already noticed. The father is concerned that the boy should retain his ability to communicate verbally, even if he cannot hear. His son's response to me made him think that I could help them.

Cindy: Are you going to do it?

Helen: Yes, I think it will be quite a challenge to keep this boy's verbal skills intact because I have to be careful that corrections are not coming across as criticism. His shyness and sadness may prompt him to retreat easily. I want to be careful not to hurt him.

Ther.:   Helen, what you just said is wonderful. You are sensitive to the boy's needs beyond the speech. You will do well with him in this challenge.

Helen: It helps me as I work on my own challenge of getting away from the victim mind-set, and it presented itself as one of the options I may have for responding to the challenge. It is the option I will take for the time being. For long-range considerations, I would like to work toward a teaching degree that would qualify me to work in places such as the school for the deaf. That will take years, but I have time.

Ther.:   Great! You have proceeded to the third station in your journey; from the "C" of the challenge, to the "O" of the options, to the "D" of the decision, and now you are ready for "A," the actions. That is excellent progress, Helen.

Ann: It seems I am still stuck at the "O." I exercised one option that we discussed here. I wrote a letter to my parents telling them that I appreciate their love and explained how I felt about being one of five equally talented children. I admitted that my yearning for being special in some way was the challenge I had to resolve by myself; I would not want to burden them with it. I encouraged them to show the letter to my siblings so that they may understand my recent outburst. It is important for me not to accuse or blame my parents for how I feel because—as I have learned in the meantime—it is my responsibility to do something that I can regard as special.

Jody: That is a very honest-sounding letter, Ann. Have your parents responded yet?

Ann: No, not yet. I just mailed it the other day. It took me a long time to think about it. It is amazing how difficult it is to change your beliefs. We have talked about it repeatedly, but I am still falling back into my old beliefs.

Ther.:   Can you give us a specific example of what you mean?

Ann: When my ex-husband lied to me about beating his previous wife I was angry—not just with him, but also with myself. I blamed myself for having been lied to.

Liz: You mean you took on responsibility for his behavior?

Ann: Yes, in a way I did. I thought that something about me encouraged him to lie. I remember reading a book then about lies men tell women and why the women believe them. I thought if there is a book about this on the market, I must not be the only one. By the time I met Ron I must have forgotten about the book, because I believed what he told me, although he did not really lie to me, unless he lied about having made the corrections in the content before he gave the pages to me. He just made it sound as if he was more interested in having me understand the content of his writing than correct the grammar and punctuation.

Jody: Did he contact you again?

Ann: Yes, we met again. He talked about how important this book will be because of new scientific discoveries. He also mentioned that the deadline was approaching rapidly. Apparently, he wants me to proofread faster. He doesn't seem to have time for anything except working on the book. We don't have any long evenings like the first time anymore. It's a quick dinner and he hands me another stack of pages before saying "good night."

Jody: That does not sound very romantic.

Ann: It's not. That's why I am upset. I have fallen for another trick, making me do things for a man without getting much in return. You would think that I would learn after a while.

Ther.:   Ann, you are blaming yourself again for possibly being the victim of someone's lies or manipulations. While Ron's behavior is his responsibility, you can decide when to quit being a victim. Perhaps you can shift your focus away from blaming yourself. We have no control whether or not people will lie to us. We do have control over how to respond. But before we can respond we have to be aware of what is happening.

Ann: Are you saying to let them lie to me?

Ther.:   If you can't prevent it. The challenge in this case may not be the prevention or elimination of being lied to—because we can't control that—but the awareness of it when it happens. Once we are aware of that we have behavioral options for responses. Awareness is a state of mind to be welcomed as a knowledge base from which to proceed with decisions and actions.

Betty: In other words, the sooner we become aware, the sooner we can do something about it.

Ther.:   That's correct, Betty.

Ann: Can we practice becoming aware sooner—as Betty said?

Ther.:   As you plan your new life to reduce the possibilities of being the victim of lies or manipulation, one way is to make sure not to blind yourself because you want the lies to be true. The next thing is to remind yourself that all behavior is purposeful—verbal behaviors as well as action behaviors. If verbal behaviors and action behaviors are not congruent, there may be more than one purpose operating. Verbal behavior often reflects wishes, hopes, dreams, as well as intentions. Actions, however—in addition to reflecting intentions—also reflect reality. To distinguish fact from fiction, a comparison of both types of behavior can be helpful.

Ann: Can you give me an example of how this works?

Ther.:   Let's say a husband is reminded by his wife to take out the garbage this evening. He responds with "I'll take it out tomorrow morning before I leave for work". The next morning he goes to work without taking the garbage out. What would you say the purpose of his verbal message was?

Jody: To get her off his back. That's exactly what I did before I invented the "zipper on my mouth." I promised to do something for others just to be off the hook for the moment and not to make them upset at me. But soon after I promised I knew that I did not really want to do these things.

Ther.:   You made quite a connection here to your own behaviors, Jody, a great insight. You are absolutely correct, in looking at the congruence between verbal and action behaviors, we can certainly apply that to ourselves, not just to the people around us. Coming back to the example, what might be the purpose in the husband's behavior when he left the garbage behind?

Ann: You could say that he did not want to take out the garbage, but I think we can also make a case for just forgetting. He could have forgotten what he promised the night before.

Ther.:   That's correct, Ann. He may have had the best intentions of taking out the garbage but may have forgotten. We are not looking at isolated behaviors but behavioral trends. If overall a person's verbal and action behaviors are not congruent, one could ask what seems to be the purpose of the person's talk and what seems to be the purpose of the person's actual behavior? How does the incongruence affect our relationship?

Ann: I think I understand what you mean. I could observe Ron's behavior over time while I still help him with the proofreading, but my decision on whether or not to continue the relationship would be best based on the congruence of his behaviors. My initial excitement for him has cooled down but I can still give him the benefit of the doubt.

Ther.:   You probably have not known him that long to make a final decision. (Turning to Jody): Jody, how are you doing with the personal space you created for yourself?

Jody: The space worked out nicely. There is enough room to start writing and close the door when I am done for the day. I have started to write a few stories, but I can't finish them.

Ther.:   Why is that?

Jody: With each story I come to a certain point and then I cannot continue to write.

Ther.:   Can you describe the feelings you have when you cannot continue to write?

Jody: Terror! All of a sudden I can hardly move because of the terror that comes over me.

Ther.:   What are the thoughts that are connected with the terror?

Jody: I can't do this . . .

Ther.:   What else? I can't do this because . . .

Jody: When it's finished I have to decide what to do with it.

Ther.:   What makes the decision difficult?

Jody: It's not good enough.

Ther.:   How do you know? Did anybody tell you?

Jody: No! I can't let anybody see it. It's too important to me, almost sacred and it needs to be perfect. This is not just like an assignment in class.

Ther   How important is it, Jody? Does it have to justify your making
         a space for yourself? Or is there a resemblance with the visit-
         ing author in that workshop long ago? How do you think
         that author overcame her difficulties?

Jody: The space is part of it. The other part is if I show it to people,
         they think that I act like a writer but don't write like a writer.
         I had this conflict before. When I thought having children
         would resolve the conflict. Now it's staring me in the face
         again.

Ther.:   Jody, in one of our earlier sessions when we discussed how
         you could obtain a space for yourself, you told us that you
         had always been interested in art and literature, but you also
         said that if you had any real talent it would have manifested
         itself before now. Recently, I read an article in one of the
         journals I subscribe to that takes an interesting view of talent
         and creativity. The author (Sternberg, 2001) proposed that
         creativity involves a decision by the individual. Although tal-
         ent and creativity are not identical concepts, I think—to vary-
         ing degrees—the author's reasoning can be applied to both.
         In the traditional view, people believe that creativity is an
         innate ability possessed only by special people. In contrast to
         this view, the author suggested that individuals can decide to
         develop their creativity—at least in part—by observing others
         and studying the attitudes that are essential to making cre-
         ative decisions.

Betty: Would this be similar to the discussions we had about observ-
         ing the behaviors of others that we admire?

Ther.:   Betty, you are making an excellent connection. Yes, it is similar.
         In fact, it parallels the work we are doing here in our group.
         The creative process starts with redefining challenges and ana-
         lyzing our ideas. We have options to find out what we love to do
         and how to do it. A significant step is selling our ideas. Although
         the author meant selling our ideas to others, the public, I be-
         lieve we have to work even harder to sell them to ourselves
         because some of us do not have the necessary confidence in our
         ideas. There will be needs to take some risks, such as exposing
         our ideas to others, along with the readiness to grow with the
         feedback. At times we must be willing to trade the comfort of
         certainty for the discomfort of tolerating ambiguity. The point
         here is not that inherited abilities do not matter, they do. But
         without the determination to be creative, the innate talents will
         most likely not come to fruition. On the other hand, a person

with a more modest level of inherited abilities can be very creative. We can take this view of creativity as encouragement and as a lesson to apply when constructing our lives. In other words, life patterns don't just have to happen; we can actively create and shape them.

GROUP PROCESS: DESIGNING A LIFE

Several women had made significant steps in the process of planning and building parts of their lives. There was an atmosphere of hope as Betty and Helen outlined their plans. Ann was more tentative in her considerations, and Jody had come to a block in her endeavors. The therapist facilitated exploration of Jody's underlying fears that contributed to the block. A moment of sadness was produced by the departure of another group member.

Significant concepts surfaced in this session. One was the notion that all behaviors are purposeful, although the intent and purposes of individuals' verbal and action behaviors may not always be congruent. Group member Ann mentioned a book that she had read about lies told to women by men (Hollander, 1995). Another concept introduced in this session dealt with the idea that creativity may be teachable and learnable. Participants' responses and interactions demonstrated that they had been able to make meaningful connections to concepts that had been discussed in previous sessions.

A small but interesting part of the group's adherence to the physical structure was revealed through members' reactions to the absence of their conference table.

SUMMARY

This chapter started with a look at the determining factors in women's lives and the query if, indeed, lifestyles have been changing significantly. Changes that evolve as women transform themselves into wives and mothers or career women were explored. Variations in family-planning strategies applied by women engaged in different professions were pointed out. An emphasis was placed on the fact that there are various forms of reinventing oneself and that the decision regarding changes can come at any time in a woman's life.

The stories told by women in the community at large were used to illustrate how some women have approached the design of their lives.

Interactions in "The Group" paralleled many of the concepts explored in this chapter.

QUESTIONS FOR CONSIDERATION

How can women learn to treasure their gifts and give them freely without censoring themselves and their behaviors? How can women decide which of their personality characteristics to preserve during the transformation from woman to wife?

Suppose your boyfriend tells you that he wants to spend the rest of his life with you. He spends some time with you, but not on a regular basis. You cannot plan ahead because you never know whether he will be with you on holidays or at certain times or whether you will be alone. Are his verbal and action behaviors congruent? If they are not congruent, which behavior should you trust? What might be the purposes behind his behaviors?

If a person's creative potential is not completely determined at birth and can be increased by learning, how would a person go about enhancing or augmenting it?

RECOMMENDED READING

Cooney, T. M., & Uhlenberg, P. (1989). Family-building patterns of professional women: A comparison of lawyers, physicians, and postsecondary teachers. *Journal of Marriage and the Family, 51,* 749–758.

> *The authors surveyed different female professionals regarding their timing of marriage and childbearing and how these events were integrated into the women's professional lives.*

Heyn, D. (1997). *Marriage shock: The transformation of women into wives.* New York: Villard Books.

> *The author describes how women change and give up some of their personality traits when they marry because they believe that they have to be different as wives. They follow their ideas of what a "good wife" should be rather than remain the persons they were prior to marriage.*

Sternberg, R. J. (2001). Teaching psychology students that creativity is a decision. *The General Psychologist, 36,* 8–11.

> *The article provides a brief history of theoretical explanations regarding creativity and proposes a different view, emphasizing the individual's role in enhancing his or her creative potential.*

CHAPTER ELEVEN

Changed Attitudes Toward Self and Other Women

"It is out of our emotional ties and identification with Mother that our basic conflict with independence and autonomy is born. And it is within our friendships with each other that this conflict is nurtured, cultivated, perpetuated"

(Margolies, 1985, p 9).

FEMALE RELATIONSHIPS

MOTHER-DAUGHTER

Probably the most complex relationship in women's lives is the mother-daughter relationship. Even in the best of those relationships, there are the dynamics of pushing and pulling over years as daughters are in the process of individuation and increasing independence. In more troubled mother-daughter constellations, some daughters are not able to liberate themselves, either because of excessive fears of being on their own or because of mothers' controlling tendencies. Mothers who consider children as their purpose in life may have a difficult time of letting go when it is time for the adolescent daughter or young woman to confront independence issues or sexual development. For boys, the breaking-away-from-mother process is much more encouraged and better defined by society than it is for girls. A woman, disappointed in her own life, may want to live vicariously through her daughter's achievements. In enmeshed families, the hazy boundaries between mother and daughter may lead to narcissistic character traits in the daughter.

Well known are the horror stories about stage mothers who invade agents' and producers' offices dragging their cute little daughters along and promising the world the reincarnation of Shirley Temple. Many of us can think of mother-daughter pairs wherein the daughter becomes like a friend or younger sister and confidante of the mother, obscuring age borders as well as role boundaries.

FRIEND-FRIEND

There comes the time in girls' lives where the mother-daughter boundaries widen, when mothers appear to their daughters as less knowledgeable than their peers. A period of various best-friends relationships develops, which mirror some of the dynamics previously played out between mother and daughter. Friend-friend bonds become close and emotionally charged. Jealousy and competition grow as some girls want to be best friends with certain popular girls and want to belong to the "right" groups. Friendships break up and become rearranged into new friendship constellations until adolescence, when competition focuses on new targets—boys. Perhaps the years spent in competition for being friends with the most popular girls provide a training ground for the fiercer rivalry that is to follow. Women who participate in these competitions end up isolated from other women. They miss the comfort and encouragement that can be such wonderful ingredients of female friendships.

DISTRUST BETWEEN FEMALES

Riane Eisler (1995) has analyzed famous fairy tales, such as "Cinderella," as to what they teach girls. Among the messages is the emphasis on female helplessness and passivity as Sleeping Beauty sleeps for a hundred years until Prince Charming finds her and awakens her with his magical kiss. Certain physical attributes, such as beauty and Cinderella's tiny feet, are important prerequisites for being worthy of the prince's attention. If the foot does not fit into the glass slipper, the prince won't even look at the girl. Another message is purveyed in describing Cinderella's chronic suffering and hard work from dawn to dusk without complaining and without rebelling—perfect training for the submissive wife. In addition, Eisler pointed to another message that "women should not and cannot trust other women, much less look to them for protection against men" (p. 271), because the only adult female, the stepmother, not only mistreated Cinderella, but she also gave bad advice to her own daughters when she suggested they cut off part of their feet in order to fit the slipper.

Eisler continued, ". . . it is also not surprising that women, like members of other socially disempowered groups, have also often learned to identify with those who dominate them . . . like the Chinese mother-in-law who was expected to terrorize her son's new wife as was once done to her, women have often themselves acted as agents for the maintenance of male supremacy. Women have also all too often helped maintain, or at least taken advantage of, the economic exploitation of other women . . . women have all too often been even harsher than men in their judgment of other women as immoral and/or unladylike" (p. 275). Women, such as the group member Helen's mother, help in maintaining exploitation of other women when they are aware that their own daughters are being molested or abused by their fathers and remain passive. Inge's mother had been instrumental in creating a lasting competition between her two daughters, which prevented the formation of close sisterly bonds between them. The mothers of group members Liz, Cindy, and Ann had failed to instill a sense of uniqueness in their daughters.

HOSTILITY BETWEEN FIRST AND FUTURE WIVES

How easy it is to find women willing to judge and blame other women could be seen in the "Great California Mommy War," when the Coalition of Parent Support realized that fathers trying to avoid increases in child support would be less compelling than second wives arguing the case (Crittenden, 2001). The women took on the cause and testified with tears in their eyes that first wives and their children were taking the food from the babies of second wives. Thus, mothers were arguing against mothers. Second wives expressed their resentment over the imagined luxuries first wives enjoyed through the generosity of child support checks. The second wives "had married only to discover that the future was mortgaged by their husbands' prior procreations. They were taking out their rage and frustration not on their husbands but on a safer target: the other woman" (p.173).

Some authors (Silver & Silver, 1985) focus their attention on the hardships of second wives, explaining that many ex-wives are vindictive and jealous of their former husbands' relationships with a new woman.

But as stories about hostile, unreasonable, and revengeful first wives, abound so do stories about hostile and inconsiderate second wives. Second wives consider their husbands and themselves to be victims of first wives who endlessly bleed them financially, whereas first wives see themselves and their offspring as victims of second wives, who through wiles and manipulation alienated the husbands' affections for the first wives to the point where they were "tossed aside like an old shoe" after they had sacrificed their best years to bear and raise that man's children.

WOMEN'S WILLINGNESS TO BELIEVE MEN MORE THAN OTHER WOMEN

Women who lose their husbands to other women in a divorce tend to blame the other woman instead of the husband as if the husband was the innocent victim of the seductive and manipulative actions of the other woman. Similar reasoning seems to occur when women listen to men's stories about previous involvements. The reader is reminded of the group member Ann who disregarded information about physical violence inflicted by her fiancé on his first wife. Ann automatically believed the man's statements that the cold and inconsiderate ex-wife was to blame—until Ann experienced similar treatment. Of course, it is reasonable to accept that women want to trust the man they are planning to spend the rest of their lives with. When the trust is based on blind believing or wishful thinking, the woman is asking for trouble. For instance, when wife number three or four of the same man does not inquire for herself why the man's previous marriages failed, she may well neglect to avail herself of valuable information. Some women may tell themselves that they understand the man better than the previous wives, that their own capacity to love unconditionally is greater than that of their predecessors, or that the poor man just encountered a string of bad luck in choosing mates—until now. Some men lie, just as some women lie; we all know that some people lie, even presidents lie.

In the face of evidence to the contrary, women often focus on the few strands that seem truthful in the incredible tapestry of fact and fantasy supplied by the man and try to weave a canvas of hope rather than reality to be able to continue believing and loving him. Why do some women prefer to believe a man's lies over preserving some degree of doubt and checking out the truth? Because men tell women what women want to hear (Hollander, 1995). Women want to be told that they are different from all other women. Whereas every other woman before them has failed to recognize the greatness or the wonderful traits this man possesses, the current woman acknowledges and nurtures them. In fact, men have reported that potential second or third wives have admired the parts in the man's makeup that had lain wasted, unappreciated, and not rewarded by first or current wives. To be the special woman in someone's life, do we have to downgrade the women who came before us?

WOMEN'S NATURE: HOW NURTURING IS IT?

Women are trained to be self-effacing and conflict-avoidant. Women's nature is nurturing. Women are socialized to sacrifice and to place the welfare of others above their own. Women believe that it is appropriate to serve others (especially husbands and children) and that it is inappropriate to put themselves at the center of their own lives. Female characteristics—in contrast to male characteristics—include emotionality, sensitivity, compassion, empathy, cooperativeness, caring for others, and similar traits. Competition is a masculine trait and therefore is not feminine. In addition, the concept of femininity stresses the notions of being fragile, of not acting as a powerful agent in one's behalf but rather waiting for the male leader to come along to give life meaning and direction. Statements such as those have been used over and over either to manipulate women into being and doing what society deems "feminine" or for women to explain their decision to refrain from self-determination. Shelves in libraries and bookstores are bulging with books written on the basis of those declarations.

COMPETITION AMONG WOMEN IN BUSINESS

If women have been taught that competition is not feminine or not ethical for females, then the teaching was only partially successful. Women may in general not compete with men but, as described earlier, they compete with other women—although not necessarily on an overt level. Even those young women who overtly compete with men for grades and future success seem to compete on a different level with their female friends. Irene's daughter, Renée (chapter 7), who found it difficult to compete on the intense level that her friends did and decided instead to give up her career plans, is an example of this.

Apparently, the relationship among the young women was not supportive enough for Renée to confide in them and ask for help.

Women in supervisory positions have talked about their difficulties with female supervisees. The women were resistant to carry out tasks as outlined in their job descriptions, tasks they had previously performed without question under a male supervisor. On the other hand, female employees have complained about the unreasonableness of their female supervisors. According to these employees, the supervisors showed no consideration for their situation and were concerned only with getting ahead in the business. They described their female supervisors as much more cold and ruthless than male supervisors they had worked for in the past.

How much of these complaints is based in reality and how much is due to negative attitudes toward and between females is difficult to determine. What is clear, however, is the fact that women can ill afford to engage in this type of competition while they are struggling to gain a standing of equality in business as well as in their personal lives. Such competition serves as another vehicle to isolate women from other women, leaving each in weaker positions than they could enjoy in cooperation with one another.

A female college professor admitted how for several years she had observed, but not warned, younger female colleagues stumble into traps laid for them by male faculty staff, whereas she herself quietly and successfully avoided those pitfalls. The young female teachers were so busy participating in the projects of the male senior staff members that by the time they were eligible for tenure considerations they had no research projects of their own to show and their contracts were not renewed.

Laura Tracy (1991) stated, "As a feminist, I wanted to believe that women could be more supportive than competitive, that we wanted to connect with each far more than we wanted to hurt each other. Not too long ago, I discovered otherwise" (pp. xi–xii). When women are taught to be feminine, usually by their mothers, they learn to be distrustful and to contrast themselves to other women, beginning with the mother who is the teacher. "Femininity fundamentally pits women against each other. Femininity separates women from each other. . . . Femininity means innocence. It means keeping the secret that most women know very well, the secret that our relationships with each other are about power, not about community" (p. 7).

Most of the women interviewed by Tracey admitted after some soul searching that the context of competition invaded their most intense relationships. Competition existed with mothers-in-law, with rivals for romantic as well as business relationships, even with their own mothers, daughters, sisters, and friends. But this competition is held in secret (Tracy, 1991).

Denise: Competition—All in the Family

This type of secret and often silent competition is not restricted to the sphere of business life. Denise, the young mother of three well-behaved children, former high school music teacher, and active member of the local school board, volunteers at a children's hospital once a week, organizes a group of neighborhood children to visit residents in a nursing home once a month, and gives free music lessons in her home to economically underprivileged children once a week. She carefully plans visits to concerts and the museum for her children. She drives them to their music lessons and ball practice. She never misses one of her daughters' recitals or her son's games. Her house is spotlessly clean and she serves well-balanced nutritious meals. In the mornings, she gets up one hour before the rest of the family to exercise and shower before preparing breakfast. Denise is extremely efficient and earns the envy of her friends and neighbors.

There is one woman who does not envy her—Denise's mother. In fact, her mother is concerned about Denise. Her son-in-law works long hours, goes on frequent business trips, and plays a role of visitor rather than head of household to his family. Denise never accompanies her husband on his trips. She does not want to leave her children behind, even though Nancy, Denise's mother, has offered to care for them. Doug, Denise's brother, confided in his mother and raised the suspicion that Denise's husband may be involved in an extramarital affair.

What are the reasons behind Denise's strivings to be the perfect mother and good citizen of her community? Doug thinks Denise is competing with their mother. Nancy, the wife of a college professor and a graphic design artist herself, worked in her studio at home when the children were small. She loved her work and never stopped her creative activities. Although sociable, community involvement was not high on Nancy's list of priorities. When the children were older, Nancy returned to teaching art classes. The dedication to her work helped her in the adjustment to her husband's premature death. Meal planning and cooking were not Nancy's strong points. She encouraged the children's participation in spontaneous food creations that were distinctly different from the meals Denise observed in the homes of her friends. Although at home with her children, Nancy's occupation with her work left the children with a lot of freedom. Doug enjoyed the freedom but Denise interpreted it as "benign neglect."

In her adult life, having more children than her mother, Denise seems intent on showing Nancy what constitutes a good mother. Rarely does she leave her children at her mother's house overnight. After a series of polite declines from Denise, Nancy has ceased to offer keeping the children for a longer stay. She has accepted the boundaries established by her daughter. There are no arguments or complaints in the silent dance of competition.

Denise's story includes similar elements of daughter-mother competition as that of Adrienne Rich who in her book *Of woman born* (1986) writes about her mother, a young woman of remarkable talent, determination, and independence, submitting her life and career to the enhancement of her husband's career. At the birth of her own son, Adrienne felt triumphant over her mother who had produced only daughters. Part of her "wanted to hold him up as a badge of victory in our tragic, unnecessary rivalry as women" (p. 223). Sadly, the victory over her mother who had *only* given birth to daughters is more than just unnecessary rivalry, it is a designation of females as being second class citizens—her own as well as all other women and parallels the opinion of Maria Callas regarding giving birth to females, as mentioned earlier. Thus Adrienne—although in competition with her mother—continued her mother's submission to males and invalidation of her own gender.

Mothers and daughters compete in other ways, too. Daughters of beautiful mothers often feel as if they are living in the shadow of their mothers, whereas aging mothers may feel threatened by the fresh beauty of their young daughters. Some daughters of mothers who have kept their slim, trim figures seem to have weight problems. Have the chubby, overweight daughters given up the competition with their mothers in resignation or are they rebelling? Often the daughters don't know. Monica, an obese 24-year-old woman with beautiful, long, reddish-blond hair and green eyes said, "My mother keeps nagging me about my weight. I hate to have dinner at my parents' house because she always makes remarks about how much I eat of the wrong things. She puts double servings of vegetables on my plate so that there will be less room for meat and pasta. When I reach for the meat platter for an additional piece she frowns and reports on the fat content of meat. She must know by now that her nagging only makes me want to eat more. In addition, she always asks me 'have you lost weight?' or 'did you put on weight?' It does not matter which one of the questions she asks; the answer is always embarrassing for me." One wonders if that is Monica's mother's way of competing. What about the mother who, with sympathy, points out to her daughter, "Dear, you worry too much; your hair has more gray in it than mine"? How much of it is genuine concern for the daughter's troublesome thoughts and how much is pride about her own younger looking hair?

Jane, who volunteered her story in chapter 2, spent most of her life in competition with her mother and probably her daughters, as well. Her daughters—in turn—competed successfully for Jane's part of her mother's inheritance.

STEREOTYPING AS A FORM OF COMPETITION

In competing for the company of men, some females complain that they don't have much in common with other women. Women, in general, talk mostly about children, recipes, and clothes, these females argue, whereas they themselves have other interests that are more in line with what men find stimulating. Other females may admit openly that they did not want to spend time with other women or be friends with them. They explain that they cannot trust women because women are sneaky. Both types of arguments used by females are examples of stereotyping; the very same thing women often accuse men of doing to women. Describing some women as being sneaky and others as being interested only in domestic affairs amounts to placing them into distinct categories, separate and distinct from the women who do the stereotyping.

Stereotyping functions as a method of control and constitutes a category-based cognitive response to another person (Fiske, 1993). In fact, it is a refusal to consider the other person as a fully individuated, many-faceted person. Controlling aspects are expressed in the descriptive and prescriptive beliefs inherent in stereotyping. Descriptive beliefs tell how people in a certain category supposedly behave and what their competencies are, whereas the prescriptive aspects determine how the people in the category should behave and what they should be competent to do. In other words, women who regard other women as interested only in domestic issues determine that these women should stick to those issues and not engage in interchanges with men that are based on other topics, because they are not competent to deal with loftier or more esoteric topics that may be discussed by males and the selected females who possess competencies comparable with men. Stereotyping is an attempt to assign negative characteristics or traits of lower value to the occupants of the categories under consideration.

Thus, females engaged in stereotyping devalue other women but they don't realize that when women devalue other women, they devalue the femaleness in themselves (Baker, 1991).

While writing this section the author received a phone call from a bright young lady who wanted to interview her on the topic of stereotyping and the effects it has on people, in particular young people in fraternities and sororities. Ashley, who is going to attend the University of Missouri in Columbia, asked about the emotional consequences that people might experience as targets of the stereotyping process. The discussion included the factors of isolation from others, the attempts to get close to the "in" group, possibly by making gifts to or performing services for the popular members of the sorority in order to be accepted, the hostile competition, and the replication of a process that many women accuse society and the community at large of doing to them. The effects of stereotyping to young women living in a sorority can be much more damaging than if they lived in the community, because they are the outsiders in a tightly knit and bordered population with no other place to go to. They feel persecuted on a daily—if not hourly—basis. Emotional consequences for the targets of stereotyping range from depression over the isolation, to anger and hatred, to anxiety and social withdrawal, depending on the particular type of emotional responses the individual is predisposed to. In addition, if successful integration appears impossible to the individual, the person may feel so homesick as to drop out of school and return home. On the other hand, automatic and easy acceptance into the special group may function to slow the development of independence and self-determination. From the protected environment of home, the young girl is transported into the narrow and protected environment of the sorority where individuation is not encouraged.

Ashley's call certainly emphasized the relevance of exploring the concept of stereotyping and competing in a hostile manner among today's young women. Her questions indicated that the topic is as germane to girls' lives today as it was in the past.

The group members Anita and Inge both disclosed that they were isolated from other women. Although they did not state directly that they might have been competing for the attention of men, one of them, Inge, innocently dismissed the isolation as stemming from other girls' envy of her looks. In the case with her younger sister, she explained that her mother's favoritism of the younger girl had estranged the two sisters. The histories of other group members also revealed instances of competition—Ann who had been silently competing with her siblings for attention from their parents, Cindy who grew up in the shadow of her two beautiful older sisters, and Liz who craved the attention that was given to her terminally ill sister. In the case of Liz, her striving for attention could easily have taken the form of competing for something negative, an illness more serious than that suffered by her sister.

COMPETITION FOR SAINTHOOD

Negative competition is practiced by people who seem to thrive on martyrdom. They sacrifice the most; they never make an overt choice in their own favor; they are the most victimized; they endure more illnesses or accidents than others in their environment. This type of negative competition is the foundation of relationships among women living in a society with only indirect access to social power. The women who engage in negative competition look for consolation from the women with whom they are competing (Tracy, 1991). Sometimes it takes the form of caring for family members, such as husbands, children, or grandchildren suffering from rare illnesses with a sudden onset and frightening outlook. However, through the wisdom and care extended by the nurturing woman, everybody recovers once again. At other times, it is the woman herself who endures serious illnesses but continues to be concerned about the welfare of her family, still cooking, ironing, and cleaning while suffering excruciating pains. The woman's heroic suffering is not to be matched by anybody else's pain.

Arlene, a woman in her late 30s, was an example of such suffering. For years she experienced severe physical pains, which left her physicians at a loss for explanations. Several surgeries were performed, and every time another surgery was scheduled Arlene made sure that she had sufficient time to cook enough meals that her husband could just heat up, that there was enough clean laundry for everybody while she was hospitalized or recuperating. Interestingly enough, Arlene's behavior was in contrast to her own sister's and her sister-in-law's behaviors, who seemed to enjoy good health and demonstrated a lower level of concern about their families' needs. Although Arlene's sister and sister-in-law expressed sympathy for Arlene's travails and the way she coped with them, they refrained from including her in many of their activities, because Arlene would be much too weak or too busy to indulge in their frivolous pastimes. Thus, Arlene became more and more isolated and lonely.

"The best reason to avoid sacrifice is that it's bad for you" (Rubenstein, 1998, p. 65). Sacrificing is the ultimate in negative competition.

Excessive sacrifice leads women to hold distorted perceptions of themselves. The self-denial they practice comes either from feeling not worthy of their own attention, or that they have to do penance for some past sins, or that serving others will guarantee them a secure place in life. Whatever the underlying reason, it does not lead to a woman's independence and self-determination. The sacrificing woman may succeed in having others depend on her, but ultimately she becomes dependent on the target of her sacrifice.

SIBLING RELATIONSHIPS

"Relationships without rules" is the term Susan Scarf Merrell (1995) used to describe sibling relationships. A great number of changes occur in the development of sibling relationships from birth to death, and there are no guidelines that govern the behaviors of adult siblings. Siblings can ignore, or help, one another. They can celebrate together or they can isolate themselves from the other. There may be periods of close connection, or of indifference, or even of heated competition. Cindy related that her two older sisters had been connected in some ways, whereas Cindy remained emotionally more distant from them. Inge and her younger sister failed to form close bonds. In Helen's family, the three sisters formed a loosely connected triangle. When Helen and her older sister suffered ongoing sexual abuse from their father, the two girls had not formed a connection, although they had later admitted their father's abuse to each other when they contemplated the fate of their youngest sister. Helen wanted to protect her younger sister but her warning came too late and it was at the price of her place in the family. Both her sisters distanced themselves from Helen when they denied that the abuse ever occurred.

SISTERHOOD ORGANIZATIONS

For Judy, the facilitator with Big Sisters of Central Indiana introduced in chapter 10, the mother-daughter roles were reversed for a period of time when Judy's father deserted the family. During that period, Judy had her friends to fall back on for emotional support, and her friends are still there for her as they now—in coordination with Judy's mother—plan and prepare for Judy's wedding while Judy is busy with her work and studies. After Judy's mother recovered from her husband's desertion, the family—consisting of Judy, her brother, and her mother—

became closer than ever. Through her work with Big Sisters, Judy is giving to other young girls what has been given to her in time of need. She and others provide support, encouragement, and education about life choices and options for young girls who are in need of positive role models. The one-to-one mentoring program is staffed with volunteers who share a significant part of their time and experiences with these young girls. Big Sisters provide more than a role model. They give hope for a better future and a sister for life.

In a similar vein, Zonta International, a worldwide service organization, is a sisterhood with programs that encourage and assist young girls through their Golden Z Clubs; female high school seniors through the Young Women in Public Affairs program; and women seeking careers in the aerospace industry, government, academe and business through the Amelia Earhart Fellowship, which was established in honor and memory of Amelia, an early member of Zonta. In addition, the organization provides worldwide assistance and education on gender equity, health-related issues, and advocacy regarding termination of violence against women.

THE GROUP: CHANGED ATTITUDES

Cindy and Liz had arrived early for the meeting. After a few words of greeting, Liz and Cindy chose seats next to each other and started talking. Ann, Helen, and Betty arrived in short succession. They were just getting comfortable in their seats when the therapist entered with Anita at her side.

Cindy: (Jumping out of her chair and turning toward Anita): Anita is back! It's good to see you. (The women got up and hugged Anita. Betty and Helen made sure Anita would sit between the two of them.)

Anita: It's good to be back. You made me feel so welcome. I admit I was a bit scared to come back, but now I am glad that I am here.

Ther.:   We are all glad that you came back to be with us. We have missed you. As I mentioned to you, Julia and Inge had to leave us. It is always sad when members have to depart before having reached the stage of resolution to their challenges.

Tina: Where have you been all this time?

Anita: (Hesitating): I have been traveling . . . I am really embarrassed, but I guess I owe you an explanation.

Helen: Anita, don't tell us more than what you feel comfortable with. We don't have to know everything right know. We are just glad you are back.

Betty: Helen is right, take your time, talk to us when you are ready.

Anita: I'll try to make it short, but I want you to know the main points. I had met this really important man. He is wealthy and very powerful. He told me that he would help me get my sons back. Of course, I was delighted. I knew he was married, but he did not talk much about his wife or his marriage. Although he didn't say so, he seemed to imply that the marriage was more or less dead. He had to go on an extended business trip to Hawaii and then to Japan. He asked me to come along; we could discuss how to get my children back while we were traveling. In order to get the business connections established, he had to stay a week or two in some of the places. I could function as a hostess for him. While we were there, he introduced me as a cousin who was helping out while his wife could not accompany him.

Ann: Now that you are back, how is he helping you with your children?

Anita: I think that was just an excuse to get me to go away with him. We did not have much time discussing the situation. Some of the other businessmen knew that I was just his mistress. Nobody really believed the cousin story, but they behaved as if they did—except for one obnoxious guy who tried to make a pass at me. I had no illusions about myself when I got into the situation. I knew that it was just going to be an affair. He seemed to be infatuated with me, and I thought he was powerful enough to be able to help me. Actually, I had a good time and got some expensive clothes and jewelry, but I became more anxious when time went by without any discussion about my sons.

Jody: What is your situation now? (Then adding in her usual hesitant voice): We probably should not ask so many questions; it's just that we care about what happens to you.

Anita: Your questions are good; they make me feel included again, actually more than in the past. I want you to know what is happening in my life and I want you to be on my side. I remember the time we were discussing how some women become isolated from other women and that was certainly true for me. I should have made myself available to your good will and help then.

Ther.: I am glad you remembered that discussion. Will you be able to stay with us now?

Anita: Yes, I want to continue with the group. I need it. When we came back from Japan, we stopped over in Hawaii again. I was told that arrangements had been made for me to stay on for a couple of days while he went back to his home. He had given me the name of an attorney and some money and that was the last he mentioned about helping me with my children. I think he wanted to make sure that he would not be seen with me on the same airplane.

Ann: Have you seen your children since your return?

Anita: Only briefly. Unfortunately, I have lost some ground in the custody situation because I was not here for my regular visitation schedule and—of course—my ex-husband has used that against me. Now I am back to only having supervised visitation with my sons again. What I thought would help me with gaining my children has really set me back.

Ann: Did you talk to the attorney? Is there anything you can do to make the man help you as he promised?

Anita: The attorney did not give me any hope. He indicated that the man I was with would not be able to give me further assistance. He is very powerful. Even if I told his wife or others, it would just be a small blemish on his reputation and he could hurt me more than I could hurt him. Besides, my ex-husband would use my going off on an affair instead of visiting my children to his advantage. I am stuck. When I realized what was happening to me, I thought about Helen and how she was surprised that I did not consider myself a victim after the sexual abuse in my childhood and the rape by my boyfriend. Perhaps I have been a victim all along and did not want to acknowledge it.

Helen: Oh Anita, don't become a victim now. You have helped Betty and me to get away from that mind-set. We can't let you fall into that trap.

Ther.: Helen has a point, feeling like a victim is not going to be as beneficial as thinking about what you can learn from this situation and what your current options are. This was a painful lesson, but it has brought you back to us. We will help with your explorations.

Anita: I have a lot to learn. While I was gone I thought if I had discussed my plans with you, I might have gotten a different perspective on the whole situation. At the time I thought there was no point in telling the group because you would not understand me and would condemn me. As you know, I was never close to other women. I didn't trust them, so I did not trust you either, although I started to feel more comfortable with you just before I left.

Cindy: Earlier we might have judged you more harshly because your values were so different from ours. We have changed since then because of what we learned.

Ther.: One of the saddest things about women is that women don't trust other women and women compete with other women for jobs, for attention, for men, for a sense of uniqueness, for a sense of power. This competition not only isolates women from other women, it also weakens the position of the individual woman.

Anita: I did feel somewhat powerful when the man offered to help me in exchange for being his mistress. I thought I could beat my ex-husband at his own game. Sexual desire for me from a powerful man has always been exciting. Because of my looks and the attention it got me from men, I considered myself more powerful than some other women and that's why they did not like me.

Ther.: Some time ago, I believe you said that in situations as you just described you feel close to the power. It reminds me of what psychiatrist Natalie Shainess (1984) called "borrowed power." She was talking about women who daydream or believe that they can overcome their helplessness by attaching themselves to a powerful male, such as a politician, a movie or sports star, or a business tycoon.

Anita: (Turning pale and talking in a low voice without looking at anyone in the room, just staring straight ahead): There is a lot of similarity with me. What I considered a strength in me—attracting admiration from men—is actually a weakness? Did the psychiatrist call those women victims? (Helen pulled her chair closer to Anita's and put her arm around Anita's shoulders.)

Ther.: Actually, because of the helplessness and passivity involved, she saw them as masochistic. It is like a fantasy of rescue. The women don't see themselves as strong or powerful enough to overcome their difficulties but plan or hope to gain the help of a powerful person by attaching themselves to that powerful person.

Ann: That seems similar to people who hang onto celebrities, groupies they used to call them. They were all competing for a place close to the celebrity.

Ther.: You are correct, Ann. The groupies cannot find their own
        sense of meaning or their own means of excitement. They
        are trying to absorb those things from the powerful celebrity
        that they attach themselves to. And you are correct, too, in
        considering the element of competition here. The brighter
        the star, the greater is the competition among the groupies.

Jody: That reminds me of something I read in a magazine some
        time ago. It was an article about a community in the East
        where many artists live. They talked about the social life, and
        one male artist was mentioned—I don't remember the name—
        but he was described as a very nice guy who always has a
        succession of gorgeous girlfriends. I remember being upset
        when I read this part of the article and I don't quite know
        why. Was he considered to be a nice guy because of the gor-
        geous girlfriends? Did he deserve the girlfriends because of
        his niceness? Then I thought it sounded almost as if he was
        wearing a series of great-looking tailor-made suits or drove
        expensive foreign cars.

Liz: Do you mean that the article turned the girlfriends into ob-
        jects or adornments attached to the man?

Jody: Yes, that's it! How would you feel if you read the article and
        you had been one of those girlfriends?

Cindy: I would not like it. I would probably feel like one of the
        groupies Ann was talking about. I wonder if the author of
        that article was aware that the sound of it could be offensive
        to women?

Jody: I have a question about what the psychiatrist called masoch-
        istic women. I don't see how this dependent attachment is
        masochistic. I thought masochism is when people like to suf-
        fer and ask to be beaten. But the women wanted to be close
        to a powerful person because they wanted protection, not
        pain. Like Anita wanted help to get her children back.

Ther.: Your question makes sense, Jody. Many people believe that
        masochists enjoy the pain and suffering. I don't think that
        Dr. Shainess shares this opinion. Protection comes at a price.
        A helpless person can't afford to negotiate the price. The
        helpless person has to pay what is demanded by the protec-
        tor. By making oneself helpless through passivity or wanting
        to be dependent, the person is instrumental in putting him-
        self or herself in the position of suffering pains or losses that
        are determined by someone else. The terms of payment are
        controlled by the protector and to a degree by other "pro-

tectees," who may be willing to raise the price in the competition for a particular protector. Whether we call the person a victim or a masochist is not as important perhaps as the emphasis on who establishes the degree of helplessness.

Jody: That sounds as if it would apply to me because I have let my husband take over and make the decisions. The water spots on the faucets were part of the price I paid for Roger's protection in other areas, and the price was too high to keep my original feelings for him alive. Instead of enjoying our sexual activity, I came to regard sex as another payment for protection and did not like it. When you said some time ago it was important for women to know themselves and be well grounded within themselves before they enter a long-term relationship like marriage, that included knowing whether we wanted to be a victim or a masochist or a self-determining person.

Ther.: Jody, you have learned a lot. How are your feelings for your husband now?

Jody: Although I had planned to leave that issue for later when I knew more about my own interests, I did mention my feelings to Roger. He seems more understanding. I think it was the way I talked to Roger that impressed him. I did not complain or accuse him. I just explained to him how I felt.

Ther.: Congratulations, Jody. You have come a long way.

Betty: We have talked so much about competition, and I have some difficulty with the idea when I apply it to my situation. When my ex-husband left me to marry his current wife, I thought she was stealing him from me. I was not in a competition because I did not know what was going on until it was too late. If I had known that she was after my husband and if I had then decided to be more fun to be with, would that have been competition on my part?

Ther.: Betty, when you thought the woman was stealing your husband from you—how did you feel about your husband?

Betty: First I thought he was a wimp, falling for the widow. But later, when I realized that he tried to cheat me out of my part of our assets, I knew he is not a wimp. He just did what he wanted to do without caring about me. It was not so much her taking him away from me. I never really had him. We married because it seemed the reasonable thing to do. We stayed together, raised our children, and worked hard because it seemed the reasonable thing to do. He probably found her to be more fun because our marriage was not fun together, it was more drudgery and I did not know that it could be different. I assumed that was life. It's strange, but— as you said earlier to Inge—at the divorce you find out what your marriage really was like.

Ther.:   Betty, you keep surprising us with your insights. Now you see your ex-husband as a different person than you did when you were married to him. And now you are ready to make your life more exciting on your own with your prospect of assistant travel agent.

Betty: Yes, that will be a great adventure. By the way, I wanted to tell you that my sons have become friendlier toward me. They even call me from time to time and the younger one asked if I ever cook his favorite dish anymore and if he could come over for dinner. He also mentioned that the relationship between their father and his new wife had become strained. The atmosphere seemed tense the last couple of times they visited. I did not comment on that but I did invite him for dinner.

Helen: Betty, would you go back to him if he asked you to?

Betty: (Laughing): I don't think so, he is not worth competing for. (Continuing after a brief pause): But seriously, I feel much happier now. I like the friendly relationship I have with Nancy. We meet from time to time for lunch on weekends. Last week she took me to the museum. Maybe she is trying to train me for the trip. I like the new experiences and I am certainly looking forward to the trip with her art study group. Although Nancy is running her own business, she does not seem to be competing with me or her employees or her customers. I never had time to have a real friend before and I was also too afraid of confrontations. This is my opportunity to have a friend.

Ther.:   As Betty has changed her attitude toward her ex-husband's new wife and is benefiting from making friends with other women, we can all learn that we gain by not competing or distrusting other women but by treating them as we would want them to treat us. How we treat other women is how we treat ourselves. We are not gaining in status by putting one of us down. We are making ourselves stronger by being proud of and encouraging one another. Anita has returned to us. We can all continue to work together in cooperation.

GROUP PROCESS: CHANGED ATTITUDES

The return of a group member set the emotional climate for this meeting. It was not easy for Anita to disclose to the group her recent experiences and reasons for leaving, especially because she had been the one who hesitated the longest to become a caring part of the group. Her past generosity toward two group members, however, had established warmer feelings toward Anita even during her absence.

Several of the women were active in self-exploration and gaining significant insights around the topic of relating to other women. The therapist introduced the concept of female masochistic behavior (Shainess, 1984) as it relates to victims and victimizing. Women who tend to isolate themselves from other women and to become dependent on a powerful male protector participate—although often passively—in and provide opportunities for their own victimization.

The interrelatedness of changed attitudes about women and benefits derived from cooperating rather than competing with other women was demonstrated by some of the members. The therapist encouraged all members to continue to work in cooperation on the solution for their challenges.

SUMMARY

This chapter traced the attitudes of women toward other women through various relationships, starting with the earliest and most complex mother-daughter relationships to friend-friend relationships and others as they develop throughout the life cycle. While many female relationships are beneficial and supportive, there are unfortunately just as many that are competitive and even destructive. Various forms of female competition were explored. Stories of women who volunteered to disclose their histories were used to illustrate the issues and dynamics inherent in the content of this chapter. The main lesson through the chapter is the message that competition among women can be destructive and weakens all women who participate in it. Cooperation and mutual encouragement are the characteristics that can enrich all of us. By making positive changes in our attitudes about other women, we are able to make positive changes in our attitudes about ourselves.

The second part of the chapter followed the group therapy process and the discussion of topics important to the group members in a path that parallels the general direction of the chapter.

QUESTIONS FOR CONSIDERATION

Women who attempt to stereotype other women—are they the same who complain about men and society at large stereotyping women? And if so, are they identifying with the aggressor when they engage in the same behavior?

Do our society and the legal system facilitate or encourage the development of hostility between first and future wives? What are examples of this process? What are possible remedies?

RECOMMENDED READING

Eisler, R. (1995). *Sacred pleasure: Sex, myth, and the politics of the body.* New York: HarperCollins Publishers.

> *The author traces the sexual politics of our time, exposing myths that have corrupted male/female relationships over time. The book reveals a whole new history of intimate relations—and how these affect and are in turn affected by all our relations.*

Hollander, D. (1995). *101 lies men tell women: And why women believe them.* New York: HarperCollins.

> *The author describes a wide range of lies that invade male/female relationships and destroy trust. The book also shows why women are more vulnerable to certain types of lies than others.*

Tracy, L. (1991). *The secret between us: Competition among women.* Boston: Little, Brown and Company.

> *The book describes how women of all ages compete covertly with other women, their mothers, their sister, and friends for jobs, for men, for status, or for the love and attention of family members. When asked about this competition, most women deny that they engage in it—even deny it to themselves.*

CHAPTER TWELVE

Was It Worth the Price?

As people face significant decisions in life, they try to estimate possible outcomes, but some decisions are made without any degree of guarantees. The best estimates and calculations remain speculations because of the unknown variables that can interfere over time and alter expected directions and outcomes. Economies change. Accidents and natural disasters occur. Illnesses can strike unexpectedly, leading to physical impairment or untimely death of people that were involved in our lives and plans. Therefore, as decisions contain various degrees of uncertainty, it is reasonable that people would stop for a moment to ask the question, "Was it worth the price?"

MOTHERHOOD HAS A PRICE

Ann Crittenden, in her book *The Price of Motherhood* (2001), mentioned listening to the radio interview of a female book author. During the interview, the writer was asked if her life had developed according to her plans. The author's answer conveyed that her life had turned out quite differently from her expectations. She had given up her academic career goals and instead had become a "soccer mom". When the interviewer inquired whether the writer had any regrets, the woman—of course—denied having regrets about the sacrifices that she had made for her children. Crittenden questioned that any woman would have said on National Public Radio with her children and husband listening that she felt sorry for having made that choice. Her question is justified considering that society is still frowning on mothers who leave their young children in paid child care to go to work when they are financially not forced to do so because they have husbands.

Few women are willing to admit that they prefer holding a job to being full-time mothers. Even fewer would admit that they had chosen motherhood over careers and felt that they made the wrong choice for themselves. "The tragedy of motherhood is that it is not a sacrifice for nothing, but an unnecessary sacrifice for something of overwhelming value" (Apter, 1985, p. 136). There are few guidelines to weigh and balance against the real value and use of motherhood.

How many women would have sacrificed their careers if they had seriously considered that under family law a married spouse has no legal claim to the other spouse's income, that after the birth of the first child her bargaining power decreases significantly when requesting that the husband take on an equal share of the household tasks, or that it will be extremely difficult to resume her career after a prolonged absence (Crittenden, 2001)? In a typical married-with-children family, in which the husband is the primary breadwinner and the wife functions as the primary homemaker, even if she also works outside the home, "these typical wives are the very ones who, if anything, are hit hardest by divorce. The middle-class professional mother who has 'done the right, responsible thing' and cut back on her career for the sake of her family quickly discovers that when it comes to divorce, no good deed goes unpunished" (Crittenden, 2001, p. 140).

The prevailing motherhood ideology is one of intensive mothering, insisting that motherhood is exclusive and completely child centered (Hays, 1996). The mother described in this ideology is devoted to the care of others and she is self-sacrificing—not a person with her own needs and interests. Caregiving and nurturing naturally fall into the woman's domain. Women's work on behalf of others, such as family members, is considered to be a labor of love that does not need economical rewards because love is its own reward.

GUIDELINES TO ASSESS A WOMAN'S LIFE: WHERE ARE THEY?

Considering questions regarding life decisions made in the past, we normally would think of individuals who have lived through significant parts of their life spans. Some of the consequences of earlier choices and decisions take time to materialize. To articulate an integrative life story, understanding and ability to use temporal, biographical, causal, and thematic coherence, which emerge at different points in individuals' cognitive development (Habermas & Bluck, 2000), are required. We would not expect a young person such as Judy, who was introduced in chapter 10, to be able to tell us how her plans worked out for her. On the other hand, Lena, in the story of the draft-dodger's bride below, had lived long enough to remember the options that were available to her at certain stages in her life and to experience the consequences of her choices. Very little information about women at midlife is available in the literature. Major studies on adult development at midlife leave the reader with the impression that only men survive past the age of 40 (Gergen, 1990). For those who do continue to live, most studies focus on the psychological effects women experience through times of transition such as menopause or postparental periods (Lippert, 1997).

In a study examining occupancy and quality of the roles of paid worker, wife, and mother in connection to midlife women's well-being, as measured by indexes of self-esteem, depression and pleasure, it was found that role occupancy was unrelated to psychological well-being except that the role of paid worker significantly predicted the level of self-esteem. Role quality was instrumental in predicting well-being, except for the quality of the role of mother, which did not significantly predict pleasure (Baruch & Barnett, 1986).

Habermas and Bluck (2000) in their studies of autobiographical memory, have identified four types of coherence in people's life stories. Out of those four—temporal coherence, cultural concept of biography, thematic coherence, and causal coherence—the authors considered causal coherence to be the most significant type. Causal coherence in a life story links events and the self in motives or causes. Individuals outline why certain actions were undertaken and how the consequences set the stage for events or situations that followed. Such reflections on life stories could facilitate the process of answering the question raised in this chapter. Being aware of their options, goals, decisions, and actions, women would be able to build their self-confidence if the outcomes are satisfactory for expenditure and gains. If expectations are not met by the outcomes, reflections of the overall process provide a basis for learning and discovering new paths in the pursuit of approaches that make "it" worth the price. However, there is a dearth of studies about the relation between life reflection and self-development (Staudinger, 2001).

Lena: The Draft-Dodger's Bride

Lena, one of the women who agreed to reveal their stories, told me that her daughter had been instrumental in her coming forward. Her daughter Marcia and I had met at a volunteer activity. When I told her about this book she said, "My mother would be a perfect person to interview for the book. I will ask her about it. She has been such a wonderful inspiration for me. I think her story should be known." A few days later I received a phone call from Lena and we scheduled to meet for an interview.

Lena, a very attractive brunette in her 50s (which no one would guess by looking at her), arrived early. She began by saying, "It's really my mother who deserves all the praise. Without her, my life would have been a lot more difficult." Then her story unfolded. Lena had been a sociology student in college during the time of the Vietnam Conflict. In one of her classes she had met Benjamin, who was about to graduate at the end of the semester. They fell passionately in love. Ben pressed for an engagement. His reasoning was that they knew that they loved each other and wanted to get married. They were meant for each other. There was some consideration about being drafted and he thought if they got married soon, he would have a better chance to avoid the draft. Lena agreed and convinced her parents who had initially been hesitant about the speed with which this relationship developed.

Her parents met with Ben and were favorably impressed by him, except for Lena's mother, who was disturbed by a comment Ben made about Lena dropping out of college so that they could move to California after a June wedding. Ben thought he would have a better chance of obtaining employment there because of his father's help and support. Ben's parents were divorced and he lived with his mother while attending college. After a year they would be able to establish residence in California and Lena would be able to continue with her college education. Although this sounded reasonable on the surface, Lena's mother was concerned that her daughter would not continue her education as planned. Her older daughter Marjorie had dropped out of college before graduating to marry a commercial artist and to move to the East coast with him. By now Marjory was the busy mother of four lovely children. College had become a remote idea, indeed. Lena carried a double major; she was interested in sociology and in nursing and had planned to become a registered nurse as well as to obtain her degree in sociology.

Although busy with her classes, Lena agreed to plan for a small, June-first wedding. Their honeymoon would be the drive to California. After discussing it with her husband, Lena's mother described the options to Lena. Due to the husband's early retirement because of health reasons, the family lived on a fixed income, but there was a fund set aside for Lena. She could either have a big wedding or a small intimate reception with relatives and close friends only as guests. The remaining money would be kept for her for future use, such as completing her studies or other career choices. Her mother made it clear that the money would not become part of a wedding gift and that she was strongly in favor of saving the money for Lena's future— although these were options for Lena to consider and exercise. Lena agreed to follow her mother's wishes because she trusted her mother to have Lena's best interest at heart. Her mother praised Lena for her wise choice and suggested that Lena put all her energies into finishing the semester with good grades while her mother would work on the wedding plans. Selection of the bridal gown would be Lena's only responsibility.

Everything went as planned. Lena's gown followed classic lines; it's simplicity and the satiny whiteness underlining and emphasizing Lena's beauty. During the last fitting sessions Lena's mother took some photographs of Lena as she was standing still for the seamstress. Ben and Lena enjoyed a few small parties during their brief engagement. She proudly showed off her engagement ring. They were very much in love and didn't always take precautions during their lovemaking. In fact, Ben thought it might even help his draft status if Lena became pregnant. Two days before the wedding, Ben and his friends went to the northern part of the state for a bachelor's party. One of his friends had a hunting lodge there and it seemed a good place for the party. They just wanted to relax and do some fishing, sit around the fire, drink beer, and exchange stories. Because of Ben and Lena's move to California, this would be the last time for a while that the friends would be together. Lena had some concerns about Ben's timely return for the wedding, but she decided to be quiet and not start their marriage as a nagging wife.

Very early on the day of the wedding, Lena's parents were awakened by the sound of the doorbell. One of Ben's friends appeared on the threshold with a letter in his hand. The letter was from Ben to Lena. The letter stated that Ben and two of his friends had gone to Canada. They had been afraid that they would be drafted and decided to disappear. Their plans were to part company and make their way individually to different parts of the country to avoid discovery. Ben would be in touch with Lena but did not know yet when and how. He asked for her forgiveness and continued faith in him. Their wedding would not be cancelled—only postponed.

At this point in her report Lena stated, "I don't know what I would have done without my mother. She took over in the most loving but firm manner. While my father seemed enraged, she planned. We notified the minister and the photographer as well as some of the people we could reach. We cancelled the bridal suite in the hotel—of course—losing the deposit. The reception was supposed to be held in our house and garden. Everything was decorated and the caterer was ready to bring the food. My mother held me in her arms without saying much. After a while, she wiped my face with a tissue and asked me to assist her in taking down the decorations and then to get dressed. She needed my help in arranging the food that the caterer was about to deliver any minute. My father heard her last words as he entered the room. He thought she had lost her senses. But she told him that several of the guests were bound to arrive, the food was on the way and could not be cancelled without losing the money. Although we could not have a wedding reception, we might as well turn it into a planning meeting because we had some thinking to do. Only later did I realize that my mother had wanted to keep me busy and distracted as much as possible to get over the shock of being jilted. Ben's mother did not attend the meeting. During all that time my mother never said a bad word about Ben. My mother was a wise woman."

As Lena continued her story she revealed her discovery that she was pregnant. She confided in her mother, who was willing to discuss various options, reassuring her that whatever option Lena chose, she would have her mother's support. Her support, however, would not be unconditional. Lena, strong in the belief that Ben would return, decided against an abortion. This was Ben's and her baby and she would take good care of it until his return.

Acknowledging Lena's decision without expressing approval or disapproval, her mother outlined the conditions of her support. Because Lena had not preregistered for the fall semester due to the planned marriage and move to California, her mother suggested that she immediately do so, even if she had to pay a penalty or could not get all the courses of her choice. While registering for the next semester, she should also try to enlist in a summer course. In other words, she should continue with her studies as soon and as long as she could. If the pregnancy progressed normally, Lena would have time to complete at least the next semester. Lena needed to get herself into a position in which she could support herself and her child perhaps for a long time, because they did not know when Ben would return or if he would want Lena and the baby to join him in Canada. Lena accepted her mother's conditions as fair.

After a year of waiting without hearing anything from Ben, Lena felt betrayed by him. Surely, he could have gotten word to her by now.

Lena found out that Ben's father had been killed in an accident shortly after their planned move to California. With Ben gone, his mother decided to move in with one of her sisters in Arizona. Lena had told her about the pregnancy and the woman promised to stay in touch with Lena because of the grandchild. Lena never heard from her. She had kept her bridal gown protected and in good condition for the "postponed" wedding. Now it became a reminder of her dead dreams. Besides, even if Ben returned, as the mother of a child, Lena did not think it would be appropriate to wear a white gown that still was considered to symbolize innocence and virginity. She did not qualify for either one now. Lena decided to sell the gown and placed an advertisement in the local paper: "FOR SALE: Wedding dress, white satin, simple style, size 10, never worn." She used one of the pictures her mother had taken of her in the gown, framed it, and placed a copy of the ad on the bottom of the picture. This served as a constant reminder for her to put her energies into a career that would ensure her independence.

Lena's relationship with her mother remained a special one. While attending school, Lena and her daughter, Marcia, lived with Lena's parents. Her mother, after years of volunteering her services at the local art museum, had been able to obtain part-time employment there as assistant to the museum's volunteer coordinator. Lena was expected to help with the chores at home, and the two women coordinated their schedules so that Marcia would be in the care of her mother or grandmother. Lena had ample opportunity to date, but she placed her daughter and her studies first. Her trust in men was damaged. She obtained her RN and a bachelor's degree in sociology. Later she obtained certification as nurse practitioner and enrolled in a master's degree program in social work. With the nurse practitioner's certificate, she was in better charge of her schedule and could work as consultant in different medical practitioners' offices. With an MSW degree, she would have options to work as therapist and could combine some degree of physical and mental care for her clients. It was an ambitious undertaking. Her mother was proud of her.

In raising her daughter, Lena followed her mother's role model. She told Marcia the story of the wedding gown picture and emphasized the importance of studying to make good grades in school because that was the best ticket for Marcia's future. From a young age, Marcia had age-appropriate assigned chores to perform. Her responsibilities grew as she progressed in age and ability. Neither her mother nor her grandmother spoiled or pampered Marcia. They treated her with respect according to her age and behavior. Marcia loved to visit with her grandmother at the museum. Usually her grandmother would save her break time for Marcia's visits and would take her to certain paintings—usually no more than two or three—in the galleries and tell her stories about the paintings. Other visits would include her mother. Marcia learned an appreciation for art early in her life.

With her own professional success progressing as it did, Lena became more confident in herself. She learned that trust in herself was vastly more important and rewarding than having trust in another person, such as a man. With that realization her bitterness receded, and she was finally able to enjoy a man's company. She knew she could stand on her own two feet, make her own decisions, set her own goals, and allow herself the pleasure of a man's company without losing anything of herself. When Marcia was about 8 years old, Lena met a young physician who was attracted by her beauty as well as her personality. They dated for a while and Lena recovered her past passionate self. Thomas proposed marriage and Lena accepted happily, but she had learned from her mother the value of putting conditions on agreements and commitments. She informed Thomas that she would be happy to be his wife but she also wanted to continue her work and her studies. She was willing to reduce her hours and progress more slowly toward her goals in order to devote time to their marriage. Thomas was disappointed; it was his plan to have Lena work with him in his medical practice as his nurse. They came to an agreement with the arrangement that Lena would work with him as a nurse and nurse practitioner as needed, but would also continue her studies with a reduced course load. Although Lena had some misgivings about working as a subordinate to her future husband in his practice, she was willing to compromise for her happiness.

Because of her responsibility for Marcia, Lena suggested that they work on a financial framework for their marriage. What would be their budget after they combined their incomes? Thomas admitted that he still had some outstanding debts from medical school and, in addition, he was paying child support to a woman who bore his child but whom he never married. He had never seen the child but he grudgingly accepted the financial responsibility. Lena's face grew pale when she heard about the child. Immediately she was reminded of her relationship with Ben. Ben had never contacted her. Did he know about Marcia's existence? Surely, his mother would have told him if he had been in communication with her. Lena could not sort out her feelings at the moment; the similarities between Thomas and Ben were too strong. Although Thomas knew about Marcia's past relationship with Ben, he did not seem to recognize the resemblance.

After Lena went home she searched her mind and emotions for answers. How could she love a man who had treated another woman the way Ben had treated her? Was the difference between the two women greater than the similarity between the two men? In other words, did the other woman have more influence or responsibility in her relationship with Thomas than Lena had had with Ben? Answers to those questions were difficult to reach. She could not ask the other woman. Lena struggled with her decision. She was strongly attracted to Thomas, and their work in the medical field gave them a common ground on which to build their future, although Lena would have liked more professional freedom and flexibility for herself than Thomas had envisioned. The life of a physician's wife would be so much easier than that of a working single mother. She reminded herself that easiness was not the overriding goal of her life but independence and self-determination were. The parallels inherent in Ben's and Thomas's decisions regarding their commitments to women and to fatherhood were determining factors. Lena chose the option of remaining a single mother.

A few years later, another opportunity for romance developed in Lena's life. This time she became attracted to a man about 15 years her senior. It was different from the passionate feelings she had experienced for Ben and Thomas. Richard's gentle smile warmed her heart. His behavior was kind and considerate. He had such a loving expression on his face when he looked at Lena that she felt secure with him. Richard encouraged her to follow her dreams. He wanted to enjoy her presence as a loving and lovable companion rather than as a submissive wife. Lena's friends expressed concerns regarding the age difference. In all likelihood Lena would be alone again toward the later part of her life. She would probably outlive Richard. Lena agreed that it would be sad if Richard died long before she did, but she did not want to sacrifice the happiness she could experience now because of worries about the future. In fact, she could afford to look for happiness now because she knew she would be able to take care of herself if and when she needed to. Shortly after their marriage, Richard adopted Marcia as his own daughter. Lena is now finishing the course work for her doctoral degree in social work. Richard has been supportive of her goals all along. He is proud of her. As she spoke about Richard and her current life, her face was bathed in a radiant glow. She had found happiness and self-determination in the same relationship and she was glad that she had not settled for less.

She concluded with "Here you asked me for my story, but it really is my mother's story. She was the biggest influence in my life. She was the best role model any woman could have—even though she was not a career woman. But she believed in a woman's self-determination and she helped me to become the master of my future. My mother was a woman who learned from her own experiences and mistakes and did not hesitate to admit them. For instance, when she provided me with those conditional options after Ben had left me, she told me that she had previously supported my older sister in her decisions. In retrospect, my mother thought she had made a mistake by not imposing some conditions on Marjorie because—although she was happily married—with four children Marjorie would have been better provided for if she had a career to fall back on, in case anything would happen to her husband. Fortunate for me, my mother was not willing to repeat that mistake.

"I have learned that options carry conditions with them—whether they are spelled out or not. Love and acceptance include conditions—even though we don't want to admit it. I have also learned that agreements and commitments contain terms that need to be specified. All these are valuable lessons about reality. The learning process and the decisions were painful at times. In retrospect, it would probably have been easier for me to decide on an abortion after Ben had deserted me. Later, marriage to Thomas seemed so desirable and promising. My friends thought I had made a big mistake when I chose not to marry him. Although my mother had approved of the marriage, after I told her everything she supported me in my decision. Today, we both know my current happiness was worth struggling and waiting for."

COMMITMENTS AND THEIR AFTERMATHS

It is interesting to think about what Lena called "valuable lessons about reality," those lessons she had learned from her mother. Indeed, people make commitments and talk about commitments but they do not specify the details included in a given commitment. We hear statements, such as "I want to spend the rest of my life with you." Or "I am always going to be there for you." Or "I want to share my life with you." Rarely do we find a definition of what "the rest of my life" means. Does it mean continuous togetherness 24 hours each day until death do us part? Or does it mean that some portion of the time the persons engage in activities or interests of their own? "Always being there for you"—does that mean whenever you need me or want me or does it mean in crisis situations and when I am not geographically distant? "Sharing my life with you"—does it mean every single event? What do we share? Everything? Some things?

People discussing and agreeing about commitments may have an idea of what they mean but rarely do they communicate the meaning in detail to the other person involved. People who ask for commitments and those who agree to make commitments may not know what the other intends the commitment to cover. Both persons just assume that they are in agreement and later on become disappointed and complain bitterly when the other person's behavior falls short of the commitment as expected but not communicated clearly.

It is remarkable—if not scary—that people are willing to commit themselves to perform or deliver behaviors for extended periods of time without being knowledgeable about the terms or details involved. This is analogous to jumping blindly into a swimming pool without knowing how much water—or if any—the pool contains. Bruises, broken limbs, or worse are likely consequences. Similarly, fractured dreams, broken hearts, bruised egos, and deaths of relationships are likely consequences of blindly committing oneself.

How much time and effort is required to communicate details of commitments? People document heir significant actions in contracts. When we purchase an automobile there is a contract. When we rent or buy a house there is a contract. When we start a new employment there is a contract. The contracts outline the details of what is being delivered or guaranteed and what items are not included in the contract. By comparison, marriages or relationships would appear to be of equal to if not more significance than purchasing a car or a house. Marriage vows (or contracts) may mention in vague and fuzzy terms behavioral characteristics of loving, honoring, obeying, and so forth in sickness and in health "until death do us part." However, the participants have rarely bothered to define what it is they commit to for the rest of their lives.

One major prerequisite to making commitments is to have extensive knowledge of oneself. Only with the awareness of what one can and is able to give without resentment and what one would like to receive to feel accepted, loved, and cared for by another person can one make a meaningful commitment. This prerequisite differs from person to person. Once individuals know what they can give and what they want to receive in order to be happy or satisfied in relationships, the first commitment would best be to themselves—the commitment not to settle for less.

Rita: Being Trapped in Undefined Commitments

Rita, a librarian at a large university, had a far-away expression on her face as she related her story. A quietly beautiful brunette with blue eyes and a soft voice, she seemed lost in the past, as if she did not know where to begin. She had been a good student and always wanted to become a librarian. From an early age she loved to read, and being around books seemed like the best work she could imagine. In college she was fascinated by history and sociology. While in her second semester in the master's program for library science, she met Rick who was pursuing a law degree. They dated and made plans for the future, which looked promising.

Their wedding was planned to follow shortly after Rita's graduation. Two months before the wedding Rita realized that she was pregnant. She talked to Rick before telling her parents. Rick seemed shocked. Although they had planned to have children, this was supposed to be in the future. Now was not a good time. He had just started to work for a local law firm and he was expected to pass the bar examination as soon as possible. Financially, a child was a burden they could not really afford at this time. In a year or two they would be in much better shape to have children. Rick pleaded with Rita to have an abortion. On their engagement they had made a commitment to help each other and make each other happy, Rick reminded Rita. Having a baby now would be a disaster. Rita agreed to have an abortion.

Rita continued by saying that she thought that she and Rick were way ahead of other young people when they made that commitment to be helpmates to each other. They were serious about the relationship, but Rita did not realize what "helping each other" could include. They had not talked about it in specific terms, and Rita never thought that an abortion would be part of it. Several years later, they tried to have children but Rita could not conceive. Her gynecologist had doubts that she would get pregnant. She did not ask if it had anything to do with the abortion—she didn't want to know. She became depressed and Rick could not help her. He was doing great in his work. After a while he did not like coming home to a depressed wife. During the day Rita's job distracted her, but at night she thought about the child she could have had. The marriage did not survive the stress. Shortly after their divorce, Rick remarried and now he has two children.

To distract herself, Rita went back to school and worked on her doctorate. Then she started writing, mostly biographies about people in history. Two years ago, she married a kind and understanding man. They are happy. Without a verbalized commitment her husband is helping her and supporting her in her endeavors, although Rita still believes that spelling out commitments is better than just making general statements. Thinking back, in Rita's opinion, the abortion was too high a price to pay for a relationship that did not survive anyway.

THE GROUP: WAS IT WORTH THE PRICE?

Helen and Betty were dressed in the same outfits they had worn on the day prior to Anita's leaving, and they wore the kerchief and necklace she had given them. Anita smiled at them and stated that the two items still looked better on them than on Anita. Both told Anita how much her gifts had meant to them as they seemed to signal a new stage in their lives. They filled Anita in on what had happened in their lives and within the group during Anita's absence. Ann, Jody, Cindy, and Liz added to the report as they each joined the group.

Ther.: At our previous meeting, Anita told us about her experiences while she was gone. (Turning to Anita): How can we help you define your current challenges and options?

Anita: My biggest challenge remains to increase the contact with my children and eventually to gain custody of them. That has not changed, but the options are different from what I had perceived them to be in the past. The powerful male protector is not an option anymore. The previous session was really helpful in demonstrating that to me. What I had seen as an option was not worth exploring. It cost me more than I could afford. My current option is to get a job. I have an opportunity to work for a builder as a sales representative. It would take a lot of weekend work, but since I don't have regular visitation with my children, I might as well work. Depending on how well I do, there are several opportunities for advancement. When I told them about my interior decorating background, they thought that might be helpful for decorating the model houses and dealing with the furnishing suppliers. Although it does not sound like a great career, I need to start with something. Becoming a real estate agent would interest me too.

Ann: I didn't know you had a background in interior decorating.

Anita: (Laughing somewhat bitterly): I took some training in interior decorating because I thought it would come in handy when I married a rich man, and it did. Our house was very elegantly furnished and decorated, and I did a lot of it my-self. Years ago pictures of the house appeared in a magazine. I took many photographs and put them into an album, like a portfolio. Perhaps I can renew some of my old contacts.

Jody: I bet your house was gorgeous. Can you show us your pic-tures or would that be too painful?

Anita: I'll bring in the album. I have to learn to live with the past and work toward a future. If you hear of anybody wanting to buy a home, think about me.

Ann: Anita, you'll be great, you have a flair for putting things together. I'll let people know about your houses. Perhaps I can visit your model home on a Sunday. I'll be more convinc-ing to others after I've seen it.

Cindy: That's a great idea, Ann. Let's all drum up business for Anita. She needs the money for a good attorney.

Anita: You are very kind to me. It's the first time I feel I belong somewhere.

Ther.:   It sounds as if you discovered an option that is workable for you, and as you go along more options may open up. How are the visits with your sons, Anita?

Anita: Painful. They ask about my absence and I cannot tell them the truth. The woman who supervises us seems to be listen-ing to every word. I have to be careful about what I say.

Jody: How long will it take until you get regular visitations with your sons?

Anita: I don't know. My ex-husband has a lot to do with that. He is in control.

Ther.:   You are taking on control over the part that you can deter-mine—to build up a stable existence for yourself and for your sons to join you when the time comes. We are on your side.

Jody: The last time, when you told us about your experiences while you were gone, I thought you were so courageous to come back to us after all that. It made me look at my own lack of courage. I sat down at my little desk and finished one of the stories I had been working on. I was anxious while I was doing it, but I calmed myself down several times and contin-ued writing. After that, I made an appointment with the writ-ing teacher from last year and asked her if she would be willing to read my story and give me feedback. I am thinking of taking another class with her.

Betty: What did she say about your story?

Jody: It's too early; I just gave it to her yesterday. Although I would want her to like it, the important point is that I overcame my fear of admitting that I want to be a writer.

Ther.: Jody, that was a big step. Before, you felt that admitting what you want and hope for would limit your chances of making it come true. Instead, you are freeing yourself now from those limitations and opening the door for further explorations of your talents. You demonstrated that you have the courage necessary for those explorations. (Turning toward Helen after a brief pause): Helen, are you still tutoring the boy who lost his hearing?

Helen: Yes, I am. I enjoy working with him; he is such a sweet child. The father is very grateful for what I am doing for his son. He has asked me if I could join him and his son on a vacation. He would pay for my room, transportation, and meals. He can't pay me for my time, except a small daily amount.

Jody: Are you going with them?

Helen: I am not sure. One reason for my hesitation is my past. I am not ready to talk to anyone else about it. With daily all-day interaction, there is more of a chance for disclosure and I don't want to lie either.

Ther.: What is your main concern about not wanting to disclose?

Helen: When I left my family and hometown I changed my name. I don't want them to know where I am; at least not until I have built a new life for myself.

Jody: Won't they be concerned about you?

Helen: I doubt that. They are probably relieved about my quiet disappearance, and that's fine with me. Some time ago, I told you that I had been in another therapy group. It was an incest and abuse survivor group.

Ther.: I remember you mentioned that the other group members did not understand that you were even more upset about your mother's behavior than about your father's actual sexual abuse.

Helen: Yes, that is correct. They turned against me because I would not forgive my mother. I told them that every time I thought of my mother, I imagined her turning us three girls into sacrificial lambs for my father to devour. She had to know what was going on, and she protected him instead of us. She may even have protected herself—perhaps she did not want to have sex with him anymore.

Ther.:   It is terrible to be abused by one parent and not receiving
          protection from the other. So much pain and loneliness comes
          from that. Did the other group members have experiences
          similar to yours, Helen?

Helen: Some may have had. I don't remember the details anymore.
          Two things stand out in my mind when I think about that
          group.

Ther.:   Do you want to share that with us?

Helen: As the other women talked about their lives, it seemed that
          several of them had been involved in abusive relationships
          repeatedly. I could not figure out whether they attracted oth-
          er abusers, or whether other people that would not normally
          be abusive considered these women to be "damaged goods"
          and therefore treated them similarly.

Ther.: That is an important observation, Helen. Victims at times be-
          have in ways that signal to abusers that they can be victim-
          ized. For instance, a woman alone in an elevator may avoid
          eye contact and look down to the floor when a man enters
          the elevator. Some criminals read this as a clear message that
          the woman will not report them if they were to be assaulted
          by the man.

Liz: If the woman looked at the man that might be interpreted as
          she wanted his attention.

Ther.:   Yes, Liz, that can be true. It depends on how she looks at him
          or how she avoids eye contact. Either way, if there seems to
          be a lack of confidence behind her behavior, a criminal will
          most likely interpret this as "victim behavior." Another test
          may be to see if the woman can be persuaded to change her
          mind, such as a woman who initially responds with "no" to a
          request but then gives in. The test may start with a small,
          rather innocent-sounding request. After the first change of
          mind has occurred, another attempt at persuasion follows
          until the intruder or perpetrator feels he is in control. This
          type of behavior has been described by Gavin de Becker (1997)
          in his book, *The Gift of Fear.* This may partially explain your
          observation, Helen. The other explanation is that the ac-
          counts of violence and abuse can have a desensitizing effect
          on some people, as you mentioned. Is that a reason for your
          hesitancy in talking about your own experiences?

Helen: That may be part of it. I want to take my time and think more
          about it before I make a decision.

Ther.: Your approach to this issue is reasonable. There are different variables to consider and it makes sense to proceed slowly. You mentioned that two things were on your mind as you thought about the previous group experience. What was the other?

Helen: The other issue was that of forgiveness. They were almost obsessed with forgiving. It was their opinion that if I did not forgive my parents and my sisters that I would not be able to progress from victim to survivor.

Liz: That sounds silly. You were already a survivor. We all survived what we went through and we want more than just to survive.

Helen: Exactly! That's the way I felt. Although at the time I didn't know what more there could be for me. The trouble I have with forgiveness is that I cannot see any reason why I should forgive them for what they did, especially my parents. I worked hard not to hate them anymore because I don't want to poison the rest of my life. (Turning to the therapist): As you said before, it is time that I won't let them hurt me anymore with it. But forgiveness—that is like saying it's all right, it's acceptable what they did. I am glad that nobody in this group has condemned me and nobody has told me to forgive.

Ther.: We have no right to tell you whether to forgive your parents or not. You are the one who endured the abuse and you decide which way to feel about it. The main point is—as you said—that you will not let it poison your life and that you move from just surviving to striving. That process you have already started. It looks like the pain of moving away from your hometown and the name change was worth what you have built for yourself so far.

Ann: Building for ourselves—I am finally understanding what you have said several times. It would be good for us to have an interest developed for ourselves, or to be "grounded within ourselves," as you called it. When you talked about it, I did not think it applied to me because I have a profession—but it does. I have decided to fade out of the relationship with Ronald and start seriously searching for myself. With my own interests and goals, I would be less vulnerable to have others take advantage of my time and good will.

Ther.: Ann, you have a great profession and you are doing well in it. But you are correct; there is more of you and more for you out there in the world. From your comments it sounds as if

	Ronald has asked you for more proofreading but not more romantic involvement.
Ann:	That's about it in a nutshell. But, fortunately, there is more to it.
Liz:	What is it? It sounds mysterious.
Ann:	I had this minor revelation. It came to me the last time Ronald and I had dinner. It is a little difficult to describe, but I'll try. It occurred to me that there were really three of us at the table.
Liz:	Who else was there?
Ann:	The book. As usual, Ronald was talking about his research and how he hoped it would stimulate other scientists to look at parts of his work and to make related discoveries. Altogether, it would serve to advance science and help mankind.
Cindy:	His work must really be important. Why do you want to stop seeing him?
Ann:	It probably is very important. But when I had this image of three chairs at the dinner table, it gave me a strange feeling. In reality there were only two chairs at opposite sides of a small table but in my 'vision' Ronald was sitting on one chair, the research or book was sitting on a chair next to Ronald, and I was sitting by myself on the other side of the table. Ronald and the book seemed like a couple and I was serving them both, but the real close relationship was between Ronald and his research. I was an outsider.
Cindy:	Wow! What a 'vision'! How did you feel Ann?
Ann:	Very strange at first; it seemed spooky. I usually don't have any imaginations like this. Then I became excited because I made my own discovery. And, actually Cindy, you were the impetus to that.
Betty:	This is becoming more and more intriguing. Tell us more of your discovery.
Ann:	Betty, you are a part of it, too. My discovery was that I had observed Ronald from a different point of view—in a way unrelated to me. Perhaps it is because women are so trained or conditioned to see their environment in relational terms to themselves or it could be part of my nurse's training. I have not sorted that out yet.
Ther.:	That is very interesting, Ann; it could be a combination of both. What made you look at it differently this time?
Ann:	Way back when we first started talking about observing others, it sounded superficial to me. And from some of the responses

it seemed others had similar thoughts. But Betty always made a connection to something deeper, and I wondered at the time how she came to those connections. I should have asked her, but I felt stupid and did not want to admit it.

Betty: I didn't always understand it either; I just tried to make sense out of it.

Ann: And you did—for yourself and some of us. When Cindy and Liz talked seriously about these observations and putting them into workshops or books, I still did not get the whole picture. Finally, when Cindy used her observations to demonstrate how we as women may contribute to the gap between the sexes and to our own detriment, it clicked. Cindy's observations became important and useful. I noticed that even though she was involved in some of the situations, her observations made her appear like a casual observer—neutral, objective. It must have impressed me more than I realized, because I was not consciously aware of using that type of observation in the situation with Ronald.

Ther.: Ann, how did you feel when you went through your "minor revelation"?

Ann: Normally, I would have been angry realizing that I was not really important to Ronald. But the funny thing was that I felt rather calm, curious in a way and—perhaps—slightly amused.

Ther.: Great! (Turning to the group): Ann and Cindy have shown us that we can get ourselves outside of the—let's call it—"relational mode" in our thinking and observing. Women are capable of being objective and don't have to conform to the myth of being only "relational creatures." We can free ourselves temporarily from the relational mind-set when it is wise to do so. This was a wonderful experience for all of us.

Ann: Cindy's work also helped me put the whole group process into perspective. Her challenge was to become visible. There were several options for her to choose from. She could have dyed her hair green or done some other outrageous things. The task of making observations opened additional options for her and she explored them and decided to use them to help and teach others, like me. She has become a very interesting person.

Cindy: Thank you, Ann; that is the best compliment I ever had. If my observations made an impression on you and Betty, that indicates the project is worth pursuing. I still think about Inge and hope that my comments did not drive her away.

Ann: Cindy, I believe that Inge left because she had decided to go
          back to Europe with her first husband. Like Jody, I think it
          was not the best choice for her. Also, I think that Inge did
          not really understand that if we want things to be different,
          then it is up to us to do something about them. In hindsight,
          it seems that Inge and I had a handicap. We both are success-
          ful in our careers, so we did not see a big problem within us
          but thought our environment was to blame.

Ther.:   You have reached a significant insight, Ann, and you have
          come a long way in a short time. In your own ways, you have
          all come to a point where you can decide if what you have
          done and learned so far was worth the effort, time, and the
          pain that is at times part of the explorations into ourselves. If
          your answer is positive, we will continue to look at our chal-
          lenges, to consider our options, and to decide on actions to
          take that will bring us closer to our goals. When we continue
          with our explorations, we will do so because we consider it a
          wise investment strategy for life.

GROUP PROCESS: WAS IT WORTH THE PRICE?

In evaluating the challenges that faced them, the options they perceived, and the decisions they made regarding which option to take—
did the group members choose the best path? Did the consequences
justify the choices and efforts? Ann revealed significant insights she
had gained through the thoughts and discussions of other members.
Most of the members had come to a point where they could evaluate
the progress they had made so far and could decide if it was worth it
to them to continue on their journey of self-knowledge, discoveries,
and assumption of personal authority.

What has become of Julia? The therapist never heard from her
again. While it is sad to assume that she once more gave up her own
dreams in return for the security of an intact family system and the
approval of her family, it is very likely that she sacrificed her goals—at
least for the years that her children were still at home. Growing up in
a family system where young girls were not encouraged to explore
paths to their own fulfillment but instead to unquestioningly accept
the decisions of men, Julia's final choice of a husband resulted in
having someone much like her father by her side. No wonder she had
felt comfortable while dating Bob; they had a lot in common. Julia was
prepared for the job as Bob's wife. She was unprepared for making a
successful transition to a life of her own, developing her own talents

and following her own dreams. Stripped of her support system, it is likely that Julia resigned herself to accept the unpleasant and reverted to "life as usual."

SUMMARY

This chapter explored the decisions women are faced with through the life cycle, the choices they make at different points and the consequences of those choices. The most significant choices for many women are those that involve careers, marriage, and motherhood. There are no guidelines and there are no easy solutions. Decisions toward one goal may require sacrifices of other goals. Relinquishing one option for another—in the end women are faced with the question: "Was the cost too high or was the outcome worth the price?"

CODA

Although this chapter is the conclusion of the book, it is not the end of The Group. The women we have met and perhaps additional group members will continue to address the challenges in their lives. They will continue to search for options and behavioral alternatives. They will weigh the options against the probable consequences, and they will decide what actions to take to reach their goals. They will recognize the significance of commitments and the need to build in definitions and details into the commitments they make. As they pursue their independence and self-fulfillment, they will remember not to isolate themselves from other women through various forms of competition, but instead they will enjoy the strength and comfort that are found in cooperation with others. Although nurturing their own individual distinctiveness, they will respect and celebrate the uniqueness of other women. Although engaged in the journey of self-determination, these women are willing to pay the price for reaching their goals, but they are the ones to determine what the fair price is.

RECOMMENDED READING

Crittenden, A. (2001). *The price of motherhood.* New York: Henry Holt.
  Using interviews and current research in economics, sociology, history, child development, and law, the author shows how mothers are disadvantaged and financially dependent while carrying out society's most important job.

References

Adler, A. (1927). *Understanding human nature*. New York: Greenberg.

Ainsworth, M. D., Blehar, M., Waters, E., & Wall, S. (1978). *Patterns of attachment*. Hillsdale, NJ: Erlbaum.

Alington, D. E., & Troll, L. E. (1984). Social change and equality: The roles of women and economics. In G. Baruch & J. Brooks-Gunn (Eds.), *Women in midlife* (pp. 181–202). New York: Plenum Press.

Allen, R. E. (1985). *Greek philosophy: Thales to Aristotle* (2nd ed.). New York: The Free Press.

Amaro, H. (1995). Love, sex, and power: Considering women's realities in HIV prevention. *American Psychologist, 50,* 437–447.

Amaro, H., & Gorneman, I. (1992). *HIV/AIDS related knowledge, attitudes, beliefs, and behaviors among Hispanics: Report of findings and recommendations.* Boston: Boston University School of Public Health and Northeast Hispanic AIDS Consortium.

Anderson, D. Y., & Hayes, C. L. (1996). *Gender, identity, and self-esteem: A new look at adult development.* New York: Springer.

Apter, T. (1985). *Why women don't have wives: Professional success and motherhood.* New York: Schocken Books.

Archer, J. (1996). Sex differences in social behavior: Are the social role and evolutionary explanations compatible? *American Psychologist, 51,* 909–917.

Arnett, J. J. (1998). Learning to stand alone: The contemporary American transition to adulthood in cultural and historical context. *Human Development, 41,* 295–315.

Arnett, J. J. (2000). Emerging adulthood: A theory of development from the late teens through the twenties. *American Psychologist, 55,* 469–480.

Arnkoff, D. B., & Glass, C. R. (1989). Cognitive assessment in social anxiety and social phobia. *Clinical Psychology Review, 9,* 61–74.

Ashby, J. S., Kottman, T., & Rice, K. G. (1998). Adlerian personality priorities: Psychological and attitudinal differences. *Journal of Counseling & Development, 76,* 467–474.

Atkinson, M., & Boles, J. (1984). WASP (wives as senior partners). *Journal of Marriage and the Family, 46,* 861–870.

Baker, M. (1991). *Women: American women in their own words.* New York: Pocket Star Books.

Bandura, A. (1977). Self-efficacy: Toward a unifying theory of behavioral change. *Psychological Review, 84,* 191–215.

Bandura, A. (1986). *Social foundations of thought and action: A social cognitive theory.* Englewood Cliffs, NJ: Prentice-Hall.

Barkley, B. H., & Salazar Mosher, E. (1995). Sexuality and Hispanic culture: Counseling with children and their parents. *Journal of Sex Education and Therapy, 21,* 255–267.

Bartholomew, K., & Horowitz, L. (1991). Attachment styles among young adults: A test of a four category model. *Journal of Personality and Social Psychology, 61,* 226–244.

Baruch, G. K., & Barnett, R. C. (1986). Role quality, multiple role involvement, and psychological well-being in midlife women. *Journal of Personality and Social Psychology, 51,* 578–585.

Bateson, M. C. (1989). *Composing a life.* New York: A Plume Book.

Baumeister, R. F. (1997). Esteem threat, self-regulatory breakdown, and emotional distress as factors in self-defeating behavior. *Review of General Psychology, 1,* 145–174.

Baumeister, R. F., & Exline, J. J. (2000). Self-control, morality, and human strength. *Journal of Social and Clinical Psychology, 19,* 29–42.

Beall, A. E. (1993). A social constructionist view of gender. In A. E. Beall & R. J. Sternberg (Eds.), *The psychology of gender* (pp. 127–147), New York: The Guilford Press.

Beattie, M. (1987). *Codependent no more.* New York: HarperCollins (reissued with a new preface in 1992).

Beauchamp, C. (1998). Developing character: Frances Marion and the silver screen. *Women in the Arts, 16,* 12–15.

Beeghley, L., & Cochran, J. (1988). Class identification and gender role norms among employed married women. *Journal of Marriage and the Family, 50,* 719–729.

Bemker, M. (2000). Why they use: Risk factors for substance abuse in adolescent females. *Report of the National Council on Family Relations, 45,* F18, 20.

Bergmann, B. R. (1986). *The economic emergence of women.* New York: Basic Books.

Berk, S. F. (1985). *The gender factory: The apportionment of work in American households.* New York: Plenum.

Bernard, J. (1975). Adolescence and socialization for motherhood. In S. E. Dragastin & G. H. Elder, Jr. (Eds.), *Adolescence in the life cycle: Psychological change and social context* (pp. 227–252), New York: John Wiley & Sons.

Bloom, C. (1996). *Leaving a doll's house: A memoir.* New York: Little, Brown and Company.

Bluck, S., & Habermas, T. (2001). Extending the study of autobiographical memory: Thinking back about life across the life span. *Review of General Psychology, 5,* 135–147.

Bohmer, C., & Ray, M. L. (1996). Notions of equity and fairness in the context of divorce: The role of mediation. *Mediation Quarterly, 14,* 37–52.

Bonett, R. M. (1994). Marital status and sex: Impact on career self-efficacy. *Journal of Counseling & Development, 73,* 187–190.

Bowlby, J. (1988). *A secure base.* New York: Basic Books.

Brayfield, A. (1992). Employment resources and housework in Canada. *Journal of Marriage and the Family, 54,* 19–30.

Brewster, K. L., & Padavic, I. (2000). Change in gender-ideology, 1977—1996: The contributions of intracohort change and population turnover. *Journal of Marriage and the Family, 62,* 477–487.

Brown, L. M., & Gilligan, C. (1992). *Meeting at the crossroads: Women's psychology and girls' development.* Cambridge, MA: Harvard University Press.

Browne, A. (1993). Violence against women by male partners: Prevalence, outcomes, and policy implications. *American Psychologist, 48,* 1077–1087.

Bruner, J. S. (1987). Life as narrative. *Social Research, 54,* 11–32.

Burke, P. (1996). *Gender shock: Exploding the myths of male and female.* New York: Anchor Books.

Campbell, W. K., & Sedikides, C. (1999). Self-threat magnifies the self-serving bias: A meta-analytic integration. *Review of General Psychology, 3,* 23–43.

Caplan, P. J. (1985). *The myth of women's masochism.* New York: E. P. Dutton.

Cassidy, J. (2000). Adult romantic attachments: A developmental perspective on individual differences. *Review of General Psychology, 4,* 111–131.

Coley, R. L., & Chase-Lansdale, P. L. (1998). Adolescent pregnancy and parenthood: Recent evidence and future directions. *American Psychologist, 53,* 152–166.

Collins, W. A., Maccoby, E. E., Steinberg, L., Hetherington, E. M., & Bornstein, M. H. (2000). Contemporary research on parenting: The case for nature and nurture. *American Psychologist, 55,* 218–232.

Colwell, L. H. (1992). *Erma Bombeck: Writer and humorist.* Springfield, NJ: Enslow.

Cooney, T. M., & Uhlenberg, P. (1989). Family-building patterns of professional women: A comparison of lawyers, physicians, and postsecondary teachers. *Journal of Marriage and the Family, 51,* 749–758.

Coontz, S. (2000). Historical perspectives on family studies. *Journal of Marriage and the Family, 62,* 283–297.

Crittenden, A. (2001). *The price of motherhood.* New York: Henry Holt and Company.

Cross, S. E., & Markus, H. R. (1993). Gender in thought, belief, and action: A cognitive approach. In A. E. Beall & R. J. Sternberg (Eds.), *The psychology of gender* (p. 55–98), New York: The Guilford Press.

Csikszentmihalyi, M., & Rathunde, K. (1993). The measurement of flow in everyday life: Toward a theory of emergent motivation. In J. E. Jacobs (Ed.), *Developmental perspectives on motivation* (pp. 57–97), Lincoln: University of Nebraska Press.

Cunningham, M. (2001). The influence of parental attitudes and behaviors on children's attitudes toward gender and household labor in early adulthood. *Journal of Marriage and Family, 63,* 111–122.

Daniluk, J. C. (2001). "If we had it to do over again . . .": Couples' reflections on their experiences of infertility treatments. *The Family Journal: Counseling and Therapy for Couples and Families, 9,* 122–133.

de Becker, G. (1997). *The gift of fear: Survival signs that protect us from violence.* New York: Little, Brown and Company.

DeLucia-Waack, J. L. (1999). Supervision for counselors working with eating disorders groups: Countertransference issues related to body image, food, and weight. *Journal of Counseling & Development, 77,* 379–388.

Demo, D. H., & Acock, A. C. (1993). Family diversity and the division of domestic labor: How much have things really changed? *Family Relations, 42,* 323–331.

Domar, A. D., & Dreher, H. (1996). *Healing mind, healthy woman.* New York: Henry Holt and Company.

Eagly, A. H., & Wood, W. (1999). The origins of sex differences in human behavior: Evolved dispositions versus social roles. *American Psychologist, 54,* 408–423.

East, P. L. (1998). Racial and ethnic differences in girls' sexual, marital, and birth expectations. *Journal of Marriage and the Family, 60,* 150–162.

Easton, C. (1996). *No intermissions: The life of Agnes de Mille.* New York: Little, Brown and Company.

Edwards, M. E. (2001). Uncertainty and the rise of the work-family dilemma. *Journal of Marriage and Family, 63,* 183–196.

Eisler, R. (1995). *Sacred pleasure: Sex, myth, and the politics of the body.* New York: HarperCollins.

Elder, G. H., Jr. (1975). Adolescence in the life cycle: An introduction. In S. E. Dragastin & G. H. Elder, Jr. (Eds.), *Adolescence in the life cycle: Psychological change and social context* (pp. 1–22). New York: John Wiley & Sons.

Engel, B. (1990). *The emotionally abused woman.* Los Angeles: Lowell House.

Erikson, E. H. (1963). *Childhood and society* (2nd ed.). New York: Norton.

Erkut, S., & Marx, F. (1995). *Raising competent girls: An exploratory study of diversity in girls' views of liking one's self.* Special report from Center for Research on Women. Wellesley, MA: Wellesley College.

Feeney, J. A., & Noller, P. (1992). Attachment style and romantic love: Relationship dissolution. *Australian Journal of Psychology, 44,* 69–74.

Fiske, S. T. (1993). Controlling other people: The impact of power on stereotyping. *American Psychologist, 48,* 621–628.

Fletcher, A. C., Steinberg, L., & Sellers, E. B. (1999). Adolescents' well-being as a function of perceived interparental consistency. *Journal of Marriage and the Family, 61,* 599–610.

Fox-Tierney, R. A., Ickovics, J. R., Cerreta, C. L., & Ethier, K. A. (1999). Potential sex differences remain understudied: A case study of the inclusion of women in HIV/AIDS-related neuropsychological research. *Review of General Psychology, 3,* 44–54.

Foxhall, K. (2000, December). Rural life holds particular stressors for women [Practice dept.]. *APA Monitor, 31,* 30–32.

Fraley, R. C., & Shaver, P. R. (2000). Adult romantic attachment: Theoretical developments, emerging controversies, and unanswered questions. *Review of General Psychology, 4,* 132–154.

Freilino, M. K., & Hummel, R. (1985). Achievement and identity in college-age vs. adult women students. *Journal of Youth and Adolescence, 14,* 1–10.

Gage, N. (2000, October). Callas's unsung lullaby. *Vanity Fair, 482,* 236–250.

Gannon, L., Luchetta, T., Rhodes, K., Pardie, L., & Segrist, D. (1992). Sex bias in psychological research: Progress or complacency? *American Psychologist, 47,* 389–396.

Geis, F. L. (1993). Self-fulfilling prophecies: A social psychological view of gender. In A. E. Beall & R. J. Sternberg (Eds.), *The psychology of gender* (pp. 9–54). New York: The Guilford Press.

Gergen, M. M. (1990). Finished at 40: Women's development within the patriarchy. *Psychology of Women Quarterly, 14,* 471–493.

Gerson, K. (1985). *Hard choices: How women decide about work, career, and motherhood.* Berkeley: University of California Press.

Gibson, D. M., & Myers, J. E. (2000). Gender and infertility: A relational approach to counseling women. *Journal of Counseling & Development, 78,* 400–410.

Gilbert, L. A. (1987). Female and male emotional dependency and its implication for the therapist-client relationship. *Professional Psychology: Theory, Research, and Practice, 18,* 555–561.

Gilligan, C. (1977). In a different voice: Women's conception of self and morality. *Harvard Educational Review, 47,* 481–517.

Gilligan, C. (1982). *In a different voice.* Cambridge, MA: Harvard University Press.

Girvetz, H., Geiger, G., Hantz, H., & Morris, B. (1966). *Science, folklore, and philosophy.* New York: Harper & Row.

Glasser, W. (1998). *Choice Theory: A new psychology of personal freedom.* New York: HarperCollins.

Glick, P., & Fiske, S. T. (2001). An ambivalent alliance: Hostile and benevolent sexism as complementary justifications for gender inequality. *American Psychologist, 56,* 109–118.

Goldman, K. W. (1993). *My mother worked and I turned out okay.* New York: Villard Books.

Gray, M. R., & Steinberg, L. (1999). Unpacking authoritative parenting: Reassessing a multidimensional construct. *Journal of Marriage and the Family, 61,* 574–587.

Green, M. R. (Ed.). (1964). *Interpersonal psychoanalysis: The selected papers of Clara Thompson.* New York: Basic Books.

Greenstein, T. N. (1996). Husbands' participation in domestic labor: Interactive effects of wives' and husbands' gender ideologies. *Journal of Marriage and the Family, 58,* 585–595.

Greenstein, T. N. (2000). Economic dependence, gender, and the division of labor in the home: A replication and extension. *Journal of Marriage and the Family, 62,* 322–335.

Greer, G. (1999). *The whole woman.* New York: Alfred A. Knopf.

Grolnick, W. S., Deci, E. L., & Ryan, R. M. (1997). Internalizing within the family. In J. E. Grusec & L. Kuczynski (Eds.), *Parenting and children's internalization of values: A handbook of contemporary theory* (pp. 135–161). New York: Wiley.

Habermas, T., & Bluck, S. (2000). Getting a life: The emergence of the life story in adolescence. *Psychological Bulletin, 126,* 748–769.

Hanmer, T. J. (1996). *The gender gap in schools: Girls losing out.* Springfield, NJ: Enslow Publishers. Inc.

Harding, S. (1986). *The science question in feminism.* Ithaca, NY: Cornell University Press.

Hare-Mustin, R. T. (1986). The impossible pursuit of perfection. In C. Tavris (Ed.), *Every woman's emotional well-being* (pp. 7–29). Garden City, NY: Doubleday.

Harter, S. (1993). Causes and consequences of low self-esteem in children and adolescents. In R. Baumeister (Ed.), *Self-esteem: The puzzle of low self-regard* (pp. 87–116). New York: Plenum.

Hays, S. (1996). *The cultural contradictions of motherhood.* New Haven, CT: Yale University Press.

Hazan, C., & Shaver, P. R. (1987). Romantic love conceptualized as an attachment process. *Journal of Personality and Social Psychology, 52,* 511–524.

Heath, C., Larrick, R. P., & Wu, G. (1999). Goals as reference points. *Cognitive Psychology, 38,* 79–109.

Heilbrun, C. G. (1988). *Writing a woman's life.* New York: Ballantine Books.

Hewlett, S. A. (1986). *A lesser life.* New York: William Morrow.

Heyn, D. (1997). *Marriage shock: The transformation of women into wives.* New York: Villard Books.

Hochschild, A. (1989). *The second shift: Working parents and the revolution at home.* New York: Viking.

Hollander, D. (1995). *101 lies men tell women: And why women believe them.* New York: HarperCollins.

Houseknecht, S. K., Vaughan, S., & Macke, A. S. (1984). Marital disruption among professional women: Timing of career and family events. *Social Problems, 31,* 273–284.

Howard, G. S. (2000). Adapting human lifestyles for the 21st century. *American Psychologist, 55,* 509–515.

Hsu, L. K. G. (1989). The gender gap in eating disorders: Why are the eating disorders more common among women? *Clinical Psychology Review, 9,* 393–407.

Jesse, K. (2001, March 25). 'Fair sex' fights for fairness [Lifestyle]. *The Indianapolis Star,* pp. J1–J2.

Kalmuss, D., & Straus, M. (1990). Wife's marital dependency and wife abuse. In M. Straus & R. Gelles (Eds.), *Physical violence in American families* (pp. 369–382). New Brunswick, NJ: Transaction.

Kane, E., & Sanchez, L. (1994). Family status and criticism of gender inequality at home and at work. *Social Forces, 72,* 1079–1102.

Karoly, P. (1999). A goal systems-self-regulatory perspective on personality, psychopathology, and change. *Review of General Psychology, 3,* 264–291.

Kefir, N. (1981). Impasse/priority therapy. In R. Corsini (Ed.), *Handbook of innovative psychotherapies* (pp. 400–415). New York: Wiley.

Kennedy-Moore, E., & Watson, J. C. (2001). How and when does emotional expression help? *Review of General Psychology, 5,* 187–212.

Kimmel, M. S. (2000). *The gendered society.* New York: Oxford University Press.

Kitto, H. D. F. (1951). *The Greeks.* London: Penguin.

Kotre, J., & Hall, E. (1990). *Seasons of life: Our dramatic journey from birth to death.* Boston: Little, Brown and Company.

Krueger, D. W. (1990). Success and success inhibition. In R. J. Sternberg & J. Kolligian, Jr. (Eds.), *Competence considered* (pp. 246–260). New Haven, CT: Yale University Press.

Langenfeld, S., & Main, F. (1983). Personality priorities: A factor analytic study. *Individual Psychology, 39,* 40–51.

Langer, C. L. (1996). *A feminist critique.* New York: HarperCollins.

Lent, R. W., & Hackett, G. (1987). Career self-efficacy: Empirical status and future directions. *Journal of Vocational Behavior, 30,* 347–382.

Lerman, H. (1996). *Pigeonholing women's misery: A history and critical analysis of the psychodiagnosis of women in the twentieth century.* New York: Basic Books.

Levine-Shneidman, C., & Levine, K. (1985). *Too smart for her own good?* New York: Doubleday.

Levinson, D. J. (with Darrow, C. N., Klein, E. B., Levinson, M. H., McKee, B.) (1978). *The seasons of a man's life.* New York: Ballantine.

Lindsey, L. L. (1990). *Gender roles: A sociological perspective.* Englewood Cliffs, NJ: Prentice Hall.

Lippert, L. (1997). Women at midlife: Implications for theories of women's adult development. *Journal of Counseling & Development, 76,* 16–22.

Lipson, A., & Perkins, D. N. (1990) *Block: Getting out of your own way.* New York: A Lyle Stuart Book, published by Carol Publishing Group.

Locke, E. A., & Latham, G. P. (1991). Self-regulation through goal setting. *Organizational Behavior and Human Decision Processes, 50,* 212–247.

Lopata, H. Z., & Barnewolt, D. (1984). The middle years: Changes and variations in social role commitments. In G. Baruch & J. Brooks-Gunn (Eds.), *Women in midlife* (pp. 83–108). New York: Plenum Press.

Lorber, J. (1994). *Paradoxes of gender.* New Haven, CT: Yale University Press.

Lucas, M. S., Skokowski, C. T., & Ancis, J. R. (2000). Contextual themes in career decision making of female clients who indicate depression. *Journal of Counseling & Development, 78,* 316–325.

Lyness, K. S., & Thompson, D. E. (1997). Above the glass ceiling? A comparison of matched samples of female and male executives. *Journal of Applied Psychology, 82,* 359–375.

Maass, V. S. (1995). Modern family life and the significance of values. In P. L. Lin & W. Tsai (Eds.), *Marriage and the family: A global perspective* (pp. 19–28). Indianapolis: University of Indianapolis Press.

Maass, V. S. (2000a, May). *The function and impact of attention throughout life.* Paper presented at the 2000 Spring Convention of the Indiana Psychological Association, South Bend, IN.

Maass, V. S. (2000b, February). *Promises for 2000: Who will keep them?* Paper presented at the Annual Conference of the Indiana Council on Family Relations, Muncie, IN.

Maass, V. S., & Neely, M. A. (2000). *Counseling single parents: A cognitive-behavioral approach.* New York: Springer.

Maccoby, E., & Martin, J. (1983). Socialization in the context of the family: Parent-child interactions. In Ph. H. Mussen (Series Ed.) & E. M. Hetherington (Vol. Ed.), *Handbook of child psychology: Vol. 4, Socialization, personality, and social development* (pp. 1–101). New York: Wiley.

Macmillan, R., & Gartner, R. (1999). When she brings home the bacon: Labor-force participation and the risk of spousal violence against women. *Journal of Marriage and the Family, 61,* 947–958.

Maltz, M. (1973). *The search for self-respect.* New York: Grosset & Dunlap.

Margolies, E. (1985). *The best of friends, the worst of enemies.* Garden City, NY: The Dial Press.

Markus, H., & Oyserman, D. (1989). Gender and thought: The role of the self-concept. In M. Crawford & M. Hamilton (Eds.), *Gender and thought* (pp. 100–127). New York: Springer-Verlag.

Martin, C. L., & Ruble, D. N. (1997). A developmental perspective of self-construals and sex differences: Comment on Cross and Madson. *Psychological Bulletin, 122,* 45–50.

Martin, L. L., & Tesser, A. (1989). Toward a motivational and structural theory of ruminative thought. In J. S. Uleman & J. A. Bargh (Eds.), *Unintended thought* (pp. 306–325). New York: The Guilford Press.

Maslow, A. H. (1968). *Toward a psychology of being.* (2nd ed.). New York: Van Nostrand Reinhold.

Mason, K. O., & Lu, Y. H. (1988). Attitudes toward women's familial roles: Changes in the United States, 1977–1985. *Gender & Society, 2,* 39–57.

Masten, A. S., & Coatsworth, J. D. (1998). The development of competence in favorable and unfavorable environments. *American Psychologist, 53,* 205–220.

May, R. (1960). The emergence of Existential Psychology. In R. May (Ed.), *Existential Psychology* (pp. 11–51). New York: Random House.

May, R. (1972). *Power and innocence: A search for the sources of violence.* New York: W. W. Norton.

Maynard, R. (1995). Teenage childbearing and welfare reform: Lessons from a decade of demonstration and evaluation research. *Children and Youth Services Review, 17,* 309–332.

McAdams, D. P. (2001). The psychology of life stories. *Review of General Psychology, 5,* 100–122.

McCrone, J. (1993). *The myth of irrationality.* New York: Carroll & Graf.

McKenzie-Mohr, D. (2000). Fostering sustainable behavior through community-based social marketing. *American Psychologist, 55,* 531–537.

McPhee, J., McPhee, L., & McPhee, M. (2000). *Girls: Ordinary girls and their extraordinary pursuits.* New York: Random House.

Melamed, E. (1983). *Mirror, mirror: The terror of not being young.* New York: Linden Press/Simon & Schuster.

Merrell, S. S. (1995). *The accidental bond: The power of sibling relationships.* New York: Times Books.

Merrick, E. N. (1995). Adolescent childbearing as career "choice": Perspective from an ecological context. *Journal of Counseling & Development, 73,* 288–295.

Milar, K. S. (2000). The first generation of women psychologists and the psychology of women. *American Psychologist, 55,* 616–619.

Miller, J. B. (1986). *Toward a new psychology of women.* Boston: Beacon Press.

Minton, H. L. (2000). Psychology and gender at the turn of the century. *American Psychologist, 55,* 613–615.

Moen, P., Erickson, M. A., & Dempster-McClain, D. (1997). Their mother's daughters? The intergenerational transmission of gender attitudes in a world of changing roles. *Journal of Marriage and the Family, 59,* 281–293.

Mohney, C., & Anderson, W. (1988). The effect of life events and relationships on adult women's decisions to enroll in college. *Journal of Counseling and Development, 66,* 271–274.

Monge, R. H. (1973). Developmental trends in factors of adolescent self-concept. *Developmental Psychology, 8,* 382–393.

Moretti, M. M., & Higgins, E. T. (1999). Own versus other standpoints in self-regulation: Developmental antecedents and functional consequences. *Review of General Psychology, 3,* 188–223.

Murray, B. (1998, November). A study links women's concern with their looks with lower math scores. *APA Monitor,* p. 7.

Nechas, E., & Foley, D. (1994). *Unequal treatment.* New York: Simon & Schuster.

Neumann, D. (1992). How mediation can effectively address the male-female power imbalance in divorce. *Mediation Quarterly, 9,* 227–239.

Norton, M. B. (1996). *Liberty's daughters (The evolutionary experience of American women, 1750–1800)* (Preface to the Cornell paperbacks edition). Ithaca, NY: Cornell University Press.

Oskamp, S. (2000). A sustainable future for humanity? How can psychology help? *American Psychologist, 55,* 496–508.

Osman, A. K. A., & Al-Sawaf, M. H. (1995). Cross-cultural aspects of sexual anxieties. *Journal of Sex Education & Therapy, 21,* 174–181.

Parcel, T. L., & Menaghan, E. G. (1994). *Parents' jobs and children's lives.* New York: Walter de Gruyter.

Park, C. L, & Folkman, S. (1997). Meaning in the context of stress and coping. *Review of General Psychology, 1,* 115–144.

Pearson, M. (2000). Reaching for higher ground: A new approach to teen sexuality. *Report of the National Council on Family Relations, 45,* F15.

Peck, T. A. (1986). Women's self-definition in adulthood: From a different model? *Psychology of Women Quarterly, 10,* 274–284.

Petersen, S. (2000). Multicultural perspective on middle-class women's identity development. *Journal of Counseling & Development, 78,* 63–71.

Phillips, D. A., & Zimmerman, M. (1990). The developmental course of perceived competence and incompetence among competent children. In R. J. Sternberg & J. Kolligian, Jr. (Eds.), *Competence considered* (pp. 41–66). New Haven, CT: Yale University Press.

Pillemer, D. B. (1998). *Momentous events, vivid memories.* Cambridge, MA: Harvard University Press.

Pillemer, D. B. (2001). Momentous events and the life story. *Review of General Psychology, 5,* 123–134.

Pipher, M. (1994). *Reviving Ophelia. Saving the selves of adolescent girls.* New York: Ballantine Books.

Price, N. (2000, June 18). A century of caring [Lifestyle]. *The Indianapolis Star,* pp. 1–3.

Pyke, K., & Coltrane, C. (1996). Entitlement, obligation, and gratitude in family work. *Journal of Family Issues, 17,* 60–82.

Rampage, C. (1991). Personal authority and women's self-stories. In T. J. Goodrich (Ed.), *Women and power: Perspectives for family therapy* (pp. 109–122). New York: W. W. Norton.

Rehm, D. (1999). *Finding my voice.* New York: Alfred Knopf.

Rich, A. (1986). *Of woman born: Motherhood as experience and institution.* (Tenth Anniversary Edition). New York: W. W. Norton.

Rodin, J., & Ickovics, J. R. (1990). Women's health: Review and research agenda as we approach the 21st century. *American Psychologist, 45,* 1018–1034.

Rose, N. (1990). *Governing the soul: The shaping of the private self.* New York: Routledge.

Ross, C. E., & Van Willigen, M. (1996). Gender, parenthood, and anger. *Journal of Marriage and the Family, 58,* 572–584.

Rothbaum, F., Weisz, J., Pott, M., Miyake, K., & Morelli, G. (2000). Attachment and culture: Security in the United States and Japan. *American Psychologist, 55,* 1093–1104.

Rubenstein, C. (1998). *The sacrificial mother: Escaping the trap of self-denial.* New York: Hyperion.

Ryan, R. M., & Deci, E. L. (2000). Self-determination theory and the facilitation of intrinsic motivation, social development, and well-being. *American Psychologist, 55,* 68–78.

Samenow, S. E. (1989). *Before it's too late.* New York: Times Books.

Sanchez, L., & Gager, C. T. (2000). Hard living, perceived entitlement to a great marriage and marital dissolution. *Journal of Marriage and the Family, 62,* 708–722.

Sanford, L. T., & Donovan, M. E. (1984). *Women & self-esteem: Understanding and improving the way we think and feel about ourselves.* Garden City, NJ: Anchor Press/Doubleday.

Schaef, A. W. (1981). *Women's reality: An emerging female system in the white male society.* Minneapolis, MN: Winston Press.

Scher, M., & Good, G. E. (1990). Gender and counseling in the twenty-first century: What does the future hold? *Journal of Counseling & Development, 68,* 388–391.

Schlegel, M. (2000) Women mentoring women [Education]. *Monitor on Psychology, 31*, 33–36.

Seligman, M. E. P. (1975). *Helplessness: On depression, development, and death.* San Francisco: W. H. Freeman.

Shainess, N. (1984). *Sweet suffering: Woman as victim.* Indianapolis/New York: Bobbs-Merrill.

Shimer, D. B. (Ed.). (1982). *Rice bowl women.* New York: New American Library.

Silver, G. A., & Silver, M. (1985). *Second loves.* new York: Praeger Publishers.

Silvia, P. J., & Gendolla, G. H. E. (2001). On introspection and self-perception: Does self-focused attention enable accurate self-knowledge? *Review of General Psychology, 5*, 241–269.

Simmons, R. G., & Rosenberg, F. (1975). Sex, sex roles, and image. *Journal of Youth and Adolescence, 4*, 229–258.

Simonds, W. (1992). *Women and self-help culture: Reading between the lines.* New Brunswick, NJ: Rutgers University Press.

Simons, R. L., Beaman J., Conger, R. D., & Chao, W. (1992). Gender differences in the intergenerational transmission of parenting beliefs. *Journal of Marriage and the Family, 54*, 823–836.

Snodgrass, S. E. (1985). Women's intuition: The effect of subordinate role on interpersonal sensitivity. *Journal of Personality and Social Psychology, 49*, 146–155.

Sommers, C. H. (1994). *Who stole feminism? How women have betrayed women.* New York: Simon & Schuster.

Starrels, M. E., & Holm, K. E. (2000). Adolescents' plans for family formation: Is parental socialization important? *Journal of Marriage and the Family, 62*, 416–429.

Staudinger, U. M. (2001). Life reflection: A social-cognitive analysis of life review. *Review of General Psychology, 5*, 148–160.

Sterling, S. F. (1995). *Women artists: The National Museum of Women in the Arts.* New York: Abbeville Press.

Sterling, S. F. (1999). The defining eye of Helen Kornblum: An interview with the collector. *Women in the Arts, 17*, 4–8.

Stern, P. C. (2000). Psychology and the science of human-environment interactions. *American Psychologist, 55*, 523–530.

Sternberg, R. J. (2001). Teaching psychology students that creativity is a decision. *The General Psychologist, 36*, 8–11.

Stroh, L. K., Brett, J. M., & Reilly, A. H. (1996). Family structure, glass ceiling, and traditional explanations for the differential rate of turnover of female and male managers. *Journal of Vocational Behavior, 49*, 99–118.

Sullivan, K. R., & Mahalik, J. R. (2000). Increasing career self-efficacy for women: Evaluating a group intervention. *Journal of Counseling & Development, 78*, 54–62.

Tanenhaus, S. (1999, November). Damsels in dissent. *Vanity Fair, 471*, 144–158.

Tavris, C. (1992). *The mismeasure of woman.* New York: Simon & Schuster.

Thompson, L., & Walker, A. (1989). Gender in families: Women and men in marriage, work, and parenthood. *Journal of Marriage and the Family, 51,* 845–871.

Thorne, B. (1993). *Gender play.* New Brunswick, NJ: Rutgers University Press.

Tichenor, V. J. (1999). Status and income as gendered resources: The case of marital power. *Journal of Marriage and the Family, 61,* 638–650.

Tracy, L. (1991). *The secret between us: Competition among women.* Boston: Little, Brown and Company.

Valian, V. (1999). *Why so slow? The advancement of women.* Cambridge, MA: The MIT Press.

Valois, R. F., Kammermann, S. K., & Drane, J. W. (1997). Number of sexual intercourse partners and associated risk behaviors among public high school adolescents. *Journal of Sex Education and Therapy, 22,* 13–22.

Volz, J. (2000, January). Women's health task force cites research needs [In Brief]. *Monitor on Psychology, 31,* 11.

Wagner, L. (1998). *Expectations: Thirty women talk about becoming a mother.* San Francisco: Chronicle Books.

Walker, B. G. (1983). *The woman's encyclopedia of myths and secrets.* New York: Harper & Row.

Walker, L. E. (1999). Psychology and domestic violence around the world. *American Psychologist, 54,* 21–29.

West, C., & Zimmerman, D. (1987). Doing gender. *Gender and Society, 1,* 125–151.

Westkott, M. (1979). Feminist criticism of the social sciences. *Harvard Educational Review, 49,* 422–430.

Wilkie, J. R., Ferree, M. M., & Ratcliff, K. S. (1998). Gender and fairness: Marital satisfaction in two-earner couples. *Journal of Marriage and the Family, 60,* 577–594.

Williams, C. (2000, November). Desperately seeking female mentors [Education]. *Monitor on Psychology, 31,* 37.

Williams, J. H. (1983). *Psychology of women: Behavior in a biosocial context* (2nd ed.). New York: W. W. Norton.

Wilson-Sweebe, K., & Bond-Zielinski, C. (2000). Project reality: A teenage pregnancy prevention program. *Report of the National Council on Family Relations, 45,* F14.

Winter, D. D. (2000). Some big ideas for some big problems. *American Psychologist, 55,* 516–522.

Yalom, I. D. (1980). *Existential psychotherapy.* New York: Basic Books.

Name Index

Subject Index